The In

By

Jules Michelet

Coming Soon
How I Stole 5.6 Million from Walmart
The Gods Return Loki's Trial
Zombie Squirrels

Loki's Publishing

Seattle, WA

The Insect

Contents

The Insect

Preface

The Insect" is one of the four remarkable works in which the late M. Michelet embodied the results of a loving and persevering study of Nature. These works are absolutely unique; the poetry of Science was never before illustrated on so large a scale, or with so much vividness of fancy, or in so eloquent a style. The aspects of Nature were never before examined with so strong an enthusiasm or so definite an individuality,—with so eager a desire to identify them with the feelings, hopes, and aspirations of humanity. Michelet approached his subject neither as philosopher nor as poet, but yet with something of the spirit of both. His philosophy and poetry, however, were both subordinate to his ardent sympathy with what he conceived to be the soul, the personality of Nature; and whether his attention was directed to the life of ocean, the bird, the insect, or the mountain-plant, he still sought for some evidence of its special and distinct existence, with thoughts and emotions, as it were, and a character of its own. It was almost as if he saw in Nature a likeness to, and a kinship with, humanity. No doubt, in expressing these views he was occasionally led into a certain extravagance, and his enthusiasm not infrequently outran or overmastered his judgment. He lacked the profound insight and sober reflection of Wordsworth, and accuracy of detail was often sacrificed for the sake of a brilliant generalization. But, after making due allowance for defects inseparable, perhaps, from a genius rather passionate and impulsive than analytic and self-composed, it must be admitted that the lover of Nature has cause to be grateful for the fine fancies, rich illustrations, and suggestive analogies crowded into the books we speak of.

A recent writer, M. Monod,[1] has pronounced upon them an animated eulogium:—"Scientific men may discover in these books errors, inaccuracies, and exaggerations; but, in spite of all, they have shown that the physical sciences, though accused of withering the soul, and robbing Nature of poetry and life of enchantment, contain the elements of a profound and varied poetry, that never loses its charm, because it is not dependent on the caprices of taste and fashion, but has its source in the unchangeable reality of things. Many have said that science will drive out religion and poetry; Michelet finds in every branch of science the demonstration of a new faith, revealing to him a harmony till then unperceived, centered in the supreme unity of the Divine mind and of the Absolute Being."

Whether the reader endorses this high eulogium or not, he will certainly, in "The Insect," as in "The Bird," find a new stimulus to the study of Nature, and a fresh proof of the power and fancy of one of the greatest of modern French writers.

Of the present translation, it is necessary only to say that it has been executed with a conscientious adherence to the original, and with an effort to preserve, as far as possible, its peculiarities of style. If it should be thought that in the attempt something of freedom and fluency has been sacrificed, it is hoped the critic will acknowledge that something of faithfulness has been gained. The author of "The Insect" took much interest in the presentation of it and its companions to the English reader in an English dress, and was pleased to express his approval of the manner in which the Translator had accomplished his task.

It remains to be added that the exquisite Illustrations, by M. H. Giacomelli, have all been specially drawn and engraved for the English edition.

W. H. Davenport Adams

---

[1] *Macmillan's Magazine*, July 1874, pp. 231, 232.

Introduction

A Home Among the Mountains

I. The Living Infinite

We have followed the Bird in all its liberties of flight, and space, and light; but the Earth which we quitted would not quit us. The sweet melodies of the winged world could not prevent us from hearing the murmur of an infinite world of shadow and silence, which, wanting the speech of man, expresses itself, nevertheless, with eloquent force, by means of a myriad mute tongues.

A universal appeal made to us simultaneously by all Nature, from the depths of Earth and Sea, from the bosom of every plant, from the very air which we breathe.

The eloquent appeal of the ingenious arts of the Insect, of its powers of love so vividly manifested through its wings and colors, in the brilliant scintillation with which it enkindles our nights.

An appeal which becomes frightful from the number of those who make it. What is the little tribe of Birds, or that of Quadrupeds, compared with them? All the animal species, all the various forms of life, brought face to face with this one family, disappear, and are as nothing. Put the world on one side, and on the other the Insect World; the latter has the advantage.

Our collections contain about one hundred thousand species. But taking into consideration that every plant at the least nourishes three, we obtain the result, according to the number of known plants, of three hundred and sixty thousand species of insects! And each, be it remembered, of prodigious fecundity.

Now call to mind that every creature nourishes other creatures on its surface, in the thickness of its solids, in its fluids, and in its blood; that each insect is a little world inhabited by insects; and that these again have parasites of their own.

The Insect

Is this all? No; in the masses men have supposed to be mineral or inorganic, animals are now revealed to us of which it would take a thousand millions to form one inch in thickness,—the which do not the less present us with a rough sketch or outline of the Insect, and have a right to be spoken of as *insects commenced*. And what are the numbers of these? A single species accumulates the Apennines out of its débris, and with its atoms has raised up that enormous backbone of America, the Cordilleras.

Having arrived at this point, we think our review is ended. Patience! The molluscs, which in the Southern Seas have created so many islands,—which literally pave, as recent soundings have shown, the twelve hundred leagues of Ocean separating us from America,—these molluscs are qualified by many naturalists with the name of *embryo insects*; so that their fertile tribes form, as it were, a dependency of the higher race,—candidates, one might say, for the rank of Insect.

This is sublime. The reason that, nevertheless, makes me regret the little world of Birds,—those charming companions which bore me aloft on their wings not long ago,—is not their harmonious concerts, is not even the spectacle of their airy and sublime life—but because they understood me!

We comprehended and we loved one another; we interchanged our languages. I spoke for the Bird, and the Bird sang for me.

Having fallen from heaven at the threshold of the sombre kingdom, and in the presence of the mute and mysterious sons of night, what language am I to invent, and what signs of intelligence? How am I to exercise my wits to discover a mode of communicating with them? My voice and gestures do but drive them away. There is no glance of recognition in their eyes; no emotion visible on their inscrutable mask. Under its warrior-cuirass the Insect remains impenetrable. Does its heart—for it has one—beat after the fashion of mine? Its senses are infinitely subtle, but do they resemble *my* senses? It seems as if they still remained apart, unknown, ay, and without a name.

It escapes us; Nature has created for it, with respect to man, a perpetual *alibi*. If she reveals it to us for a moment in a single gleam of love, she hides it for years in the depths of the shadowy earth or in the discreet bosom of the oaks. And even when discovered, captured, opened, dissected, and examined by a microscope in every detail, it still remains to us an enigma.

And an enigma of by no means reassuring character,—whose singularity almost scandalizes, while it so confuses our ideas. What shall we say of a being which breathes through its side and flanks? of a paradoxical walker, which, contrary to all other organisms, presents its back to the earth and its belly to the sky? In many respects, we may look upon the insect as a creature of contradictions.

Add, moreover, that its littleness contributes to the misunderstanding. Every organ appears to us fantastic and threatening, because our weak eyes do not see it with sufficient clearness to be able to explain its structure and utility. What is imperfectly seen always perplexes; and therefore provisionally, we kill it! And it is so little, too, that we do not trouble ourselves to be just towards it.

Jules Michelet

We are in no want of systems. We could willingly accept the definitive decree of a German dreamer, who sums up the whole matter in a word: "The good God made the world; but the devil made the insect!"

The Insect, nevertheless, does not look upon itself as vanquished. To the systems of the philosopher and the terror of the child (which are, perhaps, both the same thing), this is its answer:—

In the first place, that Justice is universal, that size has nothing to do with Right; that if one could suppose the Right to be unequal in its application, and the Universal Love to incline the balance, it would be on the side of the little.

It says that it would be absurd to judge by the figure, to condemn organs of whose uses we are ignorant, which are principally the tools of special professions, the instruments of a hundred trades; that it, the insect, is the great destroyer and fabricator, the most industrious of artisans, the energetic workman of life.

And, finally, it says (this pretension will perhaps appear most arrogant), that if we judge by visible signs, by works and results, it is It, among all beings, which loves most truly. Love endows it with wings, with a marvelous iris of colors, and even with visible flames. Love is for *it* the instantaneous or approaching death, with an astonishing *second sight* of maternity which continues over the orphan an ingenious superintendence. And lastly, the maternal genius extends so far, that, surpassing and eclipsing the rare associations of birds and quadrupeds, it has enabled the Insect to create republics and establish cities!

I admit that this weighty plea has made an impression on me.

If thou toilest and lovest, O Insect, whatever may be thy aspect, I cannot separate myself from thee. We are truly somewhat akin. For what am I myself, but a worker? What has been my greatest happiness in this world?

Our communion of action and destiny will open my heart, and give me a new sense with which to understand thy silence. Love—the divine force which circulates in all things, like an universal soul—is the interpreter through whose agency our insects discourse and understand each other without speech.

II. Our Studies at Paris and in Switzerland

In the prolonged perusal of naturalists and travelers by which we prepared ourselves for writing "The Bird," and for which nothing less was required than the patience of a solitary woman, we gathered on the way a number of facts and details which presented the Insect to our eyes under the most varied aspects. The Insect appeared to us incessantly in company with the Bird,—here like a harmony, there as an antagonism,—but too often in profile, and as a subordinate being.

I was in the middle of the sixteenth century, and while engaged for about three years in historical studies, my knowledge on this point was collected only by means of extracts, readings, and conversations every evening. The various elements of this grand study I acquired through the medium of a soul eminently gentle towards the things of nature, and generously given to love the weak; whose loyal and patient affection, indefinitely extending curiosity, picked up, so to speak, like the ant, and as so many grains of sand, the materials which we found less frequently in the more important works than in an infinity of memoirs and scattered dissertations.

To live long, steadfastly, for ever,—this it is which renders weak spirits strong. Such a perseverance of taste and affection is not less necessary when one wishes to put aside one's books, and enter upon a course of observation, of long and delicate studies of life. I am not surprised that Mademoiselle Jurine contributed so largely to her father's astonishing discoveries respecting bees, nor that Madame Mérian, as the fruit of her far-off wanderings, has bequeathed to us her wise and beautiful book of drawings of the Insects of Guiana. The eyes and hands of women, so delicate and well adapted for dealing with tiny objects, are eminently appropriate for such pursuits as these. They have also a greater respect for, attention to, and condescension towards trifling existences, than man exhibits. Though poetical, they are less poets, and impose less upon the Real the tyranny of their thought. They are more docile towards it, do not dominate over it, submit themselves to it, and do not bestow on these little beings the rapid and often disdainful glance of the higher life. And when, with all this, they are patient also, they may well become excellent observers, and miniature Réaumurs.

Feminine qualities are specially needful in microscopical studies. To succeed in these, one must become somewhat of a woman. The microscope is amusing at a first hasty glance; but if one would make a serious use of it, it demands a certain amount of dexterity, patient tact, and especially leisure,—considerable leisure,—full liberty of time,—in order that one may indefinitely repeat the same observations, and examine the same object on different days, in the pure light of morning, in the warm ray of noon, and occasionally even at a later hour. For certain objects which we must regard as a whole are best seen through a single lens; others only through a transparency, by illuminating them beneath the mirror of the microscope. Others, insignificant or commonplace by day, grow marvelous in the evening, when the focus of the instrument concentrates the light. To conclude: their study demands—what in the present age one least possesses—an isolation from the world, a point beyond time; the support of a blameless curiosity, and of a constant and reverent love of these imperceptible existences. Theirs is a kind of virginal and solitary maternity.

I was not released from my absorption in that terrible sixteenth century until the spring of 1856. "The Bird" had also made its appearance. I sought an interval of rest, and established myself at Montreux, near Clarens, on the Lake of Geneva. But this most delightful locality, awakening in me a keen perception of Nature, did not restore my tranquility. I was still too much affected by the bloody story I had been narrating. A flame burned within me which nothing could extinguish. I rambled along the roads, with my cup of fir-wood, tasting the water at every fountain—all so fresh and so pure!—and demanding of them if any possessed the property of effacing the bitternesses of the Past and Present, and which, out of so many springs, might prove to me a Lethe.

At length I found, at about half a league from Lucerne, an old convent transformed into a hostelry, where I selected for my study the parlour, a very spacious apartment, which, through its seven windows opening on the mountains, the lake, and the town—a threefold prospect—afforded me a magnificent light at all hours. From morning to evening the sun remained faithful to me, and revolved around my microscope, set in the middle of the chamber. The beautiful lake, shining in front and on every side, is not that which afterwards, when hemmed in by the heights, and furious and violent, will be called the Lake of Uri. But the firs which everywhere overhang the landscape warn you not to place too much reliance on the season,—inform you that you are residing in a cold country. In numerous things, moreover, you find a certain barbarous savagery prevailing. It is from the very south the breath of winter blows. In front of me, and my constant companion, arose, on the farther shore, the gloomy Pilatus, a barren mountain with keen razor-like edges; and over its black shoulder gleamed, at ten leagues distant, the snow-white *Virgin* and the *Silver Peak* (the Jungfrau and the Silberhorn).

The country is very beautiful and very fresh in July, but frequently, in September, is already cold. You perceive above and behind you, at an enormous elevation, an ocean of water suspended. This is the main reservoir whence issue the great European reservoirs; the mass of St. Gothard, a table-land measuring ten leagues in every direction, which from one extremity pours out the Rhine, from another the Rhone, from a third the Reuss, and towards the south the Ticino. You do not *see* this reservoir—except a little of its outline—but you *feel* it. Do you wish for water? Come hither. Drink; it is the grandest cup which quenches the thirst of humanity.

I began to feel less athirst. In the middle of summer the nights were cold, the mornings and evenings fresh. Those spotless snows, which I gazed at so eagerly and with insatiable eyes, purified me, it seemed, from the long, dusty, sun-burned, blood-besprinkled, and sublime, but also sometimes miry, revolutions of history. I recovered a little my equilibrium between the drama of the world and the eternal epopea.

The Insect

What can be more divine than these Alps? Elsewhere I have called them "the common altar of Europe." And wherefore? Not on account of their height,—a little higher, or a little lower, one is no nearer heaven,—but because the grand harmony, elsewhere vague, is palpable here. The solidarity of life, the circulation of nature, the beneficent concord of the elements,—all is visible. It kindles a glorious illumination.

Each chain filters from its glacier, as a revelation of the inaccessible zone, a torrent which, concentrated, tranquillized and purified in an ample lake,— translated into pure and azure water,—emerges as a great river, and diffuses everywhere the soul of the Alps. From these innumerable waters reascend to the mountains the mists which renew the treasure of their glaciers.

All is in such perfect sympathy, and the perspectives are so noble, that the lakes and their rivers still reflect or survey, as they wander afar, the grave assemblage of the mountains, the upper snows, the sublime virgin peaks of which they are an emanation.

They face, they explain one another, harmonize with and love one another. But in what austerity! In their mutual love we recognize an identity of the strongest contrasts,—fixity and fluidity, rapidity and eternity, the snows above the verdure, forebodings of winter in summer.

Hence results a prudent nature, a general sagacity in the things themselves. One enjoys without forgetting that one's enjoyment will not be of long duration. But the heart is not the less moved by a world of such seriousness and purity. This brevity attracts, and this austerity takes one captive. From the gleaming snows to the lakes, from the woods to the rivers and to the fresh emerald meads, a sovereign virginity predominates over the whole country.

Such localities are for all the seasons of life. Old age grows strengthened by its association with nature, and greets without melancholy the grand shadows falling from the mountains. And hearts still young, which feel only the morning and the dawn, expand to the charming joys of religious tenderness,—tenderness for the Soul of the world, tenderness for its smallest infants.

The favorite place for our walks, and our usual studio, was a small grove of firs situated at a tolerable elevation above the lake, in the rear of the rock of Seeberg. We ascended thither by two routes doubly illuminated by the mighty radiance of the splendid mirror in which the four cantons are reflected. No landscape can be more gentle, if we look towards Lucerne; none more serious or solemn, in the direction of St. Gothard and the amphitheatre of mountains. But all this grandeur and brightness terminated suddenly at the first step we took beneath our firs. It was as if one had reached the end of the world. The light lessened; sounds seemed subdued; life itself appeared absent.

Such, at the first glance, is the customary effect of the woods. But at the second all is changed. The suffocation, or at least subordination, imposed by the fir upon all those plants which would fain grow in its shade, lets light into the depths; and when the eyes have become accustomed to this kind of gloaming, we see considerably further, and distinguish much more clearly, than in the inextricable labyrinth of ordinary forests where everything acts as an obstruction.

Jules Michelet

The spectacle first presented to us under the noble funereal pillars—the pillars, may we not say? of a stately temple—was a spectacle of death; not of a saddening death, but of a death rich, adorned, and graceful, such as Nature frequently vouchsafes to plants. At every step the old trunks of trees, felled but not uprooted, were clothed in an incomparable velvety green,—a tissue superbly woven of fine mosses soft to the touch, which delighted the eye by their changing aspects, their reflexes, and their shifting gleams.

But where was the animal life of the forest? Our ears soon grew accustomed to recognize and divine its presence. I do not refer to the whistle of the tomtits, or the strange laughter of the woodpecker, the evident lord of the place. I am thinking of a different people, against whom the birds wage war.

A great hum and murmur, sufficiently loud to drown the noise of a brook, warned us that the forest was haunted by wasps. Already we had discovered their fort, whence more than one endeavored to lead us astray, suspecting our steps, and obviously ill-disposed towards us.

In the very localities least frequented by the wasps, light, hoarse, internal rustlings seemed to issue from the trees. Were these the voices of their genii, their Dryads? No, indeed; but of their mysterious enemies, the mighty populace of the shadows, which, following up the veins of the trunk and penetrating its entire extent, work out for themselves, with patient teeth, innumerable ways and channels and galleries. Sometimes nearly a hundred thousand *scolyti*[2] (for such is their name) are found in a single tree. The sickly fir is at length reduced by their teeth to the condition of a piece of delicate lace-work. Yet the bark remains intact, and deludes us with the phantom of life.

How does the tree defend itself? Sometimes by its sap, which, while preserving its strength, asphyxiates the enemy; but more frequently it is assisted by a friend, a physician, from without—the woodpecker—which carefully auscultates it, taps and strikes it with its strong hammer, and with persevering ardor watches for and pursues the nibbling colony.

Is this internal combat between the two lives, the animal and the vegetable, really understood? Of this I cannot be sure, and there are times when I think myself deceived.

In that silence which was not silence, a something—I know not what—assured us that the dead forest was in truth alive, and on the point of breaking forth into speech. We entered it full of hope, and believing that we should discover some secret. We felt certain that to our inquiring spirit a great manifold Spirit was about to reply. Though fatigued by the walk, and in an infirm state of health, I felt great pleasure in the search I had undertaken in these pallid glooms. I loved to see before me a person deeply moved, and enthusiastically smitten by their great mysteries. Stick in hand, she advanced into this fantastic twilight, interrogating the sombre forest, and seeking, as it were, the Virgilian "golden bough."

---

[2] A genus of *Coleoptera*.

The Insect

I was about to quit the scene, and seat myself in a sunny opening, when at length a more successful sounding in one of the ancient trunks brought to light a world whose existence no one would have suspected.

At the summit of this trunk, cut off within a foot of the ground, you could very easily distinguish the works wrought by the *scolyti* and weevils, the former inhabitants of the tree, in conformity to the concentric arrangement of the sap. But all this belonged to ancient history; a different condition of things now existed. These miserable *scolyti* had perished, having undergone, like their tree, the energetic action of a great chemical transformation which excluded all life.

All life, except one, and that the keenest—a consuming and burned-up life, it seems—the life of those beings powerful under an infinitely little form, in which one might have readily concluded that a black flame, shining fitfully, had consumed all that was material, and reserved only what was spiritual.

The *coup de théâtre* was violent, and the immense swarming had its effect. A vivid and unwonted joy agitated the much-moved hand that had made the happy discovery; and in proportion to the full revelation of its greatness, a wild vertigo passed from the distracted people to the author of this great ruin. The walls of the city fell down, and revealed the interior of the edifice; innumerable halls and galleries were laid bare; generally four to five inches in length, and about half an inch in height,—a height certainly quite sufficient, and even majestic, if we take into account the size of the members of the community.

A true palace, or rather a vast and superb city; limited in breadth, but to what depth may it not penetrate the earth? It is said that some have been found which, perseveringly excavated, have numbered no fewer than seven hundred stories. Thebes and Nineveh were insignificant! Babylon and Babel alone might have sustained, in their audaciously towering piles, a comparison with these shadowy Babels which continually expanded in the abyss.

But more astonishing than the grandeur is the interior aspect of these habitations: without, all damp, and mossy, and overgrown with tiny cryptogams; within, an astonishing dryness, and an admirable cleanliness—every partition firm though soft, just as if it had been tapestried with cotton velvet, very heavy and lustreless. Is this black velvet produced from the wood itself, after undergoing powerful modification, or by an extremely delicate layer of microscopic fungi which may have been established in the tree while it was still moist, and before it received its all-powerful necromancers? The agent of the transformation betrayed itself directly: each separate cell, if closely smelt, betrayed the pungent odor of formic acid, by means of which the busy race had effected the metamorphosis of its abode, had burned it and purified it with its flame, had dried it and rendered it wholesome with its useful poison.

It is this acid also which, undoubtedly, had accelerated and assisted the enormous and colossal labor, had opened the way to the tiny efforts of those indefatigable sculptors whose chisels are their teeth. Yet even in this case there can be no question but that it must have occupied a considerable time. Successive generations had very probably passed their lives in the tree, working always on the same plan and in the same direction. The image of the projected and longed-for city—the hope of creating a secure fortress, a noble and massive acropolis—had for long years sustained the hearts of the courageous citizens. Ah, what would life be worth if one labored only for one's-self! Let us look forward to the future. The first-comers who spent their lives in the tree, and from their internal reservoir drew and exhausted the juices that excavated it, could have enjoyed but for a very brief time a habitation so melancholy, and so steeped, as yet, in pestiferous damps and protracted rains; but they thought of future generations, and reverenced posterity.

Alas, I am much afraid that the sanguine dream is ended! It is not that a child's stick, held by a young and womanly hand, has penetrated to the very bottom of the structure carried so deeply into the earth; but that the exterior defenses, which protected and closed up the whole, and kept off the rains, have been removed and scattered abroad. And lo! the great autumnal floods pouring down from the Rhigi, Mont Pilate, and the St. Gothard, the father of rivers,— floating above the forests in heavy mists or descending in torrents,—will swamp for ever the internal recesses. And what flame, or what burning life, can the inhabitants oppose to these repeated invasions of the waters, to rebuild their palace and purify it again?

Seated on a fir, I eyed it steadfastly, and as I gazed I dreamed. Though accustomed to the fall of empires and republics, its ruins flung me into an ocean of thought. A wave, and then another wave rose, and throbbed in my heart. The verse of Homer hung upon my lips,—

"And even Troy shall see its day of doom."

What could I do for this ravaged world, this half-ruined city? What for this great laborious insect race, which all living tribes pursue, or devour, or despise, and which nevertheless reveals to us the strongest images of unselfish love, of public devotion, and the social sense in its keenest energy? One thing: to comprehend it,—to explain it, if I could,—to pour light upon it, and supply it with a generous interpretation.

My wife and I returned home dreaming, and understanding one another without speaking. What had previously been an amusement, a curiosity, and a study, thenceforth became a Book.

III. Our Studies at Fontainebleau

I feel no surprise that our great initiator into the Insect World, Swammerdam, recoiled in affright when the microscope first afforded him a glimpse of it.

For the name of its inhabitants is, the Living Infinite.

Upwards of two hundred years men have labored, simplifying in one direction, and complicating in another. The excellent treatises written upon this subject leave, among a multitude of partial illuminations, a certain feeling of being dazzled. Such is the impression which their study for some time produced upon us.

Ought I to flatter myself that I can render it clearer than my masters have done? By no means. But I discovered, through the incident which took place at Lucerne, and others of later date, that our enthusiastic and sympathetic ignorance could penetrate further, perhaps, into the meaning of the insect life than has been the lot of many scientific classificators.

The thought pursued me during the winter, but I could not verify any experiment at Paris; it was only at Fontainebleau that I worked out the truly simple formula about to be submitted to the reader, and obtained some tranquility of mind, so far as this subject was concerned.

The place admirably favored the then condition of my soul. All the painful circumstances of the time, by driving me back upon myself, increased my concentration. We constituted for ourselves a perfect solitude. Our chamber became for us an entire city. And outside there was nothing but a ring of wood, then tolerably small, which we traversed on foot.

This ring oppressed me a little in the great heats, when the sun shone reflected on the sandstone. But in these dry hot days the thought does not grow enfeebled. I could follow up and investigate mine with sequence and perseverance, enjoying—what is rare enough in life—a grand harmonious unity of ideas and sentiments, which I was by no means anxious to vary, but rather to deepen.

I went forth alone at noonday, and walked some distance into the dull, dumb, and sandy forest, which was without whisper and without voice. I carried thither my theme, and trusted to attain its meaning in that infinite of sand overlaid by an infinite of leaves. But how much vaster that infinite of animated life, the abyss of imperceptible organisms into which I was fain to descend!

All that says of Fontainebleau is true so far as relates to the vague dreamer who brings with him no prevailing thought. Yes; the landscape "is generally on a small scale, dull, low, and solitary without being wild." Animals are seldom met with, except in a few kids whose number is easily counted. Birds are not numerous. Few or no springs are visible; and the apparent absence of water has a specially depressing effect on the Alpine traveler, who still recalls the freshness of the innumerable fountains of the Alps, and still has before his eyes the radiance of those delightful and sublime mirrors—their lakes. There, all is clear and luminous in the waters and the snows. Here, all is obscure. This small angle, sequestered as it were from the rest of France, is an enigma. It shows you the dead sandstones without a trace of life; it shows you, particularly to-day, the newly-planted pines, which suffer nothing living under their shade. To discover what lies concealed beneath this outer mask, you must have recourse to the divining-rod, the hazel-wand. Revolve it, and you shall find. But what is this divining-rod? A study or a love; any passion which lights up the inner world.

The power of this locality does not lie in its historical, any more than in its artistic associations.[3]

The chateau distracts one's attention from the forest by its abundant variety of memories and epochs; but it fails to increase the impression. Nature is the true fairy in this strange, sombre, fantastic, and sterile region.

The Forest of Fontainebleau

Observe that wherever the forest assumes an aspect of grandeur, either through the extent of its vista or the loftiness of its trees, it resembles all other forests. The truly magnificent towering beeches of Bas-Bréau seem to me, in spite of their stately bearing and smooth shining bark, a thing I have seen elsewhere. The place is original only where it is low, gloomy rock; where it

---

[3] It contains, however, three notable things: one magnificent, the Hall of Henry II.; one marvelous, the Little Gallery of Francis I.; and one sublime, the four colossi, the incomparable relics of a lost art, that of sculpture in sandstone.

bears evidence of the struggle of the sandstone, the twisted tree, the perseverance of the elm, or the courageous effort of the oak.

Many persons have remained here fascinated and enthralled. Coming only for a month, they have lingered until death. To the enchanting scene they have addressed the lover's speech to his beloved:—"Let me live, let me die with thee!"—*Tecum vivere amem, tecum obeam libens.*

It is a curious fact that every individual finds here what he most delights in: Saint Louis, the Thébaïd of which he dreamed; while Henry IV., who cared for nothing but pleasure, exclaimed, "My delicious deserts!" The poor mystical exile, Kosciusko,[4] felt the attraction of his Lithuanian forests, and here took root. A man of stone, of flint,—the Breton Maud'huys,—saw here the image of his native Brittany, and built up, stone upon stone, the most original book written upon Fontainebleau.

It is a region of power, which you cannot enter with impunity. Some persons lose in it their wits, undergo a strange metamorphosis, and like Bottom, in Windsor Forest, see themselves adorned with ass's ears. For the forest is a *person*: has its lovers and its detractors—some curse it, others bless it. A foolish dreamer wrote of it, on a rock near Nemours, "I *will* possess thee, cruel stepmother!" And her lover, the old soldier Denecourt, who bestowed on her all that he had in the world, called her "My adored!"[5]

Some one has said to me: "Is she not the *Viola* of Shakespeare, with her dubious but always charming aspect; now a maiden, and now a cavalier? Or his young page, Rosalind, after she appears as a laughing damsel?" No: the contrasts are much greater.

For the fairy here has countless faces. She has the cold Alpine plants, and yet she shelters the most delicate flora. Austere in winter and spring, she terrifies you with the rugged rocks which, in autumn, she conceals under a crimson mantle of foliage. She has at her disposal, for a daily change, the delicate tissue of floating gauze which Lantara never fails to spread over it in all his pictures. With her belt of forest she arrests on every side the light mists, and gaily weaves them into veils, and scarfs, and girdles; into all kinds of delicate disguises. You would think the heavy masses of sandstone invariable; yet they change their aspects, their colors—I was going to say their form—every hour. The little chain, for example, known as the Rock of Avon, had saluted us in the morning with the breath of the heather, the cheeriest ray of the dawn, an enchanting aurora which tinted with rose hues the sandstone; all nature seemed to smile, and to harmonize with the innocent studies of a devout and poetic soul. When we returned there in the evening, the capricious fairy had changed everything. Those pines, which had welcomed us under their airy canopy, had suddenly grown wild and fierce, and resounded with strange noises, with lamentations of sinister augury. Those shrubs, which in the morning had graciously invited the

---

[4] The Polish hero who unavailingly struggled to secure his country's freedom, but was crushed by the power of Russia:—
"And Freedom shrieked when Kosciusko fell!"

[5] It is impossible to be grateful enough for all that M. Denecourt has done; he has rendered the place accessible by everybody, even the poorest, who are no longer in need of guides.—Author.

white robe to pause beside them and gather their berries or flowers, now seemed to conceal in their copses an undefinable something of ill omen—robbers, it might be, or sorcerers! But greater still the transformation in those rocks, which had courteously received us, and bidden us be seated. Is it the evening, or is it a coming storm, which has changed them? I know not; but there they are, metamorphosed into gloomy sphinxes, into elephants prostrate on the earth, into mammoths, and other monsters of the old worlds which have ceased to exist. They are now at rest, it is true; but are they not about to rise? However this may be, the evening comes on apace; let us advance. My wife presses close to my arm.

Does not our forest deserve the name of the Shakespearian comedy, "As You Like It"?

No; to deal justly with it, we must own that its entertaining metamorphosis, and all its changes to the eye, are absolutely external. Movable in its leaves and mists, fugitive in its shifting sands, it has a firmer foundation than perhaps any other forest, and a power of fixity which communicates itself to the soul, and invites it to grow strong; to search out and seek within its own nature whatever it possesses of the inscrutable. Do not linger too long over its fantastic accidents. *Without* it says, "As You Like It;" *within*, "Ever and for ever."

Its beauty is that of the profound, faithful, and tender heart, which does not the less vary its exquisite grace, though it may daily repeat the words of Charles d'Orléans:

> *"Who can ever weary of her?*
> *Still her beauty she renews."*

These ideas occurred to me one day as, seated upon Mont Ussy, I looked across Fontainebleau. I comprehended how, in this confined and ordinary region—in this apparent chaos of rocks, and trees, and sandstone—prevailed a tolerable degree of order, which necessarily concealed within it a mystery not obvious at the first glance.

As a whole, it is almost a circle of hills and forests, all dry on the surface; but the sandstone is very pervious, and the sand filtrates with great facility. And the unseen waters, descend in all directions to a great reservoir which occupies the depths.

Storms are frequent here, but do not spread very far. We may nearly always expect them, for the forest detains and arrests them, preserves for itself the wealth of suspended waters, transmitting them to the lower grounds after they have been sifted through the leaves, the woods, and the sands. All this occurs below, without the process ever becoming visible.

Dig, and you shall find.

There lies the charm, the vitality of the *genius loci*.

The word "genius" conveys too great an idea of fixity, and that of "fairy" is more appropriate. Who shall describe the mystery of this profound hidden basin? this simple and attractive delusion, which, while promising only dryness, faithfully stores up underneath the treasure of its waters?

The Insect

An eminent Italian artist has given expression to it in the paintings which adorn the Hall of Henry II. It is the *Nemorosa*, the Wood-Nymph, with hands full of wild-flowers, hiding beneath a rugged rock, but subdued and dreamy, and with eyes swimming tearfully.

In the course of our labors, and especially on days when fell a fine soft rain, we frequently appreciated this sentiment. It prevailed around us like a concentration of nature. In the deep silence we could hear only our beating hearts, the pendulum of the clock, or the occasional cry of the swallow passing above our heads.

Calmed, but not lulled asleep, with clearer brain and keener eye than before, we penetrated further into the shadowy world of the atom, to discover its actual nature; the light, and especially the love, which is the true legitimate sovereign of this lower world; the tongue, the eloquent voice, by which it appeals to the upper world.

IV. Our Studies at Fontainebleau (*Continued*)

Even in its hours of silence, the forest occasionally finds a voice, a sound, or a murmur, which recalls to you the remembrance of life.

Sometimes the laborious woodpecker, laboriously toiling at its task of excavating the oak, cheers itself with its singular cry.

Frequently the heavy hammer of the quarryman, falling and falling on the sandstone, resounds in the distance with a hoarse, dull echo.

And finally, if you listen attentively, you catch a significant hum, and see, at your feet, legions of ants,—countless populations, the true inhabitants of the place, speeding over the withered and falling leaves.

So many images are these of persistent toil, which blend with the fanciful a serious gravity. Each in his own way digs and digs. And do thou too pursue thy work, and exhume and stir up thy thought.

It is an admirable place to cure you of the great malady of the day—its shiftiness, its empty agitation. The time does not know its own disease; men say that they are clogged and cloyed, when they have scarcely skimmed the surface. They set out with the delusive notion that the best of everything is superficial and external, and that it is sufficient to put their lips to the cup. But the surface is frequently froth. Lower down, and within, lies the elixir of life. We must penetrate deeper, and mingle more intimately with things, willingly and by habit, so as to discover their harmony, in which lies true happiness and strength. The real misfortune, the moral misery, is our want of concentration.

I love those spots which confine and limit the field of thought. Here, in this narrow circle of hill and wood, every change is purely external and wholly optical. With so many points of shelter, the winds, necessarily, do not greatly vary. The fixity of the atmosphere furnishes us with a moral basis. I am not certain that our ideas would here be strongly stimulated; but he who comes with them fully aroused may long preserve and cherish them, without any interruption of his dream; may seize and relish all the outer accidents, as well as the inner mysteries. The soul may here put forth its roots, and find that the true, the exquisite sense of life, is not to skim the surface, but to study, and probe, and enjoy the depth.

This spot admonishes thought. The sandstone, fixed and motionless beneath the mobility of the leaves, is eloquent enough in its very silence. Since when has it been planted here? Ah, what ages ago, since, despite its hardness, the rain has succeeded in excavating it! No other force has prevailed against it. Such as it was, even so it is; and thus it seems to say to the heart, "Persevere!"

Apparently it should be strong enough to exclude all vegetable life. But the heroic oaks will not be denied, and, being condemned to live there, have succeeded in defiance of every obstacle. With their twisted roots, and with their strong talons that have seized upon the rock, they too, after their fashion, eloquently exclaim, "Persevere!" The invincible trees, struggling all the more bravely the greater the resistance they meet with, have, on the unimpeded side, plunged so much the more deeply into the bowels of the earth, and drawn from it incalculable forces. One of them, the poor old giant named *Charlemagne*, worn-out, undermined, thunder-stricken, after so many centuries and so many trials, is still so vigorous in its loins, that in a solitary branch it has all the appearance of carrying a great oak with outstretched arms.

Between this sandstone and these oaks one may profit largely. Nor is man, if you find him here at work, a less useful teacher. The valiant quarrymen whom I encountered battling against the rock with monstrous hammers which seem never made for the hand of man, I could willingly believe to possess the resistant force of the sandstone and the iron heart of the oak. And this is undoubtedly true, so far as concerns the soul and the will. But the body has less power of endurance. Few quarrymen live beyond forty years of age; and those first carried off are invariably the most skilful and ardent at their work.

All the life of the forest centres in the quarrymen and the ants. Formerly it had the bees also. They were very numerous, and may still be met with in the direction of Franchart. But they have greatly decreased in numbers since the planting of so many pines and Northern trees, which kill everything with their shade, and in many places have exterminated the heather and the flowers. On the other hand, the yellow ants, which prefer for their materials the prickles and catkins of the pines, appear to prosper. No forest, perhaps, is richer in every species of ants.

These, then, are the true inhabitants, the true soul of the desert; the ants toiling in the sand, the quarrymen working in the sandstone. Both are of the same race; the men are ants on the surface, and the ants are men below.

I admired the resemblance in their destiny, in their laborious patience, in their admirable perseverance. The sandstone is a very refractory and rebellious substance, and often splitting badly, subjects the poor workmen to severe disappointments. Those especially who are forced by a protracted winter to return to the quarry before the end of the bad weather, find the hard and yet porous blocks excessively damp and half frozen. As a result, they have numerous ill-wrought stones, and a mass of waste. However, they do not lose their courage; and without murmuring recommence their painful toil.

The ants teach us a similar lesson of patience. The breeders of birds and game incessantly damage, overthrow, and carry away the immense works which have occupied them for a whole season. Incessantly they begin them anew with heroic ardor.

Jules Michelet

We constantly paid them a visit, and learned to sympathize with them more and more. Their patient procedures, their active and concentrated life, is, in truth, more like that of the artisan than the winged existence of the bird which formerly occupied our attention. That free inheritor of the day, that favorite of Nature, soars so high above man! To what may I compare my long laborious career? I have, indeed, caught glimpses of the sky, and sometimes heard the songs of the birds above; but, on the whole, my existence, the indefatigable labor which chains me to my task, much more nearly resembles the modest communities of the ant and the bee.

At first sight, the labors of their comrades, the quarrymen, are not very agreeable to contemplate. So many spoiled and badly quarried stones, so many fragments, so much dust and sand, have in them nothing attractive. It is but a field of ruin which is displayed before you. But what does Nature think of it? To judge by the eagerness with which the plants take possession of the sand, mingle with it, and convert it into a soil for their use, Nature is happy enough to see all this substance, which, while for thousands of years retained in the sandstone, did not enter into circulation, returning into the mobility of the Universal Life. That fortunate battle between man and the rock draws, at length, the captive element from its long enchantment. The grass seizes upon it; the tree seizes upon it; the animals seize upon it. All this sand, in which the rock never fails to end eventually, becomes permeable to the activity of a vast subterranean world.

Nothing aroused in my mind a greater number of dreams, no spectacle threw me back more directly upon myself. For I, too, through some degree of poverty or sluggishness, I have long been rebellious like this sandstone, upon which, frequently, nothing can make an impression, or which, splitting cross-wise, yields but irregular, shapeless fragments and useless refuse. It needed History, with its weighty iron hammer, to disengage me from myself, to separate me from my own obstacles, to shatter and release me.

A severe enfranchisement! What have I not lost of myself, in return for the few stones I have contributed to the great monument of the future! Sometimes, doubly stricken by the past and the present, I have felt as if I were crumbling into pieces—what say I?—into powder, into dust; and at times I have seen myself, as I see the bottom of yonder quarry, a mass of sand and rubbish.

Nevertheless, it is through these elements, through an undefinable sap hidden in the bosom of the flint, that all-powerful Nature has worked out my renovation. With a little grass and heather binding up what History and the world had crushed, she has said, smilingly: "You creature, you are Time. I am Nature, the everlasting."

Thus, then, observe the rough quarry, bristling with the *débris* of ages, which grows green, once more reproduces, and attires itself in a garb of such foliage as it never knew before man applied the iron to it. "A wild winter vegetation! Black firs! Melancholy birch-trees!" But with all the gloominess mingles the white hawthorn blossom.

What I have so eagerly craved, and yearned for, in my long years of silence, when I was as an arid block and a man of stone, was the fluid nature of the sap and its capacity of expansion. My tardy youth longed to dilate my lingering soul. Yesterday, I gave to the world "The Bird," an impulse of the heart towards light. To-day, the same force compels me, on the other hand, to descend below the earth, and embark along with you on the great living sea of metamorphoses. A world of mysteries and gloom, it is true; but where, nevertheless, the most penetrating light is thrown on the two cherished treasures of the soul—Immortality and Love.

Book the First
Metamorphosis

Chapter I. Terror and Pugnance of Childhood[6]

"Winter, summer, and nearly a... ...e fine days of the year, had passed since the departure of my father for Loui... ...a, from which he was not fated to return. Our country-house had remained ... ...rted. My mother, full of sad presentiments, and fearing herself to revisit it, s... ...ne there, one afternoon, with my brothers, to gather some fruit.

"And I went,—cherishing... ...ust own, a kind of illusion, and almost believing I should be received... ...he paternal threshold by the beloved arms.

---

[6] This fragment of a domestic jou... ...as originally intended for insertion in "The Bird." [It is from the pen of Madame Michelet.]

The Insect

"Deeply agitated, I crossed the approach to the domain, and with a spring arrived opposite the door which my father had so often opened with that ineffable smile I still can see.

"A child, and yet already a young girl, at that age of the imagination when dreams are so powerful, I opposed the obstinate need of my heart to the certain fact. I waited a moment on the threshold with a strange anxiety; the strength of my faith would fain have conquered the sad reality. But the door remained closed.

"Then, with a trembling hand, I opened it myself to find at least his shadow within. But that, too, had disappeared. An obscure world, hostile to the light, had glided into that asylum, and I was, so to speak, enveloped in it.

"His little black table—a poor family relic—and the shelves of his bookcase creaked at intervals beneath the teeth of the worm. The chamber had already put on an air of antiquity. Great motionless spiders,—guardians, as it were, of the place,—had threaded and tapestried the empty alcove. Woodlice and millipeds ran and clambered hither and thither, seeking a refuge under the panelings.

"The strange and unforeseen physiognomy of the place afflicted me so keenly that I fell back upon myself, and exclaimed, as the tears flowed down my cheeks,—'O my father! where are you?'

"From that moment could perceive nothing but the desolateness of the scene; and everywhere, in the court, in the garden, I found the new and silent guests who had taken possession of our places.

"Already the gathering mist of evening mingled with the last rays of the sun, and the slugs, tempted by the warm damp air, emerged in crowds from the leaves which strewed the garden-walks. They fared forth, slowly but surely, to feast on the fallen fruit. Clouds of wasps revelled in audacious pillage, tearing to pieces with their keen teeth our finest peaches and most luscious grapes.

"Our apple-trees, formerly so productive, were covered with network woven by the caterpillars, and offered us nothing but yellow foliage. In less than a year they had grown aged.

Jules Michelet

The Childhood's Home of Madame Michelet

"I had never before been brought in contact with a world like this. My father's vigilance, and still more successfully, the assistance of the little birds, had preserved us from it. So, in my experience, and with a heart overcome by the spectacle of so much ruin, I cursed those whom one ought not to curse, because all creatures are from God.

"Later in life, but much later, I understood the designs of Providence. When man is absent the insect ought to take his place, so that everything may pass through the great crucible, to be renewed or purified."

Such is the fear, such the instinctive repugnance of the child. But we are all children, and even Philosophy, despite its longing after universal sympathy, cannot guard against similar impressions. The apparatus of fantastic weapons with which the insect is usually armed seems to it a menace against man.

Living in a world of strife, it is imperative that the insect should be born in mail of proof, and the insects of the Tropics are frequently terrible to the eye.

Yet a considerable number of these terrifying weapons, pincers, hooks, saws, pikes, augers, screws, rollers, and dentilated teeth,—the formidable arsenal which gives them the appearance of veterans setting out for the battlefield,—prove, if we examine them rightly, to be the pacific tools with which they gain their livelihood, the implements with which they do their regular work. Here the artisan carries his workshop with him. He is at once the workman and the manufacturer. What should we say of our human operatives, if they marched ever bristling with the steel and old iron they make use of in their labors? They would appear to us very strange and monstrous, and would even fill our minds with fear.

The insect, as we shall hereafter see, is a warrior through circumstances, through the necessities of self-defense or appetite, but generally he is before all and above all industrial. There is not a single species which may not be classified according to its work, and ranged under the banner of a guild of trades.

The great achievement of the artist, or, to use the language of our ancient corporations, the test-work of this workman, by which he proves himself to be a master, is the cradle. In the Insect World, as the mother generally dies in giving birth to her child, it is important to provide an ingenious asylum which shall protect and support the orphan, and supply the mother's place. So difficult a work requires tools and implements which seem to us inexplicable. This, which you compare to a medieval poignard, to the subtly treacherous weapon of the Italian bravo, is, on the contrary, an instrument of love and maternity.

For the rest, Nature is so far from sharing our prejudices, dislikes, and childish apprehensions, that she seems specially to care for and protect the gnawing species which injuriously interfere with the economy of our small farms and plantations, but which, on the other hand, lend valuable assistance in maintaining the balance of species and keeping down the vegetable accumulation of certain climates. She preserves with watchful anxiety the caterpillars which we destroy. In the case of the oak-grub, she is mindful to glaze over or varnish its eggs, so that, concealed under the withered leaf, and beaten by winds and rains, they may safely brave the winter. The crawling worms make their appearance clothed in and defended by a thick furry garb, which deceives their enemies, until, transformed into moths, they fly to and fro in happy freedom under cover of the night.

For some she invents still greater precautions. Essential agents, undoubtedly, in the transformation of life, they possess, beyond all others, the guarantees of existence which secure them, infallibly, an immortality of race.

The grubs, for instance, alternately viviparous and oviparous, spring into full life in the summer, that they may the more quickly set to work, but are produced in autumn in the shape of an egg, that they may the better endure the cold of winter. Finally, their generous mother reserves for this beloved species an unheard-of gift,—that a moment of love shall give them the fecundity of forty generations!

Creatures so highly privileged have evidently some task to execute, some great and important mission which renders them indispensable, and makes them an essential part of the harmony of the world. Suns are necessary, but so also are gnats. Grand is the order of the Milky Way, and no less so that of the bee-hive. Who knows but that the life of the stars may be of minor importance? I see that

Jules Michelet

some of them vanish, and God dispenses with them. But no genus of the Insect World ever fails to answer to the summons. If a single species of ants should disappear, their loss would be serious, and cause a dangerous gap in the universal economy.

Chapter II. Compassion

One day, into the studio of the painter Gros entered a pupil of his, a handsome and careless young man, who had thought it clever to pin to his hat a beautiful butterfly, which, having just been captured, was still struggling painfully. The artist, indignant, broke out into a violent passion. "What, wretch!" he cried, "is this your feeling for the Beautiful? You find an exquisite creature, and can make no better use of it than to crucify and kill it barbarously! Begone, begone, and return here no more! Never again make your appearance in my presence!"

This speech will not surprise those who are acquainted with the great master's vivid sensibility, and his reverence for the Beautiful. What is more astonishing is that an anatomist, a man living with the scalpel always in his hand—Lyonnet—should speak in the same sense, and so speak in reference to insects which are to ordinary observers the least interesting. That able and patient man has opened up, as we know, an entirely new channel for science by his colossal investigation of the willow-grub, from which we learn that the muscular development of the insect is identical with that of the higher animals. Lyonnet congratulates himself that he was able to bring his prolonged labors to a conclusion without killing more than eight or nine individuals of the species he wished to describe.

A noble result of study! In fathoming life by this persevering toil, far from growing coldly indifferent, he became more intensely sympathetic. The minute details of the infinitely little had revealed to him the sources of the keen sensibility which Nature has hidden everywhere. He had found it existing at the bottom of the animal scale, and thus he acquired a due reverence for every form of life.

We are sometimes disquieted, repelled, and dismayed by insects exactly in proportion to our ignorance. Nevertheless almost every species, especially in our European climates, is perfectly harmless. But we suspect the unknown; and we are apt to kill those with which we are not acquainted, by way of acquiring knowledge.

I remember that, one morning in June, about four o'clock, when the sun was already high in the heavens, I was aroused somewhat abruptly, though still much fatigued and very sleepy. I was living in the country, and my chamber, which faced the east, having neither curtain nor shutter, the sun's rays fell full upon my bed. A magnificent drone, I do not know how, had made its way into the room, and joyously fluttered and buzzed in the sunshine. I grew weary of the noise. I arose, and thinking he wished to sally forth, threw open the window. But no; such was not his intention. The morning, though beautiful, was very fresh and damp: he preferred to remain indoors, in a more genial temperature, which dried and warmed him. Without, it was four A.M.; within, it was already noon. He acted precisely as I should have done, and would not depart. Willing to give him time, I left the window open, and returned to my bed; but I could not sleep. The fresh air from without entering into the room, my drone entered further and further, and buzzed about and around. The obstinate and importunate guest excited in me an angry feeling, and I started up, determined to expel him by main force. A handkerchief was my weapon, but undoubtedly I made use of it very unskillfully. I stunned, confused, and frightened the drone; he whirled round and round in a dizzy fit, but thought less than ever of quitting the chamber. My impatience increased: I pursued him with greater, with too great impetuosity. He fell on the window-sill, and rose no more.

Was he dead, or stunned? I would not close the window, thinking that in the latter case the air might revive him, and he would fly away. Meanwhile, by no means satisfied with what I had done, I threw myself on my bed. On the whole, it was his own fault. Why did he not escape? Such was my first reflection; but afterwards I grew more severe in self-judgment, and accused my impatience. So great is the tyranny of man, he can endure nothing. Like all kings, this lord of creation is impetuous, and at the slightest contradiction breaks out into a fury, and kills.

Very beautiful was the morning; fresh, and yet, by degrees, growing almost warm; a happy mixture of temperature, proper to that delightful country and that season of the year: it was Normandy, and the month of June. The peculiar characteristic of this month, distinguishing it from all those that follow, is, that it gives birth to the innocent species which live on vegetable food, but to none of the murderous races which need a living prey,—that it breeds flies, but not spiders. Death has not yet begun, and love reigns everywhere. All these ideas occurred to me, but proved by no means agreeable; for at this blessed, sacred time, when a universal confidence prevails, I had already *killed*: man alone had broken the peace of God. The thought was very bitter. Whether the victim was great or small, mattered but little; the dead was always the dead. And it was without any serious occasion, without provocation, that I had brutally disturbed the sweet harmony of Spring, and spoiled the universal idyl.

While revolving all these thoughts, I glanced occasionally from my bed towards the window, and watched if the drone did not stir a little, if he were really dead. Unhappily he gave not a sign: his immobility was complete.

This lasted for half-an-hour, or about three-quarters; then suddenly— without, so far as I could see, the slightest preliminary movement—my drone arose with a strong and steady flight, and without the slightest hesitancy, as if nothing had befallen him. He passed out into the garden, which by that time was thoroughly warmed and filled with sunshine.

I confess that I found in his escape a happiness and a relief; but as for my drone, he had never lost heart. I perceived that he had thought in his tiny prudence that if, by the least sign, he had betrayed his returning vitality, his executioner would have finished him. Accordingly, he imitated death with wonderful fidelity, waiting until he had quite recovered his strength and breath,—until his wings, dry and warm, were fully ready to carry him away; and then, at one leap, he was off, without saying *adieu*.

It was during a journey in Switzerland,—in the land of the Hallers, the Hubers, and the Bonnets,—that we began to study seriously; no longer contenting ourselves with collections which only displayed the exterior, but determined on examining the inner organs with microscope and scalpel. Then also we committed our first crimes.

I have no need to say that this preoccupation, this emotion—far more dramatic than one would have supposed—interfered with our journey. The sublime, enchanting, and solemn scenes of Switzerland lost, no doubt, their due power over us. But life—suffering life (and we were compelled to make it suffer)—diverted our thoughts. The hymn or eternal epopea of these infinitely great could scarcely vie with the drama of our infinitely little organisms. A fly hid from us the Alps; the agony of a beetle, which was ten days dying, veiled Mont Blanc from our gaze; in the anatomy of an ant we forgot the Jungfrau.

It matters not; for who shall rightly determine what is really great or little? Everything is great, everything important, everything equal in the bosom of nature and the impartiality of universal love. And where is it more perceptible than in the infinite travail of the little organic world on which our eyes were fixed? To lift them towards the mountains, or lower them towards the insects, was one and the same thing.

Jules Michelet
EXTRACT FROM MADAME MICHELET'S JOURNAL.

"On the 20th of July, a very hot day, but freshened nevertheless by the morning breeze which disported on the lake between Chillon and Clarens, I went out for a walk alone, my husband remaining indoors to write. The sun shot athwart our valleys of the Pays de Vaud, and poured his full splendor on the opposite mountains of Savoy. The lake, already illumined, reflected the sharp ridges of the rocks, whose base, clothed in pastures, lends life and freshness to its borders.

"By-and-by the sun turned, and the scene changed. A warm ray of light penetrated beyond Chillon, the long defile of the Valais, illuminated the pointed Dent du Midi, and colored in vapour the summit of the remote St. Bernard. But to this scene of glory I preferred the morning hour, when our Montreux reposed in shadow. It was the hour of divine service at its little church, whose terrace, half-way down the slope, propped up by sharp acclivities, wooded, and therefore obscure, pours out the crystal waters on the thirsty vineyards lying below. Beneath the terrace a beautiful mossy grot, glittering with stalactites, preserves a delightful feeling of freshness. The fane above, surrounded by hospitable wooden seats; a small library (a second temple), whence the vine-dressers borrow books; and, finally, a pretty fountain, combine in a graceful little picture, austerely charming. At morning especially, in the half-misty veil which foretokens a day of heat, this beautiful spot has all the effect of a religious thought, concentrating in itself, and yet extended over that immense panorama which the mind embraces, admires, and blesses.

"I frequently resorted thither, ascending the first slope of the mountain, solitary, and enriched with flowers. I took with me a book, and yet I never read. The prospect was too absorbing. Whether the eye ranged afar over the level mirror of the lake, and the rocks of Meillerie, with their forests, meadows, and precipices; or hovered close at hand about the nest of Clarens and the low towers of Chillon; or, finally, returned to the pretty villas, with their green lattices, of our friends the physician and the pastor,[7] in whose company my husband labored;—I remained there in a kind of dream, and my heart, deeply moved, felt the sweetness of a holy harmony.

---

[7] It was our good fortune to reside, while at Montreux—the most beautiful spot on the wide earth—with a very estimable and rare individual, whom I should have thought of Italian or Spanish birth, if I had not known her to be a Genevese, and the sister of the able and enthusiastic historian of Geneva. Next door lived an eminent physician, of simple character, but all the more learned in natural studies.

The Insect

"But soon I discovered that I was not utterly alone. Bees, or drones, which had also risen early, were already at work, seeking in the cups of the flowers the honey distilled beneath the dew, penetrating into the depths of the campanulas, or skillfully gliding into the mysterious corolla of the charming Venus's Slipper. Brilliant cicindelas opened the hunt after the gnats, while more unwieldy tribes sought their livelihood at the bottom of the herbage.

"On this day, then, the 20th of July, allowing my glance to fall mechanically at my feet, and withdrawing my eyes for a moment from the too luminous picture, I saw with astonishment a scene which vividly contrasted with this attractive and holy spot,—an atrocious warlike struggle. The insect-giant which we call the stag-beetle, one of the largest of European species, a black shining mass, whose horns bristle with superb crescent-wise pincers, had seized upon a beetle of far inferior size. Nevertheless, the two enemies being equally provided with admirable defensive arms, after the fashion of the corselets, armlets, and cuisses of our ancient knights, the struggle was long and fierce. Both belonged to the murderous race which prey on little insects,—were powerful lords in the habit of devouring their vassals. Whichever had fallen victim in the fray, the Lilliputian people had certainly applauded. However, the blind instinctive movement which leads us, in such cases, to separate the combatants, induced me to interfere; and with the point of my umbrella, skillfully, delicately, and without wounding the two antagonists, I compelled the stronger of the two to release its grasp."

The captive thus secured was, without form of trial, adjudged to undergo our investigations as a punishment for his fratricidal voracity. Our system, however, is not to impale the insect,—a horrible punishment and a pitiful spectacle which has no end; for a month afterwards, ay, and more, you will see the poor transfixed wretches writhing in agony. Ether generally kills them rapidly, and apparently painlessly. Well, then, we *etherized* our prisoner largely. In a moment he spun round and fell: we thought him finished. An hour or two passed, and lo! he was once more alive, once more upright on trembling feet, and attempting to walk; he fell, and again he rose. But, to tell the truth, his gait was like that of a drunken man. A child would have laughed at it. We had no desire to laugh, being obliged to poison him a second time. A stronger dose was accordingly administered; but in vain,—he came again to himself. It was a curious circumstance; but it certainly seemed as if this kind of intoxication, while weakening and almost paralyzing the faculties of motion, had all the more keenly excited the nerves, and what we may call the amorous faculties. The use he sought to make of his vacillating step and last efforts was to join a female of his species which we had found lying dead, and placed upon the table. He felt her with his palpi and trembling arms. He contrived to turn her over, and tumbled about (very probably he could not see) to assure himself whether she was alive. He would not part from her: one would have sworn that he had undertaken, though dying, to resuscitate the dead. It was a fantastic, a gloomy, and yet, for one who knows at heart that all nature is identical, a touching spectacle.

It afflicted us greatly; we attempted to shorten it by the help of the ether, and to separate this Juliet from her Romeo. But the indomitable male laughed at all our poisons, and dismally dragged himself along. We shut him up in a large box, where he did not die until after a considerable period, and incredibly large doses. His punishment—and, reader, you may justly call it *ours*—endured for fully fifteen days.

This robust, enduring being, with his inextinguishable flame of life, threw us into a prolonged reverie.

On our first dabbling in bloodshed, Nature had wished to show us, and with a master's hand, the strange and unconquerable energy with which she has endowed life. "Love is strong as death." Where do we find this saying? In the Bible. Yes; and it is also the eternal Bible. For what more powerfully consecrates existence, and renders it sympathetic, reverend, and sacred? And how great a pity it is, then, to cut it short at the divine moment when every being has its share of God!

We excused ourselves by saying that this insect, which lives six years in a single night, could have spread its wings beneath the sky but two months longer,—just long enough to perpetuate its race. We deprived it, therefore, of a very little time—a month out of six or seven years.

Yes; but that month was the epoch to which all its life had tended. Previously it had only vegetated; but then, it could really have lived and reigned, powerful and joyous. Long an insect, in that hour it would have become almost a bird, a son of the flower-enamelled earth and the genial light. We had acted like the Parceæ, which delight in cutting the thread of our lives at the very moment of happiness!

Chapter III. World-Builders

There is a world under this world, above, below, and all around it, of which we have no suspicion.

Occasionally, indeed, we catch a faint murmur, a sound, and thereupon we say, "It is a trifle, it is nothing." But this nothing is the Infinite.

The Infinite of the invisible life, the silent life, the world of night and of the inner earth, of the shadowy ocean,—the unseen creatures of the air which we breathe, or which, mingling in the fluids we drink, circulate within us unperceived.

An immensely powerful world, which in its details we scorn, but which at intervals affrights us, when it stands revealed before our eyes in one of its grand unforeseen manifestations.

The navigator, for example, who at night sees the ocean shimmering with lustre and wreathing garlands of fire, is at first diverted by the spectacle. He sails ten leagues; the garland is indefinitely prolonged; it stirs, and twists, and knots itself in harmony with the motions of the wave; it becomes a monstrous serpent ever extending its sinuous length to thirty, ay, and forty leagues. Yet all this is but a dance of imperceptible animalcules! What are their numbers? At this question the imagination starts back aghast; it perceives in the distance a nature of gigantic force, of terrific wealth, but possessing little relation to the other, the well-ordered, and, in a certain degree, economical nature, of the higher life.

It is impossible to speak of insects or molluscs without naming these animalcules, which seem to be their rough outline, and in the extreme simplicity of their organism already foretoken, indicate, and prepare for them. With a good microscope you can discern these miniatures of the insect, which simulate their organism, and mimic their movements. When you are able to distinguish the *Rotifers*, you think that in the aggregations and in the tentacles of their mouth you recognize them as little polypes. The *Rhizopods*, though almost imperceptible, are furnished, nevertheless, with good solid carapaces, which are equally as good a protection for them as their great shells are for the molluscs, the oyster and the snail. The microscopic *Tardigradæ* are, in fact, closely connected with insects, and the *Acarina* with worms.

What are these least of the little? Simply the architects or builders of the globe which we inhabit. With their bodies and their remains they have prepared the soil now echoing under our feet. Whether their tiny shells be still distinguishable, or whether they have been decomposed into chalk, they are not the less the foundation of immense portions of our earth. A single bed of this chalk stretches from Paris to Tours; that is, for fifty miles. Another, of enormous breadth, spreads over all Champagne. Pure chalk, or Spanish white, which we find everywhere, is composed of pounded shells.

And it is these most minute of organisms which have wrought the grandest of works. The imperceptible rhizopod has built for itself a nobler monument than the Pyramids; nothing less than Central Italy, a notable portion of the chain of the Apennines. But even this was too insignificant: the colossal masses of Chili, the prodigious Cordilleras, which look down upon the world at their feet, are the funeral monument wherein this impalpable—I had almost said invisible-organism has interred the remains of its vanished race.

A bygone world, hidden beneath the present and upper world in the profundities of life or the obscurity of time!

What might it not tell us, if God would give it speech, and permit it to recall all that it has done or is doing for us! What just demands might not the elementary plants, the imperfect animals whose dust has fashioned for our use the fertile crust of the globe, that noble theatre of life, address to us! "While you were still asleep," might say the ferns, "we alone, by transforming and purifying the previously irrespirable air, created after thousands upon thousands of years the earth now blooming with the corn and the rose! We accumulated that subterranean treasure of enormous coal-beds which warms your hearth; and that one mass, among others, a hundred leagues in length, which feeds the great forge of the world from London to Newcastle."

"We," the imperceptibles might say,—the obscure and unnamed animalcules despised or ignored by man,—"we are thy guardians, have laid out thy fields, and built thy dwelling-places. It is not the great fossil rhinoceros or mastodon whose bones have made thy soil; it is *our* work—or rather, it is ourselves. Thy cities, thy Louvres, and thy Capitols are constructed with our débris. Life itself in its essence, in that sparkling beverage by which France diffuses joy over all the earth, whence comes it? From arid hills where the vine thrives in the white dust that once was *we*, and absorbs the concealed warmth of our prior existences."

The demand made upon us would be a lengthened one; restitution impossible. These dead myriads, having nourished with their lime the various articles that form our sustenance, have passed into our very being. Others also would put forth a claim. The very pebble, the hard flint, once lived, and now nourishes life.

Great was the astonishment in Europe when a Berlin professor—Ehrenberg—informed us that the silicious stone, so sharp, rough, and brittle, the *tripoli* with which metals are polished, is neither more nor less than an aggregation of dead animalcules, an accumulation of the shells of infusoria of a terrible diminutiveness. So small is the creature I speak of, that it takes one hundred and eighty-seven millions to weigh a grain.

The labors of the unseen architects of the globe, admired by our men of science in extinct species, travelers have discovered revived in living species. They have surprised, in our own day, immense laboratories in permanent activity, of beings invisible in themselves, or apparently powerless, but really of boundless capacity of toil, if we judge by its results. What death accomplishes for life, life itself relates. Numbers of tiny organisms become by their present works the interpreters and historians of their vanished predecessors.

These, like the latter, with their structures, or their débris, build up islands in the sea, and construct immense banks of reefs, which, gradually joining together, will become new lands. Without going further than Sicily, we find among the madrepores, that cover its coasts torn by volcanic fires, a little animal, the zoophyte, which has accomplished a task man would never have dared to undertake. He contrives to move forward by protecting his soft body with a shield of stone which he incessantly secretes. Continuously developing the tubes which in succession afford him shelter, he entirely fills up the empty spaces left by the madrepores or corals, bridges over the intervals between the reefs, and connects them with one another; finally, he creates a passage in defiles previously impassable. In due time this builder will have accomplished the colossal task of a causeway all around the island in its circumference of a hundred and eighty leagues.

But it is more particularly in the vast Southern Ocean that these works are prosecuted on a grand scale by the polypes of the lime, the corallines, and madrepores of every kind; an animal vegetation worthy of comparison with the labor of the mosses in a peat-moor, which continue to flourish in their upper growth while the lower are transformed and decomposed. Exactly like these vegetables, the polypes, and even their production, the coral, while still soft and tender, frequently become the nourishment of worms and fishes which feed and browse upon them like our cattle, derive their sustenance from them, and return them in the shape of chalk, without the slightest indication of a previous existence! Recently English seamen have discovered at the bottom of the sea this manufacture of chalk, which is incessantly passing from the living into the inorganic condition.

But these destructive causes do not prevent the polypes from imperturbably carrying on their gigantic labors, incessantly elevating the islands and solid barriers which are so skillfully adapted to resist the oceanic action. They divide the work among themselves according to their species. The idlest execute their share in the quiet waters, or in the great depths, remotest from the light; others, under the sunshine, among the very breakers of which they eventually become the masters.

Soft, gelatinous, elastic, adhering to their support, the stony and porous mass; they deaden the fury of the boiling waters which would wear out the granite, and split the rock into fragments.

Under the mild trade-winds which prevail in the tropic climates, the sea would uniformly flow with a tranquil tide if it did not encounter these living ramparts, which force it back upon itself, scatter its waves in spray, and vex it with everlasting torment.

That the waters should assault them is their fate. But they inflict no injury upon them; and in truth it is on their behalf they toil. Their violence does not wear *them*, but it wears the reef, and detaches in atoms the lime on which they live and with which they build. This lime, absorbed by them and *animalized*, changes into a hundred sparkling, living, active flowers, which are identical with our polypes, and form quite an analogous world enamelling the ocean-bed.

On the margin of these islands,—which are generally circular, like a ring,—accumulates a layer of vegetable wealth, which speedily grows green, and embellishes itself with the only tree that can endure salt-water, the cocoa-nut palm. This, then, is the *humus*; the life which will for ever continue to develop. The fresh springs and fountains will next make their appearance, invited and fed by the vegetation.

Such is the original type of a young world which in due time will be inhabited. The cocoa-palm will have its insects; the birds will pause on its boughs; men will gather its fruit. Wrecked ships and floating timbers, propelled by the sea, will bring there after awhile tenants of every kind.

Some of these islands, when extended, enlarged, and solidified, measure not less than twenty-five miles in circumference. Many are larger still; fertile, inhabited, and populous, like the Maldives.

The ambition of their architects might rest contented, you would think, with these vast creations. But to insure their fixity, they have increased their extent. The buttresses by which they strengthen their work at the bottom of the sea being prolonged and elevated, expand into banks, which link the isles to each other over an immense area. Along the line of burning life, in the tropic zone, these indefatigable builders have daringly intersected the sea and worked athwart its currents, and already are arresting the courses of our navigators.

New Caledonia is now surrounded by a reef of 145 leagues in length. The chain of the Maldive Islands measures 480 English miles. To the east of New Holland stretches a bank of polypes over 360 leagues, 127 of these without interruption. Finally, in the Pacific Ocean the mass known as the Dangerous Archipelago is about 400 leagues in length by 150 in breadth.

If they continue after this fashion, incessantly connecting their various piles of submarine masonry, they will perhaps realize the prophecy of Kirby, who discerned in the coral isles and reefs the possibility of a new world—a brilliant and fertile world; and in the course of centuries may accomplish the formation of a causeway, an immense bridge, connecting Asia with America.

Chapter IV. Love and Death

Above the infinite elementary life,—that quasi-vegetable life in which generation is but, as it were, a-budding,—begins the distinct, individual, and complete organism whose strongly centralized electric network of nerves is able to sympathize directly with the rapid energy of its acts and resolutions.

However humble the insect may seem in appearance, it is from the first independent of the immovable, expectant existence of all the inferior races. It is born entirely free from that communistic fatalism which merges the being of each in the life of all. It exists independently; it moves, goes, comes, advances or returns, changes its determination or its direction at pleasure, or in obedience to its wants, appetites, and caprices. It suffices for itself; it foresees, provides, defends, and boldly confronts the most unexpected chances.

In this, then, do we not discern, as it were, a first glimpse of personality?

The individual stands out from the mass. He shows himself all at once admirably provided with the instruments necessary for the support and sustenance of the individual existence. He is born greedy and *absorbent*. But this very absorbingness is exactly the service which Nature expects of him. It is his mission to purify and disencumber the world; to clear it of morbid or extinct animal matter, which acts as an obstacle to the growth of life; to save the latter from the consequences of its excessive fecundity, the danger of its abundance.

No other being, as we shall prove, exercises so great an influence upon our globe; no other throws itself into the condition of general existence with so vital an energy. But this extraordinary strength, in such disproportion to the size, bulk, and weight of the insect, is subject to a severe law; the rapid, absolute, and complete renewal, at each generation, of the individual.

Love implies death. To engender and to beget is to die. He who is born, by the very act of his birth kills.

This is a sentence common to all beings, but carried out upon none more literally than upon the insect.

In the first place, it is death for the father to love. It is indispensable that he should surrender all his powers, and exhaust the best part of his vitality; that he should perish in himself, to revive in him to whom he shall have transmitted his germ of resurrection.

And for the mother, too, in most of the insect species, the condemnation is the same. She will love, give birth, and speedily die. Love for her shall not have its prize and recompense. She shall not see her sons. She shall not enjoy the consolations of death in seeing herself survive in her image.

A great and harsh difference between this mother and the mothers of superior animals! The woman—or the female of the mammal—as a rule cherishes in her own body her beloved treasure, warms it with her own flame, and feeds it with her love. How envious would be the insect-mother, if she knew of this supreme maternal happiness! But *she* must seek of an ungenial nature, must demand of some other being—tree, plant, fruit, or perhaps the earth itself—that it will condescend to continue the work of her maternity. This is rigorous, but it is not cruel. Let us look at it seriously. If death separate the mother and the child, it is because they cannot live together; because they are strongly sundered by the opposite conditions of life and nutrition. The child, at first a lowly grub, larva, or worm, an obscure miner, a concealed nocturnal worker, must for a long time continue to feed upon the coarsest food, and sometimes even on death itself. She, the mother, who, winged and transfigured, has mounted to a higher life; and lives solely on the honied sweets of flowers,—how could she accustom herself to the shades, and the useful but abject circumstances in which her offspring grows strong? That which is salutary and vital for the tenebrous child of the earth would be fatal to an aërial mother, who has already fluttered in the warmth and genial light of heaven.

It is needful for the due development of the child that its mother should provide it with a triple or quadruple cradle, and there deposit it; not neglected, and without succor, but furnished with its first aliment—an aliment light and fitted for its feebleness, which it can find on its waking up into life. This done, she closes the door, seals it, and voluntarily excludes and interdicts herself from returning thither. Thenceforth she must cede her rights to the universal mother, who shall replace her—Nature.

That in such a cradle the child should live commodiously,—that from its own body it should draw out a silky covering to line its plastic prison,—that finally, when sufficiently strong, it should issue forth under the influence of the heat,—this is self-explanatory, and we admire without being astonished. But what really excites our wonder is, that the mother,—a butterfly, or perhaps a beetle,—after the numerous changes through which she has passed, after her numerous sloughings, transitory slumbers, and metamorphoses, should remember, for her offspring's behoof, the place or plant where formerly she herself was nourished, and grew, and took her point of departure! It is a marvel which confounds the mind. Those creatures apparently the most heedless—the fly, or light-headed butterfly—at the moment when approaching death brightens them with the radiance of love, collect, as it were, their thoughts, and seem to revive their recollections. Then, without lapse or error, they flee away; and lo! the plant which was their own early residence, their birthplace, and their cradle, shall again become their home, and protect their offspring!

The Insect

All at once they show themselves prudent, foreseeing, and skilful. To obtain an entrance to this asylum, they practice unknown arts and display incredible address. How is this? What happens? Sometimes their weapons of war, diverted to other uses, become instruments of love; sometimes new and hitherto concealed apparatus,—frequently of an extremely complex character,—make their appearance; and yet all for this solitary act, for this single day.

A curious book has been written on the mechanism and infinitely varied instrumentation with which insects are provided for the discharge of the maternal duty. Their implements are often charming from their precision, delicacy, and subtlety. It will suffice to particularize that of the rose-bush aphis,— so well described by Réaumur, as a saw whose two blades act in an inverse direction, and whose teeth are each a set of teeth.

O unheard-of power of Love! Whether this divine workman prepares for them their tiny tools, or whether he inspires them to fashion their own by the effort and vehemency of the burning maternal desire, it matters not: you see them duly fabricated, and acting when wanted in a wholly unexpected manner.

It is a simple task for the tribes of sociable insects which labor with the assistance and protection of a numerous republic; but it is infinitely arduous and painful for the solitary mothers, who, without auxiliary, spouse, or friend, undertake enormous enterprises, and frequently raise constructions which might be the work of giants,—such as the nest of the mason-wasp. One is lost in astonishment at the amount of patience and strength of will required for so colossal an edifice.

This excessive toil ages the mother in a few days. She wears herself out, yet does not enjoy the fruit. Frequently the elaborate cradle serves for another. Too frequently a usurping stranger seizes upon it, profits by the meritorious work, and establishes there its progeny, which will not only consume the provision of the rightful tenant, but feed also on the unfortunate tenant himself!

Who will not bestow a glance of pity on this great work, and a result of such uncertain character?

In the burning days of July, when the narrow belt of forests surrounding Fontainebleau concentrated upon it the summer heats, we were astonished at the incessant and continuous labor, despite the indolence of the season, of a solitary bee which was ever going and coming. Her indefatigable journeys always brought her near some vases of camelias and rose-bays. I saw her, still fair and shapely, of a beautiful brown mingled with black, returning, at regular intervals of about five minutes, with woven fragments of leaves, which she introduced through a deep aperture into the soil of the vase where she had made her nest.

For three days she worked with undiminished ardor. There were no signs that she took the least food: constantly at her work, she appeared to have already abandoned all care for her own life.

Her preoccupation was so great and her activity so eager that we were able to approach her very closely. Nothing frightened her; so that we could establish ourselves at our ease near her little nest, and observe her with as much patience as she herself brought to her work.

On the fourth morning we found the opening closed, and we saw her no more. She had completed her task. Exhausted, but rejoicing at its conclusion, she had retired undoubtedly to some obscure recess to await her destiny.

We proceeded delicately to loosen the soil around the sides of the vase, in order to examine into what she had done.

At the bottom, resembling in shape a couple of thimbles, lay two cradles, and in these cradles two little ones. All the care had been for them: so many young, so many cells.

Each was composed of six-and-twenty fragments of leaves. Réaumur, in a similar nest, counted but sixteen. Six of these fragments, which closed up the entrance, were perfectly round,—a remarkable fact, if we bear in mind that the instrument which achieved the work was by no means appropriate to it. Yet they were as accurately finished off as if done by a punch.

The other portions of leaf, cut into ovals, and carefully placed one upon another in due accordance with the contour of the nest, resembled so many roofs designed by the indefatigable mother as a protection against the wind and rain. At the bottom lay a little honey; the last and tender legacy of the mother, bequeathed by her to those whom she had abandoned for ever.

We shall enjoy the satisfaction of seeing them weave their winter shelter. It will be pleasanter for them under our roof than at the bottom of the vase. The mother's intentions will be carefully carried out. Adopted, tended, and removed to Paris, the nymphs of Fontainebleau will take, one fine morning in spring, their flight above our windows, and, as young bees, will be able to gather, if not the honey of the heather, at least that of the Luxembourg.

Chapter V. The Orphan: Its Feebleness[8]

We have told the easiest and pleasantest story to relate, the story of the privileged creature for whom its mother has duly provided, and who is nourished and clothed by her efforts. But many—in truth, the greatest number—enter life destitute and necessitous. They fall naked into the great world.

Poverty the audacious, necessity the ingenious, the severe internal travail of hunger and desire, stimulate and develop the energetic organs which come to their assistance.

What organs? The great Swammerdam, the martyr of patience, was the first to distinguish them. With a piercing eye, examining the newly-hatched egg,—that dubious foundation!—he seized the opening lineaments of life, and marked in them the profound and decisive characters which make the mystery of the insect. He saw the little creature, with its gelatinous body, push forward its mandible or jaws,—a distinct and complete organ, placed in front of the mouth, and visibly intended to nourish and protect the still feeble being.

---

[8] *La Frileuse,*—literally, "The chilly one."

Behind this active apparatus he detected on the sides of the body a passive apparatus, a series of tiny mouths or valves (the *stigmata*) which await the air, and open to receive it.

Ingenious precautions! The orphan born completely naked, and launched into life unprotected to undergo the most toilsome metamorphoses, is rendered competent for the task only by eating greedily from the moment of its birth, absorbing and devouring! It must eat always and everywhere, even in the least respirable atmosphere, and in unhealthy and deadly places. It is for this reason nature has endowed it with a slower, and, if I may so speak, a more suspicious circulation and respiration, than that of the superior creatures which live only in pure air. In these creatures, as in man, the blood continually flows to meet the air and be vivified by it. In the insect, on the contrary, the protecting apparatus which guards its lateral mouths are disposed in such a manner as to be able always to moderate, sift, and, if need be, exclude, the invading atmosphere. One is overcome with surprise by the infinite variety of the combinations designed for this end, the numerous mechanical and chemical arts of the most complicated character. To receive and yet not receive, to breathe without breathing, to preserve the control of what must nevertheless be a passive function, to trust and yet mistrust, to surrender and yet protect, is the difficult problem which life here proposed to itself, and of which it has found innumerable solutions. To give air to a grub! Behold, arrogant humanity, which callest thyself the centre of all things, the most laborious effort that has engrossed the powers of nature!

Its circulation resembles that of the embryo in the bosom of its mother. But how much less favorable the condition of the insect! The fœtus is in immediate contact with the world through the soft maternal medium. The motherless insect embryo does not swim, like the other, in a sea of milk. It is cradled in the rude mould of the universal life; it travels therein at great peril, on the rude earth, from shock to shock.

This fact the moderns have recognized,—*the insect is an embryo*. But who would suppose that this very circumstance would doom it to death? How rude a contradiction! An embryo launched into the thick of the fray, to be the victim of all—of birds, and even of insects. An embryo armed, it is true; and nothing is stranger than to see the soft grubs brandishing their threatening jaws, while their feeble body, deprived of all defense, is exposed on every side.

Flight offers them but few chances; their best protection is night. And therefore they shun the light,—they live as they can under the ground, in the wood, or at least beneath the leaf. If this be true of the larvæ, the grubs, of what we call worms, we may say the same of the insect. For its first period (that of the larva) endures a considerable time, though its life as a nymph, and finally its third period, last but a very brief while. Numerous species (May-bugs, stag-beetles, and the like) have three to six years of a tenebrous existence, and only three months under the sun.

Even the insects which live longest in the sun, like the bees and the ants, work willingly in obscurity; are partial to the shadows of their hives and ant-hills.

The Insect

We may assert as a general rule that *the insect is the child of night.*

Most insects shun the day. But how can they avoid the air? Even in hot countries, the contact of the variable atmosphere with a live nude body, whose epidermis is not yet hardened, becomes infinitely painful. In our severe climates, each breath of air must produce the sensation of piercing arrows, of a million of fine needles. What would it be, O Heaven, for a poor human fœtus to issue, after a week or a fortnight, from its mother's womb, and instead of peacefully undergoing the transformations which strengthen it, to be subjected to them in a naked condition and in open day? What would be its sensations on quitting its soft asylum, and falling into the cold air? Yet such must be those of the insect, when, soft, feeble, assailable, and penetrable everywhere, still almost floating and gelatinous to the eye, it experiences the cold, and the wind, and the shock of so many painful accidents.

Certain clothed species are a little better protected. Some are lodged in the heart of a fruit. Others (bees and ants) form a protecting community; but the immense majority are born solitary and naked.

Some of our readers, always well clothed and warmed, will say, I am sure, that cold is an excellent thing, which stimulates the appetite and strengthens the frame. But those who have been poor will very well understand my preceding observations. For my part, recollections of my childhood convince me that cold is, in all truth, a punishment; you cannot get accustomed to it; its prolongation does not render its effect less severe. How keen a joy I felt (in rigorous winters) at each thaw which released me from my agitated, terrified, and uneasy condition, and secured the happy re-establishment of the internal harmony!

I do not deny, however, that cold may not be a powerful tonic, which sharpens and braces up the mind, and draws from it fresh efforts of invention. Cold, as well as hunger—and perhaps hunger especially—is the great stimulus of the arts; hunger weakens, cold strengthens.

It is the powerful inspirer of infinite swarms of those chilly creatures which seek before all things, as soon as they are born, the means of covering themselves. They are not in want of food; nature has everywhere prepared for them an ample banquet. All the vegetable kingdom, and a great part of the animal, are at their disposal; they might live tender and indolent, as the child sleeps at its ease on the maternal placenta which nourishes its slothfulness. But the cold irritates them; the cold damp air deadens and paralyzes their entrails; finally, the light wounds them. They can enjoy no repose until they have secured a shelter. In the lowest grade of life the smallest grub becomes an artist, and by weaving, and spinning, and carving has soon contrived a robe, and, as with a second skin over her too sensitive epidermis, has covered her suffering nakedness. Happy she who finds herself placed at the outset on a prepared soil, a cloth of warm wool, a fine fur: she does not fail to make in hot haste, according to our human fashion, a pretty paletot fitted to her figure; which, nevertheless, she leaves a little loose, like economical mothers for their young growing children, in whose case the garb too large to-day will be tight and well-fitting to-morrow.

Those who on their birth come in contact with chill green leaves, and their lustrous glaze, are still more industrious. They practice arts which astonish the observer. Some raise enormous masses with imperceptible cables, and by mechanical processes analogous to those which were employed in removing and rearing the obelisk of the Place de la Concorde. Others cut out figures purposedly irregular, which the seam afterwards fits into its harmonious *ensemble.*

Every industrial corporation may be found represented in this little world: tailors, weavers, felters, spinners, miners, and the like. And in each corporation you meet with species working each after its peculiar fashion, by the various processes appropriate to it.

The tailors work from a pattern. They mark out on the leaf a suitable piece; which they remove, and lay upon another leaf; tack it, cut out a second on the first model, and stitch them together. This done, with their scaly head they flatten the ribs, just as the tailor smooths down the seams with his iron. Then they line this coat, which they carry about with them, with the very finest silk.

Others work in mosaic, others in marquetry and veneering. After having woven the robe, they disguise it by artistically gluing to it a variety of surrounding materials. The aquatic insects, for example, embellish theirs with moss, lentils, mussels, or little snails.

The miners erect galleries between a couple of leaves, and roam about in them, constructing places of exit and ingress in their subterranean abodes.

The labor is great. But among all the species an admirable justice prevails. Whoso works hard while a child, does little when an adult; and *vice versâ.* The bee, which in the larva state is richly fed by its parents, and always carried about and cradled, is destined hereafter to an exceedingly laborious life.

On the contrary, another insect which, as a grub, has toiled, and woven, and spun, will having nothing to do in its later life but whisper love-phrases to the rose. I am speaking of Sir Butterfly.

For the great majority, hard work is for infancy, for the larva or the grub; work twofold and excessive. On the one hand, the constant, urgent, and pressing search after the food craved for by an immense internal need; the necessity of recruiting and renewing its energies, of restoring the inherited organs, and developing new ones.

The existence of these poor motherless creatures is divided between two severe conditions: toil, and growth through disease.

For their moultings, or sloughings, are, in effect, a disease.

The painful moment having arrived for the little creature to change its clothing, a clothing which clings to its flesh, it is seized with illness, abandons its leaf, and creeps languidly to some solitary asylum. If you saw it in such a soft, inert, and withered condition, so different from its natural state, you would say it was on the point of death. And many do, indeed, succumb at this laborious crisis.

Passive, and suspended to a branch, it waits until nature shall complete its work,—until its epidermis be detached from the second skin beneath, recalling it to all the energies of life.

The Insect

It is then that you see the garb, which was formerly so brilliant, dry up and harden like a thenceforth useless thing, carried hither and thither by the wind.

But before it will yield and separate, the invalid, despite of its weakness, must twist in every direction, and writhe, and swell, and contract, and employ all the efforts of a being in its strongest moments.

At length it has conquered; the old sheath is rent; and I see the insect free, but bathed in sweat.

Do not touch it yet, for the slightest pressure will wound. Of this it is aware, and lies perfectly motionless. It is pale, and almost swooning; it must wait patiently, before beginning to move, till its skin is less sensitive and its limbs are much firmer. Soon, fortunately, it will be invigorated by its food; it feels a terrible hunger, which restores its strength and prepares it for another sloughing. Such is its destiny. It is condemned to deliver itself continually in a series of *accouchements*, until it finally attains its latest transformation.

If either the exertion or the pain inspire it with a transient gleam of thought, it would say, on each painful occasion: "Now it is ended! I have finished my task; I will rest in peace; this is my last change." To which Nature would respond: "Not yet! not yet! Thou art not yet engendered. What art thou? Nothing but a larva, a mask which is about to fall."

What! A mask! and yet it wills and toils, strives and suffers, and sometimes seems more advanced than will be the being produced from it! So much industry and skill imprisoned in a skin which will immediately dry up and be blown away by the breeze!

However this may be, it is seized one morning by an undefinable kind of irritability and disquiet,—by a mysterious impulse which excites it to undertake a new task. You would say that within itself another self exists, moving, and stirring, and following up a distinct purpose, and yearning to become—what? does it know? This I cannot assert; but after awhile you may see it acting, and acting sagaciously, as if inspired by a perfect knowledge. Its presentiment of the slumber which will shortly seize upon it, paralyze its forces, and surrender it helplessly to all its enemies, incites it to the sudden display of a novel activity. "Let us work well! Let us work quickly! For soon I shall sleep soundly."

Chapter VI. The Mummy, Nymph or Chrysalis

Let us respect the childhood of the world. Let us pardon the early ages for the consolations and hopes which they drew from the strange drama represented by the Insect, the thoughts of immortality which grave Egypt founded upon it. This drama tranquillized more hearts and wiped away more tears than all the mysteries of Canopus or the revels of Eleusis.

When the mourning widow, the eternal Isis, ever reproducing herself in eternal anguish, was snatched from her beloved Osiris, she reposed her hope of a future reunion on the sacred beetle, and hushed her sobs.

What is death? What is life? What is the awakening, or what the slumber? Do you not see this little miracle, this dumb confidant of the grave, which makes us the mock of destiny? It sleeps in the egg, and afterwards sleeps again in the nymph. It is thrice born; and it dies thrice—as larva, nymph, and beetle. In each of these existences the larva or mask is the prefigurement of the succeeding existence. It prepares, begets, and hatches itself. From the most repulsive sepulchre it emerges sparkling. On the dust it shines; on the gray Egyptian plain, in its season of aridity, it shimmers, and eclipses everything. Its jewelled wing mirrors the all-powerful sun.

Where was it? In the foul shadow, in night and death. A deity has summoned it forth, and will yet do much more for this beloved soul! Sweet,

tender ray! The hope was surely founded upon justice, on the impartial love of the Creator of all life.

Accordingly, the widow draws from its death the brilliant pledge of the future, and gives utterance to this woman's cry:—"Merciful Heaven! do for my husband and for me what thou hast done for the insect. Do not grant less to man; do not grant to my best-beloved less than thou accordest to this brother of the gnat!"

Has modern science swept away the ancient poesy? Has it completely eliminated the miraculous from nature?

The inaugurator of this science, Swammerdam, has discovered that the grub already contains the nymph; nay more, even the butterfly. In the grub he has detected the rudiment of the wing and proboscis of the future being.

This is not all. Malpighi saw the *nymph* of the silkworm in its virgin slumber, *already furnished with the attributes of its coming maternity,*—containing the eggs which, as a butterfly, it would fecundate.

And yet again, this is not all. Réaumur, in the oak-grub, *in a grub scarcely a few hours old, found the eggs of the future butterfly.* In other words, the infant insect, at that very stage when the grub itself, as Harvey points out, is simply a mobile egg, already possesses eggs and children.

It is the identity of three beings. It seems as if there could be no intermediary deaths; one single life is continuously carried on.

All this seems clear, does it not? The ancient mystery has perished? Man has discovered, in its fullness, the secret of things?

Réaumur does not think so; Réaumur himself, who has guided us so far. In recording his observations he does not appear satisfied, and confesses "that they still leave very much to be desired."[9]

In truth, it is a thing to confound and almost to terrify the imagination, to think that a grub, at the outset no bigger than a thread, should include in itself all the elements of its moultings and metamorphoses; should contain its triple, and even octuple envelopes; nay more, the sheath or case of its *nympha* and its

---

[9] Réaumur, "Histoire des Insectes," tome i., p. 351.

complete butterfly, all folded up one in another, with an immense apparatus of vessels, respiratory and digestive, of nerves for feeling and muscles for moving! A prodigious system of anatomy! first traced out in complete detail in Lyonnet's colossal work on the willow-grub. The twofold monster, endowed with a strong grub-stomach for the destruction of innumerable hard leaves, will possess ere long a light and delicate apparatus for extracting the honey of flowers. And yet the clothed creature, which contains in its organism a complete silk-manufactory, will almost immediately sweep away the complex system.

One knows the gentle manœuvres by which nature conducts the young of the higher animals from the embryonic existence to the independent life, adapting the old organs to new functions. Here, this is not done. It is not a simple change of condition. The destination is not merely different, but contrary, with a violent contrast. Therefore, instruments fitted for an entirely novel existence are required, and the abolition and definitive sacrifice of the primitive organism.

The revolution, which for all other beings is so well concealed, is here entirely thrown open. And we are enabled to scrutinize with our eyes this astonishing *tour de force* in numerous grubs which undergo the great change in the light of day, suspended to the branch of a tree by a silken cable.

The effort is worthy of our admiration and pity. To see yonder nymph, short and feeble, soft and gelatinous, without arms or paws, contriving, by the skill with which it expands and contracts its rings, to escape from the heavy and rough machine which it was at first, flinging aside its limbs, setting free its head, and—one hardly dares to record the fact—throwing off its body, and rejecting many of its principal internal organs!

This little body, when it has thus escaped from its long heavy mask (living, nevertheless, but a moment since, a life full of energy), will dangle, and grow dry, and skillfully ascend to its silken fastening. There it prepares to fix itself in its new "Me" as a nymph, while its former "Me," tossed about by the wind, is speedily driven I know not whither.

All is, and ought to be, changed. *The legs will not again be the legs.* It will need lighter organs. What can the child of the air, which can balance on the point of a blade of grass, do with those coarse short feet, armed with hooks, vent-holes, and so many heavy implements?

The head will not be the head; at least, the enormous apparatus of mandibles will disappear, and also that of the muscles by which they were energetically moved. All is thrown aside with the mask. A colossal change! From a masticator the animal becomes a sucker. A flexible proboscis emerges.

If anything in the grub appeared of a fundamental character, it was the digestive apparatus. Ah, well! this basis of its being is no more. The absorbing throat—the powerful stomach—the greedy entrails,—all are suppressed, or reduced nearly to nothing. What would they avail the new being which, in certain species of butterflies, dispenses with sustenance, has no mouth but by agreement, and is so completely freed from digestion that frequently it has not even an inferior orifice? It abandons without difficulty its thenceforth useless furniture, and expectorates the skin of its stomach!

The Insect

This is grand and magnificent,—no spectacle is grander! For life at such a point to change, to dominate over the organs, to rise victorious, so entirely free of the ancient *Ego*! To those who have revealed to us such a prodigy of transfiguration, from the bottom of my heart I say, "Thanks!"

How marvelous the security in this being which abandons everything, which unhesitatingly dismisses its strong and solid existence, the complicated organism which just now was *itself*, its own individuality! We call it its *larva*, its mask; but why? The personality seems at least as energetic in the vigorous grub as in the delicate butterfly. And, therefore, it is most indubitably its individual being which it courageously leaves to shrivel up and perish, to become—what? Nothing reassuring, nothing but a little, soft, whitish substance.

Open the nymph soon after it has spun its cocoon: in its shroud you shall find nothing but a kind of milky fluid, wherein you see, or fancy you see, certain dubious lineaments. After awhile you may, with a fine needle, separate these I know not what,—and figure to yourself that they are the limbs of the future butterfly. A frightful lacuna! For many species a moment occurs when nothing of the old any longer appears, and nothing of the new as yet has come. When Æson, cut in pieces, was thrown, in order to rejuvenate him, into the caldron of Medea, you would have found, on groping there, the limbs of Æson. But here there is nothing parallel.

Trustfully, nevertheless, the mummy surrounds its body with its bands, docilely accepting the shadows, the inertness, and the captivity of the sepulchre. It feels in itself a force, a *raison d'étre*, a *causa vivendi*,—a reason for living still. And what reason? What cause? The vitality accumulated by its previous toil. All that, like a laborious grub, it has accumulated, is its obstacle to death,— its incapability of perishing,—the reason why it will immediately live again; and not only live, but with a light and tender existence, whose facility is proportioned exactly to the efforts which it makes in its anterior condition of life.

Admirable compensation! When penetrating so deep down into life, I expected to encounter certain physical fatalities. And I found justice, immortality, and hope.

Yes, antiquity was right, and modern science is right. It is death, and yet it is not death; let us call it if you will partial death. Is death ever otherwise? Is it not a new birth?

Throughout my life I have remarked that each day I died and was born again; I have undergone many painful strugglings and laborious transformations. One more does not astonish me. Many and many times I have passed from the larva into the chrysalis, and into a more complete condition; the which, after awhile, incomplete under other relations, has put me in the way of accomplishing a new circle of metamorphoses.

All this from me to me, but not less from *me* to those who were *still* me, who loved me, or made me, or, so long as I lived, whom I made. These, too, have been, or will be, my metamorphoses. Sometimes, a certain intonation or gesture which I detect makes me exclaim:—"Ah! this is a gesture or a tone of my father." I had not foreseen it, and if I had foreseen it, it would not have occurred; reflection had changed all; but, not thinking of it, I employed it. A tender emotion, a holy impulse seized me, when I felt my father thus living in myself. Are we two? Were we one? Oh! it was my chrysalis. And I—I play the same part for those who shall follow me, my children, or the children of my thought. I know, I feel, that besides the bases which I derived from my father, my ancestors and masters, besides the inheritance of artist-historian which I shall bequeath to others, germs existed within me which were never developed. Another, and perchance a better, man was within me, who has not arisen. Why were not the loftier germs which might have made me great, and the powerful wings of which I have sometimes felt myself possessed, displayed in life and action?

These germs, though put aside, remain to me; too late for expansion in this life, perhaps, but in another,—who knows?

An ingenious philosopher has remarked that if the human embryo, while imprisoned in the maternal bosom, might reason, it would say:—"I see myself endowed with organs of which here I can make no use,—limbs which do not move, a stomach and teeth which do not eat. Patience! these organs convince me that nature calls me elsewhere; a time will come when I shall have another residence, a life in which all these implements will find employment. They are standing still, they are waiting. I am but the chrysalis of a man!"

Chapter VII. The Phœnix

The drama is complete. From the gray or blackish mummy which just now lay before you dried and shriveled, you see the new creature, the resuscitated, the phœnix, blithely escaping, to shine resplendent in all the glory of youth.

The very reverse of *our* destiny: commencing with bright and butterfly days, in later life we crawl and languish; while the insect commences with years of gloom, and from a long life of obscurity emerges into the youth in which it dies glorified.

Let us be present at this departure. The warm breath of spring has awakened the plants; its banquet is prepared. More than one flower, awaiting it, secretes its honey. It delays, because to-day that impenetrable envelope which ensured its safety becomes for a moment its obstacle. Enfeebled and fatigued by so great a transformation, how shall it break through the too solid cradle which threatens to suffocate it?

Some species—as, for example, the ants—experience so great a difficulty, that the captive, probably, would never effect its release but for the opportune assistance of some power which, from without, hastens to extricate it, to deliver it (so to speak), and separate it from the trammels of its swaddling-clothes.

Fortunate difficulty! which creates the bond between the two ages, attaches the liberator to the child she has delivered, and herself begins its education and society!

But, for the majority of insects, the liberator is no other than Nature. This mother, inexhaustible in tenderness and invention, gives to the little one the key which will open the barrier, pierce the prison, and introduce it to daylight and liberty.

"What key?—and how?" say you. "How can this soft and fluid being contrive to seize upon a firm, compact tissue, frequently doubled and immured by the alluvial accumulation of a protracted winter?"

The circumstance embarrasses *us* greatly, but Nature is not troubled. Means of the utmost simplicity suffice her; she eludes, and sports with, the difficulty. The butterfly of the silkworm, for instance, at the critical moment finds a file—where?—in its eye! This eye, with numerous facets, has a fine diamond point, which files through and severs the silken prison.

Another, the cockchafer, shut up underground, suddenly discovers that it is a perfect mechanician. Of its whole body it makes a lever. Its posterior extremity furnishes it with a strong-pointed auger. It sinks solidly, anchors, and makes fast. From this *point d'appui* it derives an enormous force, and with its robust shoulders uplifts the heavy clod, enlarges the aperture, finds at length the light, extends its unwieldy apparatus of wings and wing-cases, and flies as a gnat.

Another deformed (or shapeless) miner, the mole-cricket, would never reach the surface if, to reascend from the depth of the earth, it had not two enormous hands, or rather two powerful rakes, which open up its way. Though hideous, it is not the less sensitive to the influence of spring, but it takes the precaution of never exposing its strange figure save to the doubtful rays of the moon. Its plaintive cry singularly affects the female; she yields to it, and makes her appearance, but to return again into the night and confide to the protecting shade the hope of her posterity.

A frail aquatic insect, the gnat, on this important day assumes the daring mission of the navigator. It makes fresh use of its demitted envelope, and turns it into a bark. In this it stands upright, extends its new wings for sails, glides along the wave, and very frequently without shipwreck reaches the shore; where, when dried, the same wings will bear it off to the chase and the pursuit of pleasure. In an hour it appears a complete master of all these novel arts. It is the peculiarity of love to know without having been taught.

Love is winged. Mythology is perfectly in the right. This is verified in the proper sense and without metaphor. In one brief moment, Nature displays a restless anxiety to fly towards the beloved object. All creatures rise above their own level, all mount towards the light, on the pinions of desire. The internal fire is also revealed in glowing colors. Every one decorates his person, every one wishes to please.

The butterfly apparently looks upon you with the great velvety eyes which adorn its wings. Beetles of every species, like mobile stones, astonish by their brilliant reflexes, their burning vivacities. Finally, from the bosom of the shadows bursts the flame of love, naked and unveiled, in flashing stars!

At such a moment it accomplishes the strangest transformations, and from the humblest masks issue, in violent contrast, the superbest individuals.

A dull larva of the morass, which lives only by stratagem, becomes the brilliant amazon, the agile winged warrior, called Demoiselle (*libellula*). It is the only creature of its tribe which expresses the complete liberty of flight, holding the same rank among insects as the swallow among birds. Who has not followed with attentive gaze its thousand varied movements, its turns, and returns, and the infinite circles which it makes with azure and emerald wings on the meadow or over the waters? A flight apparently capricious; but not really so, for it is a chase, a rapid and elegant extermination of myriads of insects. What seems to you a pastime, is the greedy absorption with which this brilliant creature of war feeds its season of love.

Do not believe that these riches are simply the gifts of genial climates; that these glittering festal garments which they assume to love and die in are only the sheen of the sun, the all-powerful, decorator, which with its rays intensifies the enamel and gems we admire upon their wings. Another sun—a sun which shines for the whole earth, even for the ice-regions of the pole—profits them far more considerably. It exalts in them the inner life, evokes all their powers, and, on the given day, calls forth the supreme flower. Yonder scintillating colors are their visible energies which become speaking and eloquent. It is the pride of a complete life, which, having attained its climax, displays its energy in triumph, wishes to expand and diffuse; it is the tradition of desire, the imperious prayer and urgent appeal to the beloved objects.

In pale and temperate climates, you will meet with those brilliant liveries which one would think belonged to the tropics. Who, under our gloomy and variable sky, has not seen the sparkling Spanish fly? Even in the fatal deserts where summer beams but for an instant, as if in despite of the sun,—in despite of the poor and naked earth,—love supports some beings of a sumptuous splendor, of opulent raiment and rich decoration. Miserable Siberia sees the princes and great lords of the Insect World simultaneously displaying their grandeur. The tyrannical Russian climate cannot prevent enormous beetles, pitiless hunters, fiercer than Ivan the Terrible, from appearing in green, black, violet, or deep blue morocco, shaded with purple sapphires. While some, usurping the ancient copes consecrated to the czars and the porphyrogeniti, stalk to and fro in robes of purple, broidered with Byzantine gold.

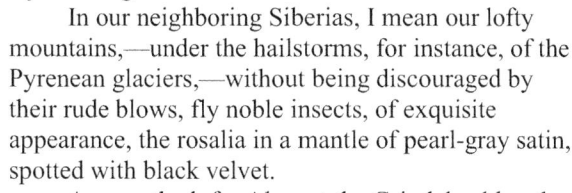

In our neighboring Siberias, I mean our lofty mountains,—under the hailstorms, for instance, of the Pyrenean glaciers,—without being discouraged by their rude blows, fly noble insects, of exquisite appearance, the rosalia in a mantle of pearl-gray satin, spotted with black velvet.

Among the lofty Alps, at the Grindelwald,—the formidable descent where that glacier comes to us, and you may touch its *aiguilles*, and its keen breath freezes you—I once admired a timid but touching protestation of love. Among some miserable birches, martyr trees, which undergo an eternal chastisement, a poor little plant, elegant and delicate, persists in flowering, with a rose-hued blossom, but a violet rose, not unworthy of the mournful region. The brother of this tragical rose is a very tiny insect which, all feeble as it is, mounts higher than any other species, and is found shivering among the lofty snows of Mont Blanc. There, above you, is only the heaven, and, beneath, the vast shroud of ice. The poetic creature has assumed exactly two tints: the celestial blue of its wings, incredibly delicate, seems lightly kindled with the white powder of the hoar-frost. The storms and avalanches which overthrow the rocks awaken in it no sensations of terror. Under the breath of the terrible giant, in his ice-bristling beard and formidable frown, it, the little one, flies daringly, as if conscious that this king of the everlasting winters would hesitate to destroy the last winged flower of love which, in his realm of death, preserves for him a reflection of heaven.

Book the Second
Mission and Arts of the Insect

Chapter I. Swammerdam

What was known of the Infinite prior to 1600? Nothing whatever. Nothing of the infinitely great; nothing of the infinitely little. The celebrated page of Pascal, very frequently cited upon this subject, is the frank astonishment of a humanity so old and yet so young, which begins to be aware of its prodigious ignorance, opens its eyes to the Real, and awakens between two abysses.

No one forgets that in 1610 Galileo, having received from Holland a magnifying lens, constructed the telescope, elevated it in position, and saw the firmament. But it is less generally known that Swammerdam, seizing, with the instinct of genius, on the imperfect microscope, directed it to the lower world, and was the first to detect the living infinite, the world of animated atoms! These great men succeeded one another. At the epoch of the famous Italian's death (1632) was born the Hollander, the Galileo of the infinitely little (1637).

Jules Michelet

An astounding revolution! The abyss of life was unfolded in its profundity with myriads upon myriads of unknown beings and fantastic organizations of which men had not even dared to dream. But the most surprising circumstance is, that the very method of the sciences underwent a total change. Hitherto men had relied upon their senses. The severest observation invoked their testimony, and they thought that no appeal could lie from their judgment. But now behold experiment and the senses themselves, rectified by a powerful auxiliary, confess that not only have they concealed from us the greater part of things, but that, in those they have laid bare, they have every moment been mistaken!

Nothing is more curious than to observe the very opposite impressions produced by these two revolutions upon their authors. Galileo before the infinite of heaven, where all appeared harmonious and marvelously ordered, felt more of joy than of surprise; he announced his discoveries to Europe in a style of the greatest enthusiasm. Swammerdam, before the infinite of the microscopic world, seemed overcome with terror. He recoiled before the spectacle of Nature at war, devouring her very self. He grew perturbed; he seemed to fear that all his ideas and beliefs would be overthrown: a melancholy and singular condition, which, added to his incessant labors, shortened his days. Let us pause awhile to dwell upon this creator of science, who was also its martyr.

The eminent physician Boerhaave, who, a hundred years after Swammerdam's time, published with pious care his "Bible of Nature," gave utterance to a surprising observation, which sets one a-dreaming:—

"He had an ardent imagination of impassioned melancholy, which raised him to the sublime."

Thus, this surpassing master in all the works of patient inquiry, this insatiable observer of the most minute details, who pursued Nature so far into the imperceptible, was a poetic soul, a man of imagination, one of those mournful spirits who groan after nothing less than the infinite, and die because they fail to conquer it.

His was a remarkable combination of mental endowments which, at the first glance, seem opposed to one another: a love of the great, and a taste for the subtlest researches; a sublimity of aim, and that obstinacy of analysis which would subdivide the atom, and yet never cry, "Hold, enough!" But, in reality, are these qualities of so contradictory a nature? By no means. Men whose hearts are filled with the love of Nature will declare that they harmonize admirably. Nothing great and nothing little. For the lover a simple hair is worth as much as, frequently more than, a world.

He was born in a cabinet of natural history; and his birth decided his destiny. The cabinet, formed by his father, an apothecary of Amsterdam, was a pell-mell, a chaos. The child wished to arrange it, and drew up a catalogue of it. A modest ambition led him from point to point, until he became the greatest naturalist of the century.

His father was one of the zealot collectors who then became common in Holland—insatiable treasurers of diverse rarities. It was not with pictures—though Rembrandt was then in his glory—it was not with antiquities, that he filled his house. But all that the ships brought back from the two Indies of minerals, plants, fantastic and extraordinary animals, he acquired at any cost, and heaped up in piles. These marvels of the unknown world, contrasting by their splendor and tropical magnificence with the gloomy climate which received them and the pale sea of the North, aroused in the young Hollander's mind a lively curiosity and a passionate devotion to Nature.

A very good Dutch painter has drawn a charming picture of the young Grotius: a universal scholar at twelve years of age, surrounded by folios, maps, charts, and all the appliances of learning. How much I should have preferred that the same artist—or rather the all-powerful magician, Rembrandt—had revealed to us the mysterious study, that brilliant chaos of the three kingdoms, and the young Swammerdam endeavoring to grasp the grand enigma!

The crowds and prodigious movement of Amsterdam favored his solitude. The Babylons of commerce are for the thinker profound deserts. In that dumb ocean of men of mercantile activity, on the border of sluggish canals, he lived almost like Robinson Crusoe in his island. Isolated even in the midst of his family, who could not comprehend him, he seldom emerged from his cabinet, and descended on the fewest possible occasions into the paternal shop.

His sole recreation was to go in search of insects in the little soil which Holland offers above the waters. The melancholy meads, covered with Paul Potter's herds, possess, in the moist warmth of the summer, a great variety of animal life. The traveler is much impressed when he sees the crane, the stork, and the crow, elsewhere hostile, reconciled here by the abundance of their food, which they frequently hunt in company on terms of perfect accord. Hence the landscape acquires a peculiar charm. The cattle assume an air of placid security which they do not elsewhere exhibit. The summer is short, and early assumes the gravity of autumn. Man and Nature—all appears of a pacific character, harmonized in a great moral sweetness and remarkable seriousness of mood.

Enthusiastic collector as his father was, he grieved to see the youth of Swammerdam thus employed. It had been his ambition to make of his son a renowned minister who should shine in controversy, and an eloquent preacher. But his son seemed daily to grow more dumb. The chagrined father lowered his views from glory to money. In that golden city, so feverish and so diseased, no career is more lucrative than that of a physician. But here arose another difficulty. Swammerdam threw himself heartily into his medical studies; but on condition that he created them—as yet they did not exist. Therefore, the basis on which he desired to rest them was the preliminary creation of the natural sciences. How cure the sick man unless you understood the healthy? And how understand the latter without studying side by side the inferior animals which translate and explain disease? But can one see into such delicate mysteries with the eye alone? Does not the feebleness of the sense of vision lead us astray? The serious creation of science would suppose a reform of our senses and the creation of optics.

A veritable creation! Look at the microscope. Is it a simple spy-glass? To the eyes which the instrument possessed, Swammerdam added two arms, one of which bears the glass and the other the object. He himself says, in reference to his more difficult investigations, "that he had attempted to obtain the assistance of another person, but that such assistance proved, in fact, an obstacle." It was for this reason that he organized a dumb man of copper, a discreet servant ready for every work; thanks to whom the observer disposes of supplementary hands and numerous eyes of different degrees of power. In the same manner as the birds expand or contract their visual organs, either to grasp objects in a whole or to scrutinize with searching glance the smallest detail, Swammerdam created the method of successive enlargement; the art of employing lenses of different sizes and varying curvature, which permit the observer to see *en masse*, and to study each separate portion, and finally to survey the whole for the purpose of properly replacing the details and reconstituting the general harmony.

Was this all? No. To observe dead bodies, time is required; but then time robs us of them. Death, which seemingly conduces to study by its immobility, is deceitful; it fixes the mask for a moment, and the object beneath melts away. Now came a new creation of Swammerdam's. He not only taught us to see and investigate, but he devised means for our permanent investigation. By preservative injections he fixed these ephemeral objects; he compelled time to halt, and forced death to endure. The Czar Peter, who, a long time afterwards, saw in the dissecting-room of one of Swammerdam's disciples the beautiful body, supple and fresh, of a little child, with its exquisite carnation tint, thought that the rose was living, and could not be prevented from embracing it.

All this is soon said; but it was long to do. How many attempts! What miracles of patience, of delicacy, of skilful management! In exact proportion as one descends the scale of littleness, the insufficiency of our means proves more and more embarrassing. We can touch nothing without breaking it. Our large fingers will hold no more: they cast a shadow, they throw obstacles in our way. Our instruments are too coarse to seize upon such atoms; therefore we refine them. But then how can we put the invisible point in an invisible object? The two terms in sight avoid us. Only one single passion—the unconquerable love of life and Nature, the undefinable, indescribable tenderness, a feminine sensibility directed by a masculine, scientific genius—could succeed in so great an aim. Our Hollander loved the tiny creatures. He dreaded wounding them so much that he spared the scalpel. He avoided as far as he could the steel, and preferred the firm but nevertheless the delicate ivory. He fashioned in it infinitely small instruments, sharpened by aid of the microscope, which would not work rapidly, and compelled the student to make his observations with due patience.

His tender respect for Nature found its reward. While still a youth, and a simple student at Leyden University, he had two strong holds upon her in her highest and lowest manifestations. He was the first to see and understand the maternity of the insect and the human maternity. The latter subject, so delicate and yet so grand—in which he labored conjointly with his master at Leyden—I put aside: let us dwell upon the former. He dissected and described the ovaries of the bee: found them in the pretended "king;" and proved that she was a queen, or rather a mother. In like manner he explained the maternity of the ant; an all-important discovery, which revealed the true mystery of the superior insect, and initiated us into the real character of these societies, which are not monarchies, but maternal republics and vast public nurseries, each of which raises up a people.

The most general fact in the life of insects, and the great law of their existence, is the Metamorphosis. Changes which in other creatures are obscure, are in them exceedingly conspicuous. The three ages of the insect appear to be three creatures. Who would have dared to assert that the grub, with its heavy luxuriance of digestive organs and its great hairy feet, was identical with a winged and ethereal being, the butterfly?

He dared to say, and by the most delicate anatomy he demonstrated, that the larva, the pupa, and the butterfly represented three conditions of the same individual, three natural and legitimate evolutions of its life.

How did learned Europe welcome this novel science of metamorphoses? That was the question. Swammerdam, young and without authority, without any position in the academy or university, lived in his cabinet. Scarcely anything of his works was published during his life, nor even fifty years afterwards, so that his discoveries might circulate and advantage all, rather than himself and his fame.

Holland remained indifferent. Eminent professors in the University of Leyden were opposed to him; and took umbrage at the fact that a simple student placed himself by his discoveries on a level with them, or even above them.

The miserable and necessitous condition in which his father left him was not calculated to recommend him greatly in a country like Holland. In his costly labors he was supported by the generosity of his friends. At Leyden it was Van Horn, his professor of anatomy, who defrayed all his expenses.

At this epoch two illustrious academies were founded,—the Royal Society of London and the Académie *des Sciences* of Paris. But the former, specially inspired by the genius of Harvey, a pupil of Padua, turned its gaze towards Italy, and addressed its inquiries to the distinguished and very accurate observer, Malpighi, who furnished at its request the anatomy of the silkworm. I know not why the Englishmen turned aside from Holland, and did not also interrogate the genius of Swammerdam.

He was honored only in France. It was here, in the neighborhood of Paris, that he made the first public demonstration of his discovery. His friend Thévenot, the famous traveler and publisher of travels, collected around him at Issy different classes of *savants*, linguists, orientalists, and, before all, inquiring students of Nature. Such was the origin of the Académie *des Sciences*. One might justly say that the revelation of the illustrious Hollander inaugurated its cradle.

Jules Michelet

A Frenchman rescued from the hands of the Inquisition the last manuscript of Galileo. A Frenchman also—Thévenot—supported Swammerdam with his purse and credit. He was desirous of establishing him at Paris. On the other hand, the Grand-Duke of Tuscany invited him to Florence. But the fate of Galileo was too strong a warning. Even in France there was little safety. The mystic Morin was burned at Paris in 1664; the very year in which Moliére performed the first acts of his "Tartuffe." Swammerdam, who was then residing there, might have been present at both spectacles.

He himself, notwithstanding his positivism, showed very singular tendencies towards mysticism. The more deeply he entered into details, the more eagerly did he long to reascend to the general source of love and life; an impotent effort which consumed him. Already, at the age of thirty-two, excessive toil, chagrin, and religious melancholy brought him to the grave. From his early years he had suffered from the fevers so common in Holland, that land of swamp and morass, and had not paid due attention to them. He studied with his microscope every day from dawn till noon; the remainder of the day he wrote. And for his studies he preferred the summer days, with their strong light and burning sunshine. Then he would remain, with his head bare that he might not lose the smallest ray, frequently until deluged and bathed in sweat. His eyesight grew very weak.

He was already in a feeble condition when, in 1669, he published in a preliminary essay the principle of the metamorphosis of insects. He was sure of being immortal; but so much the more in danger of dying of hunger. His father thenceforth withdrew from him all assistance. Swammerdam by his discoveries (as of the lymphatic vessels and hernias) had very considerably promoted the progress of medicine, and even of surgery; but he was not a physician. From a spirit of obedience he had attempted to practice: he could not continue, and fell ill. He was now without a home. His father shut up his house, retired to live with his son-in-law, and bade Swammerdam provide for himself, and lodge where he would. A wealthy friend had often solicited him to reside with him. When expelled from the paternal roof, he made an effort to seek out this friend and remind him of his offer; but he remembered it no longer.

Misfortunes now accumulated upon his head. Poor and infirm, and dragging himself along the streets of Amsterdam with a large collection which he knew not where to store away, he received another terrible shock—the ruin of his country. The earth sunk under his feet.

It was the fatal year of 1672, when Holland seemed crushed by the invasion of Louis XIV. Assuredly his fatherland had not spoiled Swammerdam; but nevertheless it was the native home of science, of free reason, the asylum of human thought. And lo! she sank, engulfed by the hosts of the French; engulfed in the ocean which she had summoned to her assistance. She lived only by committing suicide. Did she live? Yes; but to be thenceforth no more than the shadow of her former greatness.

The Insect

The infinite melancholy of such a change has had its painter and its poet in Ruysdaël, who was born and who died in Swammerdam's time, and, like him, at the age of forty. When I contemplate in the Louvre the inestimable picture which that Museum possesses of him, the one leads me to think of the other. The little man who followed the gloomy route of the dunes at the approach of the storm reminds me of my insect-hunter; and the sublime marine picture of the palisade in the red-brown waters, chafing so terribly, and electrified by the tempest, seems a dramatic expression of the moral tempests which poor Swammerdam experienced when he wrote "The Ephemera"—"among tears and sobs."

The Ephemera is the fly which is born but to die, living a single hour of love.

But Swammerdam did not enjoy that hour; and it seems as if he spent his too brief life in a state of complete isolation. At the age of thirty-six he was already drawing near his end. The depths of imagination and universal tenderness in his nature could not be alimented by the barren controversies of the age. In this condition there accidentally fell into his hand an unknown work,—a woman's book. This sweet voice spoke to his very soul, and somewhat consoled him. It was one of the *opuscula* of a celebrated mystic of that age, Mademoiselle Bourignon.

Poor as was Swammerdam, he undertook a pilgrimage to Germany, where she resided, and went to see his consoler. He found in the journey a very real assistance in escaping at the least from his contention with the *savants*, his rivals, in forgetting every collision, and in remitting to God alone his defense and his discoveries.

He longed to withdraw himself into a profound solitude. For this purpose it was necessary he should dispose of the dear and precious cabinet on which he had spent his days, in which he had enshrined his heart, and which had at length become a portion of himself. He must tear himself from it. At this cost he calculated that he would obtain a revenue sufficient for his wants; but the very loss and separation he longed for he could not undergo. Neither in Holland nor in France could buyers be found for the cabinet. Perhaps the wealthy amateurs, who think of nothing but empty *éclat*, did not find in it the glittering species which give us a child's pleasure. The great inventor's collection offered things more serious: the logical order and arrangement of his discoveries; that eloquent and living method which had guided his genius to new achievements. Alas! it perished, scattered abroad.

Jules Michelet

Having been for a long time ill, in 1680, either through weakness, or a disgust for life and men, he shut himself up, and would not go out any more. He bequeathed his manuscripts to his faithful and life-long friend, whom, when dying, he himself styled the "incomparable,"—the Frenchman Thévenot. He died aged forty-three.

What really killed him? His own science. The too abrupt revelation wounded and seized upon him. If Pascal saw an imaginary abyss opening before him, what would happen to this Dutch Pascal, who saw the real abyss and the limitless profundity of the unexpected world? It was not a matter of a decreasing scale of abstract greatnesses or of inorganic atoms, but of the successive envelopment and prodigious movements of beings which are the one in the other. For the little we see, each animal is a tiny planet, a small world inhabited by animals still more diminutive, which in their turn are inhabited by others very much smaller. And this, too, without end or rest, except from the powerlessness of our senses and the imperfection of optical science.

All men now began to fathom, and incessantly toil in, that infinity which the hand of Swammerdam had opened up to them. From that time Europe labored therein with diverse aims. Leuwenhoek, precipitating himself upon it, discovered and conquered new worlds. The Italian positivist, Malpighi, showed perhaps the highest boldness. He proved that the insect has a heart—a heart which beats like man's. One has not far to go to endow it also with a soul. Swammerdam, who was living then, was terrified by the fact. He drew back affrighted from the declivity; he wished to keep his footing, and was fain to doubt the existence of the heart.

It seemed to him that the science to which he had given the first impulse, which he had launched on the flood of his discoveries, was conducting him to something great and terrible which he shrank from seeing: like one who, adrift on the enormous sea of fresh water which dashes headlong in the Niagara Falls, perceives himself impelled by a calm but invincible and mighty movement—whither? He will not, and he dare not, think!

Chapter II. The Microscope:—Has the Insect a Physiognomy

Armed with that sixth sense which man has achieved for himself, I can move forward, at pleasure, in any direction. It is in my power to track out, to reach, to compute the spheres, and gravitate with them in their vast orbits. But I feel much more strongly attracted towards the other abyss—that of the infinitely little. In its atoms I discover an intensity of energy which charms and astounds me. And I myself, what am I but an atom? Neither Jupiter nor Sirius, those enormous globes at so great a distance from, and possessing so little sympathy with me, will teach me the secret of terrestrial life. But these, on the contrary, surround and press upon me, injure me or lend me their assistance. If they are not of my own kind, they are at all events associated with me.

Ay, fatally associated.

And yet I cannot fly from them: swarms haunt the very air which I breathe,—what do I say? float in the fluids of my body. It is my interest to know them. But my sovereign interest is to escape from my deplorable and wretched ignorance, and not to quit this world until I have peered into the infinite.

Jules Michelet

Full of such ideas, I addressed myself to one of the philosophers of the present day who have made the greatest and most successful use of the microscope,—the celebrated Dr. Robin. Under his direction, I purchased from the skilful optician Nachet an excellent instrument, and planted myself before my window on a very beautiful day.

I have said it,—the microscope is much more than a mere magnifying glass. It is an aid, a servant who has hands to supplement your own—eyes, and movable eyes, which by their changes enable you to see an object at a suitable magnitude, and either in detail or as a whole. One perfectly understands the all-absorbing attraction which it exercises; however great the fatigue it causes, one cannot separate one's-self from it. Its *début*, as we have seen, was signalized by its slaying its creator, Swammerdam. How many workmen has it not since deprived, if not of life, at least of sight? The first of the two Hubers became blind at a comparatively early age. The illustrious author of the great work on the cockchafer, M. Strauss, is nearly so. Our pallid but enthusiastic Robin is already on the same descent, but pursues his studies without pause. The seduction is too potent. Who can renounce the truth, after once beholding it? Who can willingly return into the world of errors wherein men exist? Better not to see at all, than always to see things falsely.

Behold me, then, face to face with my little man of copper. I lost not an instant in interrogating the oracle. And its first and somewhat rough reply respecting the two objects I presented was:—

One was the human hand, white and delicate,—the left hand, the idler, and that of a person who did no work.

The other, a spider's foot.

To the naked eye the former object seemed agreeable enough; the other, a tiny, obscure blade, of a dirty brown, and somewhat repulsive.

In the microscope the effect was precisely the opposite. In the spider's foot, easily cleansed of a few downy spots, appeared a magnificent comb of the most beautiful shell, which, far from being dirty, by its extreme polish was rendered incapable of being soiled; everything glided off it. This object would seem to serve two ends: that of a very delicate hand, through which the spinner, in rising or descending, suffers its thread to glide; and that of a comb, with which the attentive laborer holds its stuff, while at work, in the required position, until the woven threads—more like a cloud—grow firm and strong, are dried by the air, and no longer fall back floating and wavy, but useless.

As for the human hand, the part exposed under the microscope seemed, even with the smallest lens, a vague and immense substance, incomprehensible through its very coarseness.

Even with a medium lens, of only twelve or fifteen times magnifying power, it seemed to be a yellowish, reddish tissue, coarse and dry, ill-woven,—a kind of wiry taffeta, in which each mesh was irregularly puffed up.

Nothing could be more humiliating!

This pitiless judge, pitiless even in its treatment of the flowers, behaves with terrible severity towards the human flower. The freshest and most charming will act wisely in not attempting the experiment. She would shudder at herself.

The Insect

Her dimples would deepen into abysses! The light down of the peach which crowns her beautiful skin with the bloom of delicacy would show like rough thickets, or rather like savage forests.

After my first experiment, I felt that the too truthful oracle not only altered our ideas of proportion, but of appearances, colors, forms—transfiguring everything, in fact, from the false to the true.

Let us be resigned. Whatever the organ of truth may tell us, I thank it, and I will welcome it though it declare me to be a monster. But such is not the case. If it change with some severity our notions of the surface, on the other hand it reveals to us worlds of truly unbounded beauty beneath it. A hundred things in anatomy which seem horrible to the unassisted sight, acquire a touching and impressive delicacy, and a poetical charm which approaches the sublime. This is not the place for discussing such a subject. But a mere drop of blood, of a brickdust-red by no means agreeable to the naked eye, heavy, thick, and opaque, if you look at it when dry, under the magnifying glass, presents to you a delicious rose-bloom arborescence, with delicate ramifications as fine and subtle as those of the coral are coarse and dull.

But let us keep to our insects. Let us select the most miserable—the wonderfully little butterfly of the clothes-moth, that dirty white butterfly which seems the lowest of created beings. Take only his wing. Nay, far less, only a little dust, the light powder which covers his wing. You are astounded at seeing that Nature, exhausting the most ingenious industry in order that this offcast of creation may fly at his ease, and without fatigue, has scattered over his wing, not dust, but a multitude of tiny balloons. Or, if you prefer it, so many parachutes, most convenient instruments for flight, which, when opened, sustain the little aeronaut without fatigue and for an indefinite period; which, as they are more or less expanded, enable it to rise or sink; and when folded up, permit of its remaining quiet. The least of the butterflies, thus supported, has a faculty of flight as unlimited as the noblest bird of heaven.

One grows keenly interested in these curious apparatus, which have anticipated our human inventions. One observes their strange and surprising modes of action, as one would observe the inhabitants of another planet, if he were miraculously transported thither. But what one most yearns to see, what one burns to detect, is some reflection from *within*, some gleam of the torch which is concealed in their inner existence, some appearance of thought. Have they a physiognomy? Can I seize in their strange visage any trace of an intelligence which, judging by their works, so closely resembles our own? Of the expression which touches me in the eye of the dog, and of other animals related to me, shall I detect nothing in the bee, the ant, in those ingenious beings, those creators, which accomplish so many things the dog cannot accomplish?

A clever man once said to me: "As a boy I was very partial to insects; I searched about for caterpillars, and made a collection of them. I was especially curious to look in their faces, but never succeeded. All that I could distinguish was confused, dull, melancholy. This discouraged me. I left off making collections."

Jules Michelet

I was but a child in this new study; that is, I was fresh to it, and curious. My special anxiety was to interrogate the countenance of the dumb little world, and to surprise there, in default of voice, the silent thought. Thought? At least, the dream, the obscure and floating instinct.

I addressed myself to the ant; an humble being in form and color, but endowed with a prodigious amount of social instinct and of the educational capacity; not to speak of its quickness of resource, of the promptitude with which it confronts perils, and chances, and embarrassments.

I take then an ant of the commonest species—a neutral ant—one of the workers who are relieved from the wants of love, and in whom therefore the sex, diminished to a minimum for the advantage of labor, develops so much more powerfully its extraordinary instinct; who alone perform all the diverse trades of the little community, and are purveyors, nurses, architects, and inventors.

I selected a very fine, serene, and luminous day—not luminous with the glare of summer, but the calm radiance of autumn (1st September 1856). I was alone, in a state of perfect silence and repose, and in that complete forgetfulness of the world which is so rarely obtained. After the manifold agitations of the past and present, my heart for a moment was at peace.

Never was I more ready to hear the mute voices which do not address themselves to the ear, to penetrate in a calm and benevolent spirit the mystery of the little world which on every side surrounds us, and yet has hitherto remained out of our reach and apart from our communications.

Alone with my ant, armed with a tolerably good lens, with a magnifying power of twelve, I placed it delicately on a large sheet of fine white paper which covered nearly the whole table.

With the microscope I could have seen but a part and not the whole. A very considerable enlargement would also have exaggerated the merely secondary details—such as the scanty hairs with which the ant is provided. Finally, its mobility would not have suffered me to keep it in the focus of the microscope; but the lens, as easily shifted as itself, followed it in all its motions.

Not, however, without some difficulty. It was lively, alert, disquieted, and impatient to quit the table. I was looking at it in the middle of the sheet, when it was already nearly at the edge. I was obliged to *etherize* it a little, so as to stupefy it, and render it less uneasy.

It appeared very clean, and highly varnished. Though a neuter, and not a female, its belly was rather large, and was joined to the chest by two small swellings. From the chest the head, which was strong and nearly round, detached itself cleanly and distinctly.

This head, seen as it were *en masse*, resembled a bird's. But instead of a beak it had a circular prolongation, in which, on attentive examination, I detected the reunion of two tiny crescents joined at the point. These were its teeth, or mandibles, which do not operate like ours, from above to below, but horizontally and sideways. The insect employs its mandibles for the most widely different purposes; they are not only its weapons and instruments of mastication, but the tools it uses for every art, supplying the place of hands in masonry, plastering, carving, and in lifting and transplanting burdens which are frequently of enormous weight.

It was well for it that its body was wrapped in a complete coat of mail. The ether affected it but slightly, and only stupefied it. After a moment's immobility it partly recovered, and made a few movements like those of an intoxicated person, or as if it were affected with a fit of vertigo. It seemed to say, "Where am I?" and endeavored to make out the ground where it was walking, the great sheet of white paper. It attempted a few tottering steps, tumbling first on one side and then on the other. It carried before it a couple of instruments which at first I took to be feet, but which I found, on more careful inspection, were wholly different.

They sprang from a point near either eye, and, like the eyes, were evidently instruments of observation. These antennæ, as they are called, long, delicate, yet robust, and vibrating at the slightest touch, are fleshy, articulated in twenty pieces, and disposed one in another. They form an instrument admirably adapted for feeling and groping. But it is useful in many other ways: by means of it the ants transmit in a second very complicated advices, as, for instance, when they change their course and retire, or suddenly take a wholly different road; evidently they have a language like that of the telegraph. This supposed marvelous organ of touch is more probably a species of hearing apparatus, and so mobile that it quivers at the slightest vibrations of the air, and feels every wave of sound.

The perfect accord of every movement of the delicate and subtle tactile and telegraphic apparatus, the strong head, in fine, which seemingly *thinks*, completed the illusion. Its attitudes, its gropings, its efforts to obtain a knowledge of the situation, showed precisely what we should have been under similar circumstances. Shakespeare's Queen Mab, in her nut-shell chariot, occurred to my mind. And more, the chronicles of the Hubers; those impressive and almost terrifying narratives which would lead us to believe that the ants are far advanced in a knowledge of good and evil.

It turned its back upon me obstinately, as if it dreaded to see its persecutor. It looked upon me as a horrible giant, and, despite its semi-intoxicated condition, made constant and energetic efforts to escape me, and place itself in security.

I brought it back very softly and cautiously. But I could not make it show me its face. Its antipathy and its terror, undoubtedly, were too powerful. I therefore decided to take hold of it with a small pair of pincers, and to keep it on its back, using as little pressure as possible. The pressure, though light, acting on the small lateral orifices (or stigmata) through which it breathes, was infinitely painful, to judge from the resistance it offered. With its minute claws and mandibles it held the pincers so firmly that I could hear the air vibrate with every motion. I hastily profited by the painful position in which I had placed my ant; I looked it in the face.

That which is most disconcerting, and gives it a peculiar appearance, are the teeth or mandibles placed outside the mouth, and springing, one on the right side, the other on the left, in a horizontal direction, so as to meet together: ours are vertical. These projecting teeth seem to offer battle, though, as I have said, they are also used for pacific purposes, and *serve as hands*.

Behind the teeth may be seen several little threads or palpi at the entrance of the mouth; which are, in reality, the *little hands of the mouth*,—feeling, and handling, and turning over whatever is brought there.

In front emerge the antennæ, the *other* hands; but these are set externally, are mobile and susceptible to an excess,—in a word, *electric hands*.

Behind the head, at the chest, commence the paws or feet, two in front of great dexterity, and rightly named by Kirby the arms.

An apparatus of such complexity, placed in the fore part of the body, cannot fail to obscure and overcloud its physiognomy. What would be the case with our own, if from our eyes and mouth six hands started, to say nothing of those which proceed from the shoulders, and of four others placed lower down?

The whole is intended for action and defense. The face which the insect shows is its resisting skull, its bony case, which cannot move. This frames, encloses, and fixes the eyes, which are also immovable; but, being exterior and multiple, motion is not necessary: those of the ant are divided into fifty facets, which reveal everything to it either in front or rear. Thus, then, its sight is admirable, but it cannot *look*. No external muscle sets the mask in motion. And, therefore, it has no physiognomy.

But, in compensation, its pantomime was extremely expressive,—I may even say, very pathetic. On discovering that it was so feeble and incapable of walking, it did exactly what prudent and sagacious man would have done, and attempted to recover its energies by the very means which we should have employed. It commenced a methodical friction of its entire body, from above to below. Seated like a little monkey, it skillfully made use of its arms or anterior feet in such a manner as to rub its back and side. Occasionally it returned to its head, took it between its two hands, as if it would fain have shaken it clear of the fatal intoxication which rendered it so little able to provide for its own safety. One would have said it was questioning itself, collecting its thoughts, and saying, as we do after a bad dream, "Is it true, or is it false?—Poor head!—Alas! what ails thee, then?"

At that moment I felt that we were living in two worlds, and that there were no means of understanding each other. How could I reassure it? My language, that of the voice; its, that of the antennæ. Not one of my words could obtain access to the electric telegraph which served as its organ of hearing.

The continuous bony case which envelops its body isolates the insect from us, and conceals us from the insect. It has a heart which beats like ours; but we cannot see its pulsations beneath its thick coat of mail. It does not even command that wordless language which touches us in so many dumb beings. It is wholly wrapped up in mystery and silence.

It breathes, or rather imbibes air, through the sides, not through the face or head. No palpitation or respiratory movement can be detected in it. Therefore, how should it speak, how complain? Of all our languages it has not one; it makes a sound, but does not possess a voice.

Is the fixed and immovable mask, thus condemned to perpetual silence, that of a monster or a spectre? No. After watching its movements, its numerous actions indicative of reflection, its arts so much more advanced than those of the larger animals, we are not unwilling to believe that in this head exists a personality. And from the highest to the lowest in the scale of life, we recognize the identity of the soul.

Chapter III. The Insect as the Agent of Nature in the Acceleration of Death and Life

The insect has not my languages. He neither speaks by voice nor physiognomy. In what manner, then, does he express himself?

He speaks by his energies.

1st. By the immense destructive influence he exercises on the superabundance of Nature, on a swarm of lingering or morbid lives which he hastens to sweep away.

2nd. He speaks also by his visible energies, especially in the moment of love, his colors, his fires, his poisons (many of which are among our therapeutic agents).

3rd. He speaks by his arts, which might fecundate our human inventions. This is the subject of our second book.

Let us first attack the point where he wounds us most, and seems the auxiliary of death: his immense, ardent, and indefatigable work of destruction. Let us contemplate him in history, and begin at the remotest epoch.

In answer to our littlenesses, our disgusts, our terrors, to the narrow and egotistical judgments which we bring to bear upon such subjects, we must recall the great and necessary reactions of Nature.

It has not advanced with the order of a continuous flood, but with refluxes and recoils back upon itself, which have enabled it to compass a perfect harmony. Our short-sighted survey, frequently arrested by these apparently retrograde movements, grows alarmed, takes fright, and misconceives the character of the whole.

It is peculiar to the Infinite Love, which is continuously creating, to raise every created thing to the Infinite. But in this very infinity, it stimulates a creation of antagonisms which shall reduce the extent of the preceding. If we see it produce monstrous destroyers, be sure that they are destined, as a remedy and a repression, to check some monsters of fecundity.

The herbivorous insects have had the task of keeping under the alarming vegetable accumulations of the primeval world.

But these herbivora exceeding all law and all reason, the insectivorous insects were created to confine them within limits.

The latter, robust and terrible, the tyrants of creation by their weapons and their wings, would have been the conquerors of the conquerors, and have driven to extremities the feebler species, if, above all the insect world and its weak powers of flight, had not risen on mighty wing a superior tyrant—the Bird. The haughty libellula was carried off by the swallow.

By these successive agencies of destruction, however, production has not been suppressed, but restrained, and the species balanced in such wise that all endure and live. The more a species is pruned, the more fertile it becomes. Does it exceed? Immediately the superabundance is equilibrized by the new fecundity which is given to its destroyers.

Ye men of this lingering epoch,—sons of the lean and sober West— brought up in the little, close, carefully tended, pared, and picked gardens, which you call "wide cultivation,"—enlarge, I pray you, your conceptions; extend them, and endeavor to imagine something greater than these petty corners, if you would comprehend anything of the earth's primitive forces; of the abundance and superabundance which she displayed when, soaked with warm mists, her bosom heaved with the glow of her first youth.

The hotter countries of our present globe still show something of this profusion, though in a pale decay. Africa, which over the greater portion of its area has lost its waters, preserves as a souvenir in its happier zones that enormous and swollen herb, or herbaceous tree, the baobab. The inextricable forests of Guiana and Brazil, in their labyrinthine chaotic confusion of wild plants which, without rule or measure, envelop and choke the colossal trees, corrupt them, and bury them in their débris, are but imperfect images of the great ancient Chaos. The only beings impure enough to endure its impurity and breathe its deadly exhalations, are great-bellied reptiles, unwieldy frogs, green caymans, and serpents swollen with filth and venom. And such would have been the inhabitants of earth. Unable to draw breath in the horrible suffocation, she could never have given forth that pure air in which man alone can live.

Accordingly, from on high pounced down the bird, and, plunging into the gulf, carried back to the sky on the tops of the lofty forests some one of these monsters. But its incessant struggle would have been vain against their abominable fecundity, if, from below, myriads of nibblers had not lightened the accumulation, cleansed the frightful lairs, and thrown open to the arrows of the sun the filth under which earth was panting. The humblest insects accomplished the gigantic work which made earth inhabitable: they devoured chaos.

"Small means," you say, "and great results! How could these little beings come to the aid of an infinity?" You would not cherish the doubt, if you had been ever a witness of the awakening of the silkworms, when, one morning, they are hatched with that vast hunger no abundance of leaves can satisfy. Their proprietor has supposed himself in a position to content them with a rich and beautiful plantation of mulberry-trees; but it counts for nothing. You supply them with forests, and they still ask for more. At a distance of twenty or thirty yards you hear a strange uninterrupted buzzing; a murmur like that of brooks incessantly flowing, and incessantly grinding and wearing out the pebbles. Nor are you mistaken: it is a brook, a torrent, a boundless river of living matter, which, under the grand mechanism of so many minute instruments, sounds, and resounds, and murmurs, passing from the vegetable life to that of insects, and softly but invincibly bases itself on animality.

To return to the primeval age. The most terrible destroyers, the most implacable assailants, which penetrated the lowermost rottenness of the great chaos, which at a higher level delivered the tree from the pressure of its parasites, and finally mounted to its branches, and brightened up the livid shadows,—these were the benefactors of species yet to come. Their uninterrupted work of unconquerable destruction reduced within reasonable limits the excess in which Nature was almost lost. They opened up splendid, free, and unencumbered spaces; and the monsters, banished from the gulf where they swarmed, grew more and more barren, and by that great revelation of the forest were exposed to the child of Light,—the Bird.

A profound agreement and genial fellowship were established between the latter and his protagonist, the child of Night, the Insect, which had thrown open the abyss, and delivered into his power the enemy. Consider, moreover, that in proportion as an exuberant nourishment fortified and exalted the insect, when its blood was intoxicated by so many burning plants, a ferocity previously unknown prevailed, and the fiercer and bolder species no longer limited themselves to undermining the *retreats* of the monsters, but attacked the *monsters* also. Stings, augers, cupping-glasses, trenchant teeth, sharpened pincers, an arsenal of unknown and as yet unnamed arms, came into existence, were elongated and whetted for assault upon the living matter. They were needed. They proved to be the lancet which cut the putrescent sore of the rising world. This latter had nourished and multiplied the feebly animalized myriads of torpid worms and pale-blooded larvæ, a ghastly and also the lowest life, which gained by passing through that burning crucible of keen existence, the superior insect-race.

I know nothing upon earth which seems stronger, firmer, more durable, and more formidable than those miniature rhinoceros-like cuirassiers, which traverse earth as quickly as the great mammal traverses it heavily and slowly. The carabi, the galeritas, the stag-beetles, which carry with so much ease armor far more formidable than that of the Middle Ages, reassure us only by their size. Here strength is relatively formidable. Were a man proportionally strong, he might take in his arms the obelisk of Luxor.

The Insect

Vast energies of absorption, concentrating in these insects enormous foci of forces, translated themselves into the light by the energies of color. To these, in species where life was more elevated, succeeded the moral energies. The superbly barbarous heroes, the *scarabæi*, were exterminated by the modest citizen-species, the ants and bees, in which the secret of beauty was harmony.

Such is the whole history of insects. But to whatever height our inquiries may conduct us, let us not mistake the point of departure, —the useful nibblers and miners, which have elaborated and prepared the globe.

Is their work terminated? By no means. Immense zones remain in what may still be called an ancient condition, condemned to a terrible and unwholesome fecundity. In the centre of America the richest forests of the world seem ever to repel the approach of man, who enters them only to die. His arms, enfeebled by fever, have not even strength enough to collect their treasures. If a tree fall across his path, it becomes an insurmountable obstacle to the indifferent adventurer. He turns aside, and you may trace his circuit through the tall herbage. Fortunately the termites do not recoil so easily. If they find themselves confronted by a tree, they do not avoid it, do not turn its flank. They attack it bravely in the front, set to work as many laborers as are necessary—millions, perhaps: in two or three days the tree is devoured, and the road open.

The great law of nature, and in these countries the law of safety, is the rapid destruction of everything decaying, languishing, stagnant, and therefore injurious; its ardent purification in the crucible of life. And that crucible is, before all things, the insect. We must not blame its fury of absorption. Who thinks of accusing the flame? The flame is worthy of reproach only when it does not burn. And, in like manner, that living fire, the insect, is created to devour. Necessity demands that it should be eager, cruel, blind, and of an implacable appetite. It can have no sobriety, no moderation, no pity. All the virtues of man and of superior beings would be nonsense which one cannot even imagine. Can you conceive of an insect with the sensibility and tenderness of the dog? which should weep like the beaver? which should nourish the aspirations and poetry of the nightingale? or, finally, the compassionateness of man? Such an insect would be incapable; thoroughly unfit for its profession as the anatomist, dissector, and destroyer—we may say, more justly, the universal medium of nature, which, precipitating death by suppressing long periods of decay, in this way accelerates the brilliant return of life. Thus disembarrassed and free, it says, with a savage pleasure, "No maladies, no old age! Shame upon all decay! Hail to eternal youth! Let every creature die which lives beyond a day!"

Observe that the furious eagerness of the winged insects, which seem to be the agents of death, is frequently a cause of life. By an incessant persecution of the sick flocks, enfeebled by hot damp airs, they ensure their safety. Otherwise they would remain stupidly resigned, and hour after hour grow less capable of motion, gloomier and more morbid in the bonds of fever, until they could rise no more. The inexorable spur knows, however, the secret of putting them on their legs; though with trembling limbs, they take to flight; the insect never quits them, presses them, urges them, and conducts them, bleeding, to the wholesome regions of the dry lands and the living waters, where, growing discontented, their furious guide abandons them, and returns to the pestilent vapours, to its realm of death.

In the Soudan, in Africa, a little insect, the Nâm fly, directs with a sovereign authority the migrations of the flocks. In the dry season it rages against the camel; it audaciously ventures into the ear of the elephant. The giant is resistlessly driven forward by its winged shepherds, to escape the fires of the south, and to seek the fresh winds of the north. On the other hand, the oxen, through its management, remain with their Arab master peacefully in the genial southern pastures.

The most terrible of insects—the great Guiana ants—are valued precisely for their devouring power. Without them, no effectual means would exist of thoroughly cleansing the homes of man of all the obscure broods which infest the shadows, and swarm in the timbers and framework, in the most imperceptible crevices. One morning the black army appears at the door of the house: an army of sanitary inspectors. Man retires, gives place to them, and evacuates his dwelling. "Enter, ladies; come and go at your pleasure; make yourselves quite at home." It would not be safe for the owner to remain, since it is a law with these scrupulous visitors to leave no living thing in the track of their march. In the first place, every insect,—the largest as well as the minutest,—and their eggs, however well-concealed, perish. Then the smaller animals—frogs, adders, field-mice;—none escape. The place is thoroughly cleansed, for the smallest remains are conscientiously devoured.

The great spiders of the Antilles, without piquing themselves on accomplishing a work of purification so terrible and so complete, labor nevertheless very industriously to secure the cleanliness of human habitations. They will not suffer any disgusting insect to exist. They are excellent servants—much cleaner than the slaves. Therefore men value them, and purchase them as indispensable domestics. Markets exist where spiders are regularly bought and sold.

In Siberia, the spider enjoys the consideration to which it can everywhere put forward so many claims. That region of the farthest North, whose very brief summer is not the less infested with gnats and flies, finds a benefactor in the useful insect which industriously hunts the swarms for man's advantage. Its consummate prudence, its superior ability, its prescience of atmospheric variations and climatic phases, have so exalted the idea which the Siberians have formed of it, that many of their tribes refer the creation of the world to a gigantic spider.

Chapter IV. The Insect as Man's Auziliary

A hunter of small birds, in an ingenious academical memoir, gives utterance to the following paradox: "Their recent multiplication is the cause of the disease in the vine and the potato."

How should this be? The disease, which first broke out in September 1845, is produced, says the author, by microscopic animalcules and parasitical vegetation previously destroyed by the insects. But these insect-protectors of agriculture perished, devoured by birds, in 1844. The fatal law passed in the May of that year, for the protection of the birds, must have multiplied them to such a degree, that the insects, driven out and destroyed by them, could no longer afford to our plants the succor which defended them against their invisible enemies.

This hypothesis, supported with much wit and ability, and apparently grounded on facts and dates, rests wholly on one basis, and if it fails, crumbles to the ground.

It supposes that the birds have been efficaciously protected by the law, and that, in twelve years, they have been so able to multiply as to become masters of the field, the tyrants and exterminators of the useful insect-species, and that, in fine, the latter have unfortunately almost disappeared.

To this three replies may be given:—

Jules Michelet

1st. The birds have *not* multiplied. We must not go for the truth to the *Bulletin des Lois* (the Statute-book), but to fowlers and bird-catchers. And they reply:—"So many birds have been destroyed since the enactment of the law for their benefit, that in certain countries sport has actually become impossible, because there are no more to kill."

In Provence, in the very localities where the gnats are insupportable (and the birds, therefore, most precious),—in the Camargue,—the sportsmen, in default of edible birds, now kill the swallows. They place themselves on the watch at the points where the winged legions pass in files, and slaughter several victims at one discharge.

2nd. The insects have by no means been destroyed by the birds. Ask of the agriculturists what species has disappeared. Let them search ever so keenly, and they will not find that a solitary species has diminished. On the contrary, in the years referred to we have seen them increase, and grow, and flourish, and nothing prevents them from making war at their pleasure on the invisible animalcules.

Not an insect-species is wanting; but, on the contrary, some careful observers tell us, in their books on Hunting or Natural History, that numerous species of birds will soon become extinct.

3rd. Birds are not, as the author of the memoir calls them, "unintelligent assassins." Far from this, they kill by preference the most injurious insects. The time at which they carry on a really murderous war is when they are feeding their young. But what do they feed them with? With very few insectivorous insects; the latter, armed and mailed—carabi and stag-beetles—covered with metallic scales, equipped with hooks and pincers, of an indestructible vitality, would be a horrible food for the young of the warbler, who, before such a provision, would assuredly take to flight. This is not the kind of aliment the sagacious mother seeks for her offspring; but soft and, as it were, milky insects, fat and succulent larvæ, fine little tender caterpillars,—all herbivorous, fructivorous, and leguminivorous animals; exactly those which do the greatest mischief in our fields and gardens.

Accordingly, the great labor of the bird against the insect precisely coincides with the labor of the husbandman.

The Insect

For the rest, we are far from saying, as the author referred to makes us say, that the bird is the sole purifier of creation. One must be blind, and indeed senseless, not to see that he shares this mission with the insect. The action, too, of the latter is undoubtedly more efficacious in the pursuit of a world of living atoms, which the insect, whose eyes are microscopes, detects and pounces upon in numerous obscure corners, inaccessible to the bird. The bird, on the other hand, is the essential purifier of everything demanding long-sightedness and the power of flight,—as, for example, the frightful clouds of invisible animalcules which float and swim in the air, and therefore pass into our lungs.

As a rule, the equilibrium of species is desirable. All are more or less useful. We willingly join with the author of the paper referred to in the wish that those insects which prey upon the smaller species might be specially distinguished and spared. The peasant destroys them indiscriminately, without knowing that by killing, for instance, the dragon-fly (or *libellula*)—the brilliant murderess which slays a thousand insects daily—he is helping the latter: becomes the auxiliary of the insects, the preserver and propagator of the enemies which devour his substance. The terrible cicindela does not fly so high, but with its crossed daggers, or rather the two scimitars which serve it for jaws, accomplishes a swift and almost incredible havoc among the smaller insects. Take care, then, and respect it. Do not listen to the child who is dazzled by the beauty of its wings, nor, to please him, impale on the needle-point your admirable insect-hunter, the efficacious auxiliary of the agriculturist!

The carabi,—immense warrior-tribes armed to the very teeth, and displaying an ardent activity beneath their heavy coats of mail,—are the true guardians of your fields; and day and night, without holiday or repose, protect your crops. They themselves never touch the smallest blade or seed. Their sole occupation is to capture thieves, and they ask for no other reward than the thieves' bodies.

Others toil underground. The innocent lobworm, which pierces and stirs up the soil, gets ready in a marvelously excellent manner the muddy and clayey earths which are deficient in evaporation. Others, in company with the mole, hunt far down in the depths the cruel enemy of agriculture, the horribly voracious larva of the destructive cockchafer, which, for three years, has been preying on the roots beneath the surface.

The insectivorous insects put forth undeniable claims to the protection of man, whose allies they are. But even among the herbivora there are useful destroyers of harmful plants. The useless, pungent, and in every sense disagreeable nettle, which scarcely a single quadruped will deign to touch, fifty species of insects, in fellowship with ourselves, labor to destroy.

A very beautiful class of insects, some rich in outward garb, and others in intelligence, are the *Necrophori*, which render us the important service of clearing away all dead matter from the soil. Nature, which finds them so useful, has treated them truly as her favorites, honoring them with splendid costumes, and making them both industrious and ingenious in the discharge of their functions. It is a remarkable circumstance that, notwithstanding their sinister office, they are far from being wild, but are very sociable if the need arises, and understand how to unite their forces, combine their energies, and act in concert. In brief,—these honest undertakers and grave-diggers are the brilliant aristocracy of the insect nation.

It is evident that Nature's ideas are not the same as ours. She loads the most useful with rewards, whatever the nature of their work. For instance, the *Geotrupes*, which clears away the dung, is clothed in sapphire in payment of its service. The celebrated *Coleopteron* of Egypt, the sacred *Ateuchus* of the tombs,[10] appears glorified with an emerald aureola.

Who shall describe all the services rendered by these scavengers? Yet we are not just in our dealings with them. It happened to me, one April, when I was about to transplant to my garden some dahlias which had passed the winter in the orchard, to discover that the humidity of the air of Nantes, and the compact and imporous clayey soil, had rotted the tubers. A bevy of insects were at work upon them, and usefully engaged in purging this shocking centre of dissolution. The gardener was very indignant, and ready enough to accuse them of the evil which they were endeavoring to remedy.

The enemy of damp gardens, the snail (*Helix*), is pursued by an insect,[11] the *Drylus*, which lies in wait for it, and, the better to hunt it up, mounts on its back, and makes it carry him, seizes a favorable opportunity, and on the snail re-entering its shell, enters also, lives with it and upon it. A snail lasts him about a fortnight. Then he passes on to another and a larger, and then to a third still larger. He requires three in all. In the third, as he is about to change into a pupa, the drylus makes the place clean, and, to sleep conveniently, seizes on the substantial house of the enemy which has nourished him.

There could be no more useful task than to enlighten the peasant on the distinction that ought to be made between insects useful to agriculture and insects which are noxious; or those which may be turned to advantage in various sciences,—and especially in Chemistry,—which, it is probable, will yet discover unexpected resources in beings endowed with so copious and intense a vitality. In this respect, a very honorable work of initiation has been undertaken by the eminent naturalist who has so skillfully organized the museum at Rouen. All his pupils have preserved a grateful recollection of their teacher; and it is to one of them I owe the following summary of an original and instructive lecture on the Insect as Food.

"A prejudice much to be regretted, and a ridiculous fastidiousness, has debarred our Western peoples from one of the richest and most exquisite sources of nourishment. What right have they who devour tainted game, and unclean birds,—what right have the lovers of the oyster, that slimy mollusc, to reject the nourishment supplied by the Insect World?

"Burgundy has the good sense to profit, without any feeling of silly disgust, by the excellent mollusc which peoples its vineyards,—I mean the snail,—which is very good with butter and salads, and a dish as wholesome for the chest as it is agreeable to the mouth and profitable to the stomach.

---

[10] The *Ateuchus sacer*, or Sacred Scarabæus of the Egyptians.
[11] The larva of the *Drylus flavescens*.

The Insect

"A celebrated *savant*—Lalande—dared to take a step further in advance, and to venture upon the caterpillar, rising thus another step above our prejudices. It is to him we owe our knowledge of the fact that the caterpillar tastes like almonds, and the spider like hazel-nuts. He addicted himself to the latter, which he found more delicate."—I should think so. In every sense, the spider is a superior being.

"Many insects are so nutritious and savory that they have been specially selected by ladies as a diet likely to renew their life, beauty, and youth. The Romans of the Later Empire recovered the ample outlines of the Cornelias of the Commonwealth by the use of the *Cossus*.[12] The sultanas of the East, of those voluptuous lands where love seeks the rounded, swelling figure, make their slaves bring them a supply of *Blaps*,[13] and idling in their gardens, to the music of leaping fountains, imbibe from the succulent insect an eternal youthfulness.

"In Brazil, the Portuguese extracts from the Malalis of the bamboo, when the tree wears its nuptial flower, a kind of fresh butter for the table; and eats the ants in sweetmeats, at the moment that their wings uplift them on the breeze like an aspiration of love.

"But generally the insect, apart from its real value, has been hunted by the peasants whose tillage it destroyed. It plundered them of their food, and, in revenge, they themselves have fed upon *it*. The terrible locust, whose vast increase has so often imperilled the East, has been, on that very account, the more eagerly pursued and devoured by the Orientals. The story runs that the Caliph Omar, when seated at his family table, observing a locust alight there, read inscribed upon its wing:—'We hatch nine and ninety eggs; if we laid a hundred, we should devastate the world.'

"Fortunately the locust is the manna of Asia. Who does not know that the prophets, musing in the caves of Carmel, ate nothing else? The Mohammedan anchorites adopted the same *régime*. One day a person said to Omar:—'What think you of locusts?' 'That I would fain have a basketful.' Soon afterwards the supply failed him. It was with difficulty his servant found a single insect; whereupon he, delighted and grateful, exclaimed, 'Allah is great!'

"Even at the present day locusts are sold throughout the East, and are eaten in the café as a dessert and a delicacy. Ships are loaded with them, and they are bought and sold by the cask.

"Here, then, we have insects exceptionally nutritious and substantial. What prevents us from making use of them? What scruple hinders us from active and useful reprisals against them?"

At this part of his discourse, the orator found his audience, consisting mainly of intelligent Norman peasants, wrapped in deep attention, as at those points of the debates of the British Parliament when the accustomed cry arises of "Hear! Hear!"

He had foreseen such a moment; and having loaded his table with some of the insects most dreaded by agriculturists, he seized them, crunched them, and

---

[12] The Goat-Moth Caterpillar
[13] The women of Egypt, it is said, eat the *Blaps sulcata* cooked with butter.

swallowed them gravely, with this strong speech, which will not be without fruit:—"They have eaten us: let us eat them!"

Chapter V. A Phantasmagoria of Light and Color

If the insect does not and will not speak to us, are we to suppose that it does not express the burning intensity of the life within it?

No living creature reveals itself more clearly; though only from itself to its kind, from insect to insect. They are bound up in themselves; are a sealed world, which has no outward expression, and no language except for its own members.

For all ordinary purposes, an electric telegraph exists in their antennæ. But the great, the eloquent language is manifested among them towards the close of their existence,—for one brief moment, it is true,—a moment announcing the approach of death, yet the grand festival of love.

They speak through the rare attractions with which they are invested,—through the wing, the flight, the airy existence,—through the fancy which possesses them (says good Du Tertre) of becoming birds. They speak through their brilliant hieroglyphics of colors and fantastic designs, their strange coquetry of extraordinary toilets. They speak in their very lustre, and some species reveal their inner flame by a visible torch.

They lavish with royal magnificence their last days. And wherefore should they economize, when to-morrow they die? Break forth then, O life of splendor! Sparkle, ye gold and emeralds, and sapphires and rubies! And let that incandescent ardor, that torrent of existence, that cataract of profuse radiance, be poured out in one common, rapid flood!

There is not space in our museums for the proper display of the prodigious, the unbounded variety of decoration with which Nature has, mother-like, sought to glorify the hymeneal of the insect and to emparadise its nuptials. A

distinguished amateur having had the patience to show me in due succession genus after genus, species after species, the whole of his immense collection, I was astounded—in truth, I was stupefied—almost terrified by the inexhaustible energy—I was going to say fury—of invention which Nature displayed. I was overcome—I closed my eyes, and begged for a truce; my brain was dizzied and blinded, and became confused. But she, she would not let me go; she inundated and overwhelmed me with beautiful beings, with fantastic beings, with admirable monsters, with wings of fire, and cuirasses of emerald, clad in a hundred kinds of enamel, armed with singular apparatus—no less brilliant than formidable; some in embrowned steel, shot with yellow— others in silken hoods, embroidered with black velvet; these with fine dashes of tawny silk on a rich mahogany ground; those in pomegranate-colored velvet lit up with gold; others in luminous, indescribable azures, relieved by jet-black beads; and others, again, bright in metallic streaks alternating with heavy velvet.

It was as if they wished to say:—

"We in ourselves are the whole of Nature. If she perishes, we shall enact a drama, and personate all her creations. For if you look for rich furry garb, behold us here in mantles such as a Russian czarina never wore. Do you wish for feathers? behold us radiant in plumage which the humming-bird cannot equal; or if you prefer leaves, we can imitate them so as to deceive your eye. Even wood—in fact, all kinds of substances—there is nothing which we cannot imitate. Take, I pray you, this little twig, and hold it in your hand,—it is an insect!"

Then I was fairly conquered. I made a humble reverence to a people so redoubtable; with a burning brain I issued from

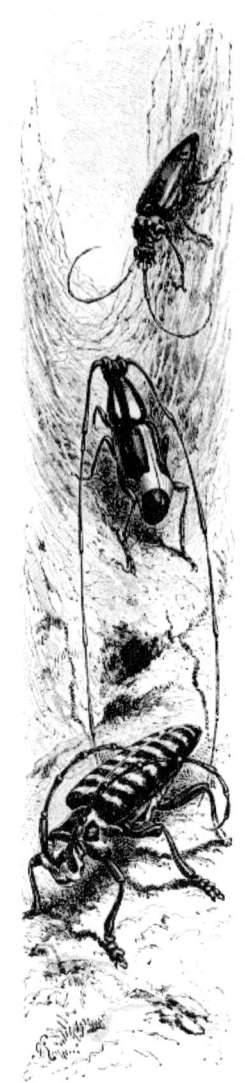

the magic cave; and for a long time afterwards the sparkling scintillating masks danced and whirled around me, pursuing me, and maintaining on my retina their wild, strange revel.

And yet I had seen them only in cases and in boxes, as dead as in nature they were ardent and restless. What would have been my impression if I had seen them alive, and in motion,—especially in the burning climes where they abound and superabound,—where everything is in harmony with them,—where the air, the water, the flora, impregnated with prolific flames, rival the keen ardor of the animal hosts in the madness of love, of production precipitated and incessantly renewed by impatient death?

The American forests of Brazil and Guiana are the formidable furnaces in which the great exchange of life is uninterruptedly carried on. The fantastic faëry of the vegetable kingdom is in accord with that of the animated forces. Savage, harsh, and plaintive cries— not songs—form the woodland concert. Strange voices of birds, in the woods and the savannahs, relieve each other,—hoarse and vibrating, but regular, as if to mark the hours. They are the clock of the desert. Some by day, others by night; and perfectly distinct also at each of the three periods of the day,—morn, and noon, and evening. They disquiet the traveler, inasmuch as they reproduce our human voices or sounds, and seem ironical or mocking. One cries, another whistles, another sighs. This strikes like an alarm, that like a hammer, while a third imitates the tones of a bagpipe. The vast plains re-echo the mighty voice of the cariama. And that of the serpent-conqueror, the courageous kamichi, harsh and strong, echoing over the marshes, makes the savage tremble, for he thinks he hears the spirits passing.

At evening, with the song of the grasshoppers, the croaking of the frogs, the shriek of the owls, and the lamentations of the vampires, mingles the howl of the apes; until a hiss, which seems drawn from a wounded bosom, silences all, and spreads a universal terror, because it indicates the presence of the sharp-clawed prowler, the swift jaguar.

In these forests there is nothing to reassure you. Yonder green and peaceful waters, whence ever and anon proceeds the sound of half-choked sighs,—you place your foot upon them, and with terror discover that they are solid! that the surface is composed of great alligators, with their greenish backs resembling breadths of moss or aquatic herbs! Let a living creature appear, and immediately they raise their heads and put themselves in motion; you behold the strange assemblage rise from the slime in all their horror! But is this all?—Even these monsters which reign on the surface have their tyrants over them. The piranha, or razor-fish, as swift as the cayman is unwieldy, severs with its saw-like teeth the latter's tail, and carries it off before it can wheel round. The cayman, nearly always, mutilated in this manner, would perish, if its cuirass did not prevent its enemy from dissecting it. The same terrible anatomist, with a flash of its scalpel, cuts down as it passes the bird which skims the waves. Aquatic birds which have been wounded by it are frequently caught. And what, then, of the quadrupeds? The most powerful are devoured. A horrible combat is waged without pause in the deep waters,—in the waters living and overflowing with life, but with death also,—where is realized to the letter a rapid and furious suicide of Nature,— Nature devouring in order to re-create itself!

The insects in fury and beauty are worthy of this scene. The exalted vitality, revealed among the gadflies and the mosquitoes, by their thirst of blood, is shown in other species by their enchanting colors, their caprices of design, their singularities of form, which either astonish us or terrify. The *Buprestis imperialis*, proud of its green cuirass powdered all over with dust of gold, seems to have passed through the bowels of the metalliferous earth, and enriched itself on the way. The *Buprestis chrysochlorus*, of a yellower green, flutters to and fro like a mounted gem. The *Arlequin* of Guiana,—a gigantic mower, armed with tremendous antennæ and prodigious legs to traverse the innumerable obstacles offered by the tall herbage,—is marked with black commas on a yellow ground, with inexplicable hieroglyphs,—a being doubly strange and doubly enigmatic. It singularly reminds us of the texture of Indian stuffs, where, for the sake of harmonizing colors not usually brought side by side, the artist traces a number of wavy and broken lines, which soften and blend them into complete accord.

Those gentle and social insects, the butterflies, covering the banks with their winged tribes, transform the whole prairie into an enchanting flowery carpet. The butterfly of butterflies, the glorious butterfly of Brazil, of a rich azure lit up by shifting gleams, softly hovers, in the warm hours, above the waters crowned by the imperial dome of the blossomy forests. A pacific and splendid creature, it seems the innocent king of all the puissant nature. Others, scarcely less beautiful, follow in its train; and ever and ever more the glorious host, in floating azure, follows the current of the stream.

Such, then, are the tongues of Love; for the boundless rainbow of all these colors is simply its varied expression. And for what purpose, if love itself ought to appear without an intermediary?

Already, in our colder lands, the timid glow-worm, motionless under the hedgerow, suffers its little lamp to shine and guide through the night the lover to his love.

In Italy it moves to and fro, and its flame has acquired wings. I was much struck by it, at the hot springs of Acqui, in Piedmont, where sulphur everywhere prevails; the wild dance of the tiny lights seemed stimulated by the fires lurking in the entrails of the earth. In Brazil the very leaves overflow with phosphorus. How should aught be wanting for the illumination of the bridal-joy of the insect?

The Insect

That marvel, under the tropics, glitters everywhere and enchants everything. Two hundred species are known, which Nature has gifted with the poetic faculty of breathing forth flame, and charming their great festival with the poesy of light.

A graceful German lady, Mademoiselle Mérian, having been transplanted to these zones of fire, has related in naïve language the alarm which she experienced on seeing their insect wonders. The daughter and grand-daughter of excellent and laborious engravers, herself an artist and of well-informed mind, she has produced, in Latin, Dutch, and French, an admirable and picturesque work on the Insects of Surinam. The learned lady, in an exemplary life of misfortunes and virtues, had but one weakness (who has not one?)—the love of Nature. She quitted Germany for Holland, attracted by its unique and brilliant collections of the treasures of the two worlds. Then, as these did not suffice her, she visited Guiana, where she painted for several years. She combined in the same picture,—an excellent method,—the insect, the plant on which it lives, and the reptile which lives on the insect. Thoroughly conscientious, she sought out and posed her formidable models, of which, nevertheless, she was much afraid. Once, when the Indian savages had brought her a basket of insects, she was sleeping after her work. But in her chaste slumber she was disturbed by a strange dream. She thought she heard a harp, a melody of love. The melody grew inflamed; it was no longer a song, but an intoxication. All the room seemed filled with fire. She woke, and found her dream was true. The basket was the lyre, the basket was the volcano. She quickly saw that the volcano did not burn. The captives were fire-flies (*fulgores*); their song was an epithalamium, and their flame the flame of love.

In the tropical countries the stranger generally travels by night to avoid the heat. But he would not dare to enter the populous shadows of the forest-depths, were he not reassured by the luminous insects which he sees dancing and fluttering in the distance, and anon planted on the neighboring bushes. He takes them for his companions, and fixes them in his shoes, partly to show him the path, and partly to keep off serpents. And when the morning breaks, he gratefully and carefully replaces them among the thickets, and restores them to their amorous work. There is a pretty Indian proverb: "Carry away the fire-fly, but return it to the place from which thou carriedst it."

Who can fail to be affected by their flame? It follows the movement of life, it flares and wanes in cadence with the ebb and flow of our respiration; it beats in exact accord with the rhythm of our heart. It expands or contracts in harmony with it, and the trouble of its emotion agitates also that tremendous torch.

What lies at the bottom? the visible desire, the effort to please and to be loved, translated in a hundred different manners by the eloquence of light. One, of an unrivalled blue, with a head of rubies, outvies with its scintillation the red-hot coal. Another, of a more melancholy cast, plunges into a sombre red. A third, of flame-colored yellow, fading and passing into green, seems to express the languors, swoons, and storms of the violent loves of the South.

Jules Michelet

The ardent daughter of Spain, rendered more impassioned by the American sky, puts her hand on the creature of the flame, and seizes upon it as her own. She makes it a talisman, a jewel, and a victim. Burning, she places it on her burning bosom, where it must soon perish.

There is no purpose to which she does not turn it. By a triumph of audacious coquetry, linking the insects with silk, or imprisoning them in gauze, she wreathes the animated flames in glowing necklaces, and rolls them around her waist in girdles of fire. The queens of the ball are crowned with an infernal diadem of living topazes, of throbbing emeralds, which flicker or gleam (through suffering or love?). A brilliant but funereal decoration, of sinister magnetism, whose charm is enhanced by a sentiment of death. They dance; the waning flame associates its tender gleams with the languishing glances of a deep black eye. They dance; without end and without reason, without pity or remembrance of the amorous light dying and fading on their bosom, and having no power to say: "Replace me where you captured me!"

Chapter VI. The Silkworm

"The ideal of the human arts of spinning and weaving,"—said to me one day a Southerner (a manufacturer, but a man of imagination),—"the ideal which we always follow is a woman's beautiful hair! Oh, how far are the softest wools or finest cotton from approaching it! At what an enormous distance does all, and ever will all, our progress leave us! We drag ourselves onward, a long, long way in the rear, and enviously regard that supreme perfection which Nature daily realizes as a mere matter of pastime.

"That delicate, yet strong and tenacious hair, vibrating with an exquisite sonority which goes from the ear to the heart, and yet withal so soft, warm, luminous, and electrical—is the flower of the human flower.

"Men fruitlessly dispute respecting the merits of color. What does it matter? The brilliant black contains and promises the flame; the blonde displays it with the splendors of the Golden Fleece. The sunny brown appropriates the very sun, makes use of it, blends it with its mirages, floats, and undulates, and incessantly varies in its streaming reflexes, now smiles with light, now deepens into gloom, always deceives, and, whatever we may say, deceives us most delightfully.

"The principal, the infinite effort of human industry, has combined all possible means for the improvement of cotton. Between the Vosges and the Rhine, the rare agreement of capital, machinery, the arts of design, and the chemical sciences, has produced those splendid Indian products of Alsace, to which England herself does honor by purchasing them. Alas! all this cannot disguise the original poverty of the ungrateful tissue which men have so richly embellished. If the woman who in her vanity clothes her form in these materials, and thinks her beauty heightened by them, would loosen her tresses about her, and unroll their waves over the indigent richness of our most sheeny cottons, what would occur? How they would be humiliated!

"Sir, we must own the truth; there is only one thing worthy of being placed side by side with woman's hair. Only one manufacturer can contend against it. That manufacturer is an insect,—the modest silkworm."

A peculiar charm attends the labors of the silkworm; it ennobles everything which surrounds it. In traversing our rudest provinces, the valleys of the Ardèche, where all is rocky,—where the mulberry and the chestnut seem to dispense with earth, to live upon air and pebbles,—where low stone houses sadden the eyes by their gray tints,—everywhere I saw at the door, under a kind of arcade, two or three charming brunettes, with ivory teeth, who smiled on the wayfarer, and continued spinning their silken gold. The wayfarer said to them in a low voice, as the carriage bore him away:—"What a pity, innocent fairies, that the gold may not be for you! That instead of being disguised with a useless color, and disfigured by art, it does not retain its natural hue, and shine on the person of its beautiful spinners! How much better the royal tissue would become you than the *grandes dames*!"

A mere glance at the silkworm convinces you that it is no more a native of Europe than any other sweet thing. All that is soft and exquisite springs from the East. Our West, that hardy soldier, blacksmith, and miner, is good only to dig. It is good mother Asia, disdained by her rude son, who has bestowed upon him the treasures which seem to concentrate the essence of the globe. With the Arab horse and the nightingale, she has given him coffee, and sugar, and silk,—the revivifiers of existence and the true ornament of love.

When silk first arrived at Rome, the empresses felt that previously they had been no better than plebeians. They compared it, as far as its soft lustre was concerned, to the pearls of the Orient, paying for it, without haggling, the price of pearls and gold.

China esteemed it of such high value, that, to preserve the monopoly, she inflicted the penalty of death on any persons who dared to export the silkworm. It was only at the utmost peril, and by concealing it in a hollow cane, that men succeeded in carrying it to Byzantium, whence it passed to the West.

In the Middle Age, the age of indigence and barren disputes, when wool was the luxury of the rich, and the poor wore serge in winter, no attention was paid to silk, and its manufacture was exclusively confined to Italy.

It is the gold of the silkworms of Verona which, in Giorgione, at the mighty outcome of the Venetian art, and in the strong Titian, the master of

masters, enriches with a ruddy radiance their beautiful blondes and brunettes, the sovereign beauties of the world.

On the other hand, in an age of decadence, when Spain and Flanders had waned, the melancholy artist who preferred to paint the beauty which years had marked,—the fading flower,—the fruit too early pierced and unnaturally ripened,—Van Dyck, clothed with white silk, like a consoling beam of moonlight, his languishing and drooping signoras. Under the soft folds of their satins they still trouble hearts with vain dreams and regrets.

The woman who possessed the secret of preserving her charms to the last decline of old age, whose cypher everywhere inscribed teaches us that Love can conquer Time, Diana de Poitiers, in her profound art, did exactly the opposite of what our imprudent ladies do, who, incessantly changing, as if to amuse the passer-by, leave no trace upon the soul, and produce no permanent impression. She permitted the Irises to delectate themselves with their fugitive rainbow; but, like the celestial Dian, always wore the same costume, black or white, and invariably of silk.

It was to please her that Henry II. wore the first pair of silk stockings, and the fine silken close-fitting vest, which indicated all the gracefulness of a muscular yet slender figure. We know how ardent an enthusiasm Henry IV., at a later period, showed in promoting the growth of the silk-manufacture, planting mulberry-trees everywhere,—along the highways, in the market-places, in the courts of his palaces, and even in the gardens of the Tuileries. colored silks, for decoration and furniture, and silks with flowered designs, were soon afterwards manufactured at Lyons, which provided all Europe with them.

Shall I say it, however? These colored and ornamented silks do not by any means produce a great and profound effect. Silk in its natural state, and not even tinted, is in much more intimate sympathy with woman and beauty. Amber and pearls, the latter slightly yellow, with rich falls of lace, the latter not too yellow, are the only suitable accompaniments of silk.

For silk is a noble and in nowise pretentious attire, which lends a subdued charm to the exuberant liveliness of youth, and clothes declining beauty with its most tender and touching radiance.

A genuine mystery attends it which is not without attraction. color or gloss? Cotton has its peculiar gloss, and, when fitly prepared, often acquires an agreeable freshness. Silk is not properly glossy, but luminous,—with a soft electrical light, which harmonizes naturally with the electricity of the woman. A living tissue, it embraces willingly the living person.

Oriental ladies, before they foolishly adopted our Western customs, wore but two kinds of stuff: underneath, the real cashmere (of so fine a texture that a large shawl might be passed through a ring); and above, a beautiful tunic of silk of a pale blonde, or rather straw color, with a gleam or flash of magnetic amber.

These two articles were less garments than friends,—gentle slaves,— supple and charming flatterers: the cashmere warm, caressing, and pliant, enfolding the bather lovingly when she emerged from her bath; the silk tunic, on the contrary, light and aërial, only not too diaphanous. Its blonde whiteness agreed most admirably with the color of her skin; one might indeed have very justly said that it had imbibed that color through its constant intimacy and accustomed tenderness. Inferior to the skin, undoubtedly, yet it seemed related to it; or rather it became in the end a part of the body, and, as it were, melted into it, like a dream which informs our whole existence, and cannot be separated from it.

Chapter VII. Instruments of the Insect: And its Chemical Energies, as in the Cochineal and the Cantharides

Have I insisted too much upon my theme? No; I have reached its very depths, its most important details.

Silk is not a particular, but a general view or aspect of it, for nearly every insect produces silk.

Hitherto we have dealt with only one kind of silk,—that of the bombyx, and indeed that of a species of bombyx which is not very fertile. Let us hope that the meritorious Society of Acclimatization will introduce here the Chinese bombyx (*Attacus*), which lives on the dwarf oak, whose strong and cheap silk might be used as clothing for the poor. All classes thenceforth might wear a material warm, light, impervious, solid; and not only so, but beautiful, brilliant, and noble. Such a change would be equivalent, in my eyes, to the general ennoblement and transfiguration of the people.

Réaumur long ago asserted that numerous chrysalides would furnish a beautiful silk. The spider would yield a substance both delicate and tenacious,— as witness the admirable veil of spider's silk preserved in the Paris Museum.

Jules Michelet

The delicate Arachne, whose light thread resembles a fleecy cloud,—which is nevertheless so strong, as it issues from the spinnerets,—Arachne is pre-eminently the spinner. But, as a general rule, the insect is the weaver, and wholly devoted to that feminine art. I was about to say, the insect is a woman.

In our vocabulary "feminine" means feeble; but in the Insect World it is the synonym of strength and energy. It is,—as is the case with maternity everywhere,—it is for the purpose of defending and nourishing the child, of provisioning the cradle in which the orphan will remain alone,—it is for this purpose specially that the insect is a warrior, and furnished with formidable weapons.

As far as concerns the instruments which pierce, and cut, and saw, the insect, in spite of all our progress, is perhaps a little in advance of man to-day. The instinct of maternity, the need of providing for its child—the future orphan—the protecting shelter of the hardest bodies, has evidently inspired it to make extraordinary efforts for the development and refinement of its tools. A few, in their fantastical character, have as yet no analogues in any of our factories.

Long before Réaumur organized the thermometer, the ants, for the protection of their delicate, hygrometrical, and susceptible eggs, divided their habitations into a series of thirty or forty stories,—lowering or raising the tiny creatures to the degree of warmth, dryness, or humidity, which the temperature of the day and of the hour of the day rendered necessary. Thus they formed an infallible thermometer, on which one might rely with as much certainty as on that of the philosophers.

In the comparisons between human and insect industry, the differences which we remark belong not so much to the methods as to the speciality of their wants and situation. The insect aptly varies the application of its arts. For example: the spider which, in its network-trap, improvised every day, lightens its work by a mixture of gluing and spinning, follows quite a different process in the important labor of fabricating the soft, warm, and durable cocoons which are intended to receive its young. The nest would seem to be partly spun and partly felted, like the majority of birds' nests.

We know that from the water-spider man derived the idea of the diving-bell; but it is *not* generally known that an ingenious Norman peasant has succeeded in imitating perfectly the operations of the larva of the syrphes, which, by means of an extremely prolonged respiratory apparatus, preserves a communication with the pure and wholesome air, even while working at the bottom of the most putrid waters.

It seems, then, that in the Insect World exist a complete pharmacy, chemistry, and perfumery. Have our sciences been sufficiently attentive to this fact? The potent vitality which gives an extraordinary force to the muscles of such tiny creatures, seems also to endow their liquids with active properties and burning energies which the large animals do not possess. Many, for defensive purposes, are gifted with caustic secretions—which they eject the moment you approach—or with fulminating powders. Others with poison, which flows as soon as the sting has been thrust in. Some possess, in addition, an art of magnetizing or etherizing their enemy; and others, like certain ants which work in damp, woody places, season their abodes by burning them, as it were, with potent formic acid.

The entire genus of the *Cerambyx* (or Long-horned Beetle) exhale a strong, rose-like odor, which is smelt at a distance, is lasting, and endures after the creature's death. Even among the Carnivora, ay, and among the Coprophagi, we meet with perfumed insects, or, at all events, with insects which, when in danger of being captured, endeavor to deceive you, or implore pity, by emitting agreeable odors.

Others shine with admirable colors. The deep reds of the Nopal Coccus have furnished the purple of kings.

By a skilful mixture, we also obtain from the cochineal the pre-eminently gay and radiant color, carmine, with its innumerable tints and rosy shades.

A sovereign art with the insect is to carry on its sting, and concentrate at a particular point, the liquids which flow in the plant, in the living being. It is the very art of irritation. Its applications are innumerable in medicine and industry; tints, paintings, varied ornaments, a hundred fantastic and beautiful things come to us from the sting of the galls, the excrescences and gibbosities which they so skillfully raise.

The cochineal insect, while engaged in extracting by this process from exotic vegetables the envelope of solid green in which it will spend its prolonged period of rest, furnishes us with the red of reds, the scarlet of lake, which will color varnishes, and wax, and a multitude of objects.

In health or illness, the stings of insects upon the living flesh are violent irritants for disturbing or re-establishing the course of life. In these there is nothing mediocre. A few, without sting, burn you by their internal acridity.

Who has not seen on the dusty plain, before the thirsty harvest, the cantharides, with its emerald enamel, abruptly crossing the footpath with a wild and agitated movement! Burning elixir of existence, where love transforms itself into a poison,—it is not with impunity that we make use of it medicinally. That medieval pharmacy, which was so dangerous to man, is not without peril, it seems, for the animals themselves. A very intelligent but eccentrically ardent cat, which I kept for a long time, among its other caprices of violence loved to hunt the cantharides. It seemed attracted by the acridity of the beautiful insect, as the moth is by the flame. It was an intoxication. But when, hunting it through the flowers, she had seized and crushed her dangerous victim, the latter appeared to take its revenge.

The inflammable feline nature, stimulated by the fiery sting, broke out in cries, in excesses of fury, in strange leaps and bounds. She expiated her orgie of fire by terrible sufferings.

But, on the contrary, another insect, the bamboo-worm, or *malalis*, provides you, if you first remove its head, which is a deadly poison, with an exquisite cream, the sweet and soporific influence of which, say the Brazilian Indians, lulls love asleep. For two days and nights, the young maiden who has tasted of it, crouching under the blossomy tree, feels all the more powerfully in her soul the depth of the virgin forests, and the mystery of those fresh glades which have never seen the sun, nor echoed to the step of man, nor known any intruder but the lonely great blue butterfly. And yet she is not alone: love quenches her thirst with the most delicious fruits.

Chapter VIII. On the Renovation of our Arts by the Study of the Insect

The Arts properly so called, the Fine Arts, should profit much more than the Industrial, by the study of insects. The goldsmith and the lapidary would do well to seek in them models and instruction. The soft insects, the flies, specially possess in their eyes truly magical irises, with which no casket of gems can bear comparison. In passing from one species to another, and even, if I mistake not, from one individual to another, new combinations may be observed. Remark that the flies with brilliant wings are not always the most richly endowed, as far as their optical organs are concerned. Take the dull, gray, dusty, odious horse-fly, which lives on warm blood; its eye, to the magnifying-glass, offers the strange faëry spectacle of a mosaic of jewels, such as all the art of Froment-Meurice has scarcely invented.

If you descend still lower, insects which do not live, like this fly, upon living but upon dead matter, ordure, and decomposition, astonish us by the richness of their reflections, which our enamel ought to endeavor to reproduce. The dunghill beetle, an ungainly black insect if we look only at the upper part of

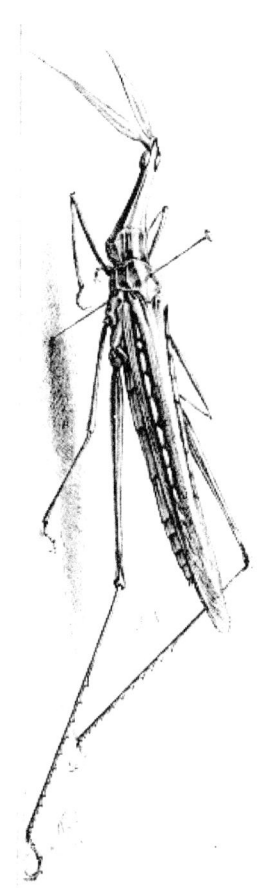

its body, is, underneath, of a deep sapphire-blue which no kingly diadem ever equalled! And what shall we say of the son of the dead, of the Egyptian scarabæus,—a living emerald, but far superior to that jewel in the gravity, opulence, and magic of its lustre? The imagination is impressed, and one does not feel astonished that a people so tender and devout, so in love with death, so full of the dreams of eternity, took for a symbol the little miraculous animal,—a burning jet of life springing from the grave!

A certain skill in examination, and a choice of day and of light, are necessary. You cannot properly study the insect of the tropics and that of our colder climates on the same day or at the same hour. The former should be examined only in favorable weather, under a pure sky and a strong sun,—a vivid and genial ray, analogous to the light which bathes it in its own country. The other, frequently uninteresting to the naked eye, but of great beauty under the microscope, may reserve its grand illuminating effects for the evening, or for artificial light. Little is promised by the cockchafer, at first sight so coarse and prosaic in appearance. Yet its scaly wing, when submitted to the focus of the microscope, and well lighted up beneath the little mirror, so that it is seen by transparency, presents a noble winter stuff, a dead leaf, where meander veins of a very beautiful brown. And in the evening it becomes quite another thing: the yellowish part of the scale has got the best of it, and in the light shines forth like gold—(a poor comparison!)—the strange, magical gold of paradise, which we dream of for the walls of the heavenly Jerusalem, or for the robes of light worn by saints and spirits before the Throne! A sun softer and tenderer than the orb of day, and one which, we know not why, charms and affects the heart.

A strange mirage! And yet nothing but a cockchafer's wing!

Perhaps it may next be an insect which neither by day nor night, neither to the naked eye nor under the microscope, could excite a feeling of interest; but if you take the trouble to lift up, with a delicate and patient scalpel, the laminæ which compose the thickness of its scaly wing, you will find there, in most instances, a variety of unexpected designs, sometimes vegetable curves,—sometimes airy ramifications,—sometimes angular striated figures, like hieroglyphics, which remind you of certain Oriental languages; and compose, in truth, a genuine necromancer's book, that can neither be referred to, nor compared with, any known form.

The Insect

These singular characters, while strongly attracting the eye and disquieting the mind, are fully worthy of the interest they excite. What they express, and give utterance to, in their emphatic language, is the circulation of life. Some are tubes through which the air enters the wing, and distends it for flight; others are tiny veins where circulate the powerful liquids that endow the imperceptible organism with its colors and its energy.

The most attractive forms are living forms. Take a drop of blood, and submit it to the microscope. This drop, as it spreads, rewards you with a delightful arborescence,—with the delicacy and lightness of certain winter trees, when revealed in their actual figure, and no longer encumbered with leaves.

Thus, Nature's infinite potency of beauty is not limited to the surface, as antiquity supposed. It does not trouble itself about human eyesight, but labors for its own behoof, and on its own work. From the surface to the interior, it frequently increases in beauty as in depth. It invests with surpassing loveliness things which are absolutely hidden, and which death alone can unveil. Sometimes, as if to contradict and confound our ideas, it clothes in ravishing forms the organs which, from our point of view, accomplish the vilest functions. I am thinking of the exquisite beauty and delicate tenderness of that coral-tree which incessantly pours out the chyle of our intestines.

To return to the insects: beauty abounds in them both externally and internally. One need not search far in order to discover it. Take an insect, not very rare, which I constantly meet with on the sandy soil of Fontainebleau, in localities well open to the sun. Take—but not without precaution, for it is well armed—the brilliant cicindela. Even to the naked eye it is an agreeable object; but under the microscope it appears to be perhaps the richest and the most varied which art could study. These are truly surprising creatures! Each individual differs; all are enamelled, and decorated to an excess, without resembling one another. In each, if taken and separately studied, new discoveries may be made.

It is the ardent and murderous hunter of other insects, and endowed with formidable weapons,—having for its two anterior mandibles a couple of sickles which close in upon one another, and transfix deeply, on both sides, their unfortunate victim. Its rich and living aliment apparently communicates to the cicindela its glowing colors. Its entire body is embellished with them. On the wings, a changeful besprinkling of peacock's eyes. On the fore parts, numerous meanders, diversely and softly shaded, are trailed over a dark ground. Abdomen and legs are glazed with such rich hues that no enamel can sustain a comparison with them; the eye can scarcely endure their vivacity. The singular thing is, that beside these enamels you find the dead tones of flowers and the butterfly's wing. To all these various elements add some singularities, which you would suppose to be the work of human art, in the Oriental styles, Persian and Turkish, or as in the Indian shawl, where the colors, slightly subdued, have found an admirable basis; time having gradually lent a grave tone to their sweet harmony.

Frankly, is there aught approaching such a degree of excellence in our human arts? How great the necessity that, in their apparently fatigued and languid condition, they should gain life and strength from these living sources!

In general, instead of going straight to Nature, to the inexhaustible fountain of beauty and invention, they have solicited help from the erudition, the history, and the antiquity of man.

We have copied ancient jewels; sometimes those of the barbarous peoples which first procured them from our own merchants. We have copied the old robes and the stuffs of our ancestors. We have copied, especially, the painted-glass windows of Gothic architecture, whose colors and forms have been selected hap-hazard, and transplanted to objects utterly discordant and unsuitable,—as, for instance, to shawls!

If we were desirous of comprehending and rehabilitating these ancient windows, we might have taken a lesson from the enamels of certain scarabæi. Seen beneath the microscope, they present very analogous effects, simply because they possess the same elements of beauty. The thirteenth century glass-windows (you may see them at Bourges, and especially in the Museum of that city) were double. The light therefore remained in them, did not pass through them, gave them the magical effects of precious stones. And of a similar character are those insect wings composed of numerous leaves, between which you may detect, with the microscope, a network of mysterious hieroglyphics.

Gothic, so little in harmony with either our wants or our ideas, has passed out of our furniture, but it still lingers in the shawl-manufacture; a rich and costly industry, which, having once adopted the fantastic method of imitating in opaque wools those windows whose transparency was their special merit, can hardly emancipate itself from the bondage.

Men have not consulted women. In order to weave complex designs, heap up a medley of arches and oriels, and condemn our wives to carry churches on their backs, men have provided a heavy groundwork of the stoutest wools; the whole being despatched from London and Paris to be servilely woven by the Indians who have unlearned their own arts.

Our intelligent Parisian merchants, who have reluctantly followed in the path traced out for them by the great producers, may very well escape from these *rich* and heavy styles. Let some one lose patience, and turning his back on the copyists of antique absurdities, go to Nature herself in search of advice,—to the great insect collections and the conservatories of the Jardin des Plantes.

The Insect

Nature, being feminine, will tell him that if he would fitly decorate his sister in the soft and airy tissue of the ancient cashmere, he must delineate thereupon—not the towers of Notre-Dame,[14] but a hundred charming creatures—that little, but, if you will, very common marvel of the cicindela, in which all styles are combined;—or the purple scarabæus glorified in its lily;—or the emerald chrysomela, which this very morning I found sensually reposing at the bottom of a rose.

Do I mean that you should copy these? Not at all. I should call these living creatures, in their robe of love, from which they derive all their charm, an animated aureola, which cannot be translated. We must be content to love and contemplate them, to draw our inspiration from them, to convert them into ideal forms, and new rainbows of colors, and exquisite posies of blossoms. Thus transformed, they will become, not what they are in Nature, but fantastic and wonderful,—as the child who pants for them sees them in its slumber, or the maiden yearning after a beautiful attire, or as the young pregnant wife when dreaming of them in her hours of longing.

<hr>

[14] Notre-Dame is the metropolitan cathedral of Paris.

Chapter IX. The Spider—Industry—The Stoppage

Before we pass on to those insect communities with which the latter portion of this volume will be occupied, let us speak here of a solitary individual.

Higher, and yet lower, than the insect, the spider is separated from it by its organization, but connected with it by its instincts, wants, and food.

A being strongly specialized in two particulars, it is excluded from the great classes of the animal kingdom, and stands isolated, as it were, in creation.

In the fertile countries of the tropics, where game abounds, it lives with its fellows. Some are said to weave around a tree one immense net, common to all, whose avenues they guard in perfect agreement. Nay more: having frequent occasion to deal with powerful insects, and even little birds, they co-operate in the hour of peril, and lend each other, as it were, a helping hand.

But this gregarious mode of living is wholly exceptional, confined to certain species, and peculiarly favored climates. Everywhere else the spider, through its organism and the fatality of its life, assumes the character of the hunter, of the savage, who, living upon uncertain prey, remains envious, mistrustful, exclusive, and solitary.

But remember that it does not resemble the ordinary hunter, who gets quit with his journeys, his exertions, and his activity. The spider's hunt costs it dearly, if I may venture to say so, and demands an incessant outlay. Every day, every hour, it must draw from its own substance the essential element of the network which is to provide it with food and renew that substance. Accordingly, it starves in order to nourish, and exhausts in order to recruit itself; it grows lean on the dubious hope of afterwards growing fat. Its life is a lottery, remitted to the risk of a thousand unforeseen contingencies. Hence, it cannot fail to develop into an unquiet creature, sympathizing but coldly with its kind, in whom it sees possible competitors,—in a word, it is a fatally egotistical animal. And were it not so, it would perish.

The worst of it is, as far as the poor creature is concerned, that it is profoundly ugly. It is not one of those which, ugly to the naked eye, are rehabilitated by the microscope. The overwhelming speciality of its career has the effect, as we see among men, of attenuating one limb, exaggerating another, and prevents anything like harmony: the blacksmith is frequently a hunchback. In the same manner the spider is pot-bellied. Nature has sacrificed everything to its function, its wants, and the industrial apparatus which will satisfy those wants. It is an artisan, a rope-maker, a spinner, and a weaver. Do not look at its figure, but at the product of its art. It is not only a spinner, but a spinning-mill.

Concentrated and circular, with eight feet around its body, and eight vigilant eyes in its head, it causes astonishment by the eccentric prominency of its enormous belly. An ignoble feature, wherein the careless observer reads the result of gormandising! Alas, it is just the contrary! This big belly is its workshop, its magazine, the pouch where the rope-maker carries in front of it the material of the thread which it winds and unwinds; but as it fills this pouch with nothing but its very substance, it enlarges only at the expense of itself, and by dint of extreme sobriety. And you shall often see it, though emaciated in every limb, retaining full and expanded the treasure which is the indispensable element of its labor, the hope of its industry, and its only chance of a future. A true type of the man of industry! "If I fast to-day," it says, "I shall eat perhaps to-morrow; but if my material runs short, all is over,—my stomach must rest and fast for ever!"

My first relations with the spider were nothing less than agreeable. In my poverty-blighted childhood, while I toiled alone (as I have said in my book on "The People") in the then ruinous and desolate printing-office of my father, the temporary workshop was in a kind of cellar, sufficiently well lighted,—being a cellar in the boulevard where my family resided, but on the ground-floor so far as concerned the adjoining street. Through a large grated window the mid-day sun obliquely lighted up the sombre case where I put together my little leaden letters. There, at the angle of the wall, I distinctly perceived a prudent spider, which, supposing the stray sunbeam would bring some imprudent fly for its breakfast, drew near my case. This sunbeam, falling not in its corner but nearer me, was a natural temptation to invite its closer approach. In spite of my innate disgust, I admired the progressive ratio of timid, slow, and prudent experiment by which it ascertained the character of him to whose mercy it virtually confided its very existence. It watched me closely with all its eight eyes, and propounded to itself the problem, "Is he, or is he not, an enemy?"

Without analyzing its figure, or very clearly distinguishing its eyes, I felt that I was observed and watched; and apparently this observation, in the long run, proved favorable to me. By the instinct of work, perhaps (which is very great in its species), it perceived that I was really a peaceful laborer, and that I was busy, like itself, in weaving my cobweb. However this may be, it abandoned its stratagems and precautions with a quick decision, as if adopting an adventurous and somewhat perilous step. Not without grace it descended upon its thread, and planted itself resolutely on our respective frontier—the edge of my case, favored, at that moment, with a golden ray of the sickly sun.

I was divided between two sentiments. I confess that I did not relish so close an intimacy,—the figure of such a friend pleased me but little; on the other hand, this prudent and observant being, which certainly did not lavish its confidence, seemed to say to me: "Wherefore should I not enjoy a little of thy sun? So different in nature, we have nevertheless arrived together from our necessitous toil and cold obscurity at this sweet banquet of light. Let us take heart, and fraternize. This ray which you permit me to share, receive it from me, and preserve it. In another half century, it will kindle up your winter."

As the little black fairy said this in its own language, whispering low, very low—in fact, it could not be lower (for it is thus that fairies speak)—I marked the effect of it vaguely, and it slumbered in my mind. The circumstance, however, was recalled for a brief while some years ago; and again, after a long interval, it has been revived on this very day, when for the first time I record and explain it.

On the former occasion, after a domestic affliction, I was spending my holidays in Paris, and I went daily alone to walk in my little garden in the Rue des Postes. My family were in the country. Mechanically I remarked the beautiful concentric stars which the spiders had woven round my trees, and which they repaired and remade incessantly with a laudable industry, giving themselves immense trouble to preserve my small stock of fruits and grapes, and relieving myself from the importunity of flies and the stings of gnats. They reminded me of the black domestic spider which, in my childhood, had entered into conversation with me. These latter were very different. Daughters of air and light, always exposed, always before the eyes of men, without other shelter than the surface of a leaf, where they may easily be captured, they are unable to cultivate the reserve or diplomacy of my old acquaintance. All their work, is visible, all their little mystery open to the wind, and their persons at everybody's discretion; they have no other protection than what may be afforded them through compassion, or in consideration of a well-understood interest in the positive services which they render.

Those which suspend their nests to the branches of trees, like those which suspend them to our windows, display an evident design to place themselves in the wind, where a current of air may waft the insects to them, or in the path of a ray of light in which the gnat may float and whirl. The web does not fall vertically, for such a position would restrict it to one current; the spider, like an able seaman, gives it a great obliquity, and thus secures a couple of currents, or even more.

From the extremity of its belly, four screw-plates or tubercles, which can be drawn in or out (like telescopes), eject by their movement a very little cloud, that increases in size from minute to minute. This cloud is composed of threads of an infinite tenuity; each tubercle secretes a thousand, and the four, by combining together their four thousand threads, make the unique and tolerably strong thread of which the web is woven.

Mark well, that the threads of the intelligent manufacturer are not all alike, but of different strength and quality according to their destination. Some are dry for warping, others viscous for gluing. The tissues of the nest intended for the reception of the new-born are of a cottony material, while those which will enwrap the cocoon containing the eggs possess all the resistant power necessary for the safety of the latter.

When the spider has produced a sufficient quantity of thread to undertake a web, it voluntarily glides from an elevated point, and unwinds its skein. There it remains suspended, and afterwards reascending to its starting-point by the assistance of its tiny cordage, moves towards another point; and continues to trace in this manner a series of radii all diverging from the same centre.

The skein stretched, it is busied next in weaving the woof by crossing the thread. Running from radius to radius, it touches each with its tubercles, which fasten to it the circular border. The whole is not a compact tissue, but a veritable network, so geometrically proportioned that all the meshes of the circle are invariably of the same size.

This web, woven out of itself, living and vibrating, is much more than an instrument; it is a part of its being. Itself of a circular form, the spider seems to expand within this circle, and prolong the filaments of its nerves to the radiating threads which it weaves. In the centre of its web lies its greatest force for attack or defense. Out of that centre it is timid; a fly will make it recoil. The web is its

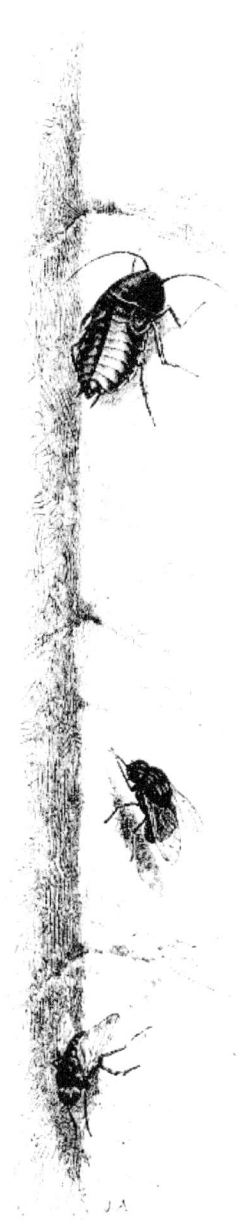

electric telegraph, responding to the lightest touch, and revealing the presence of an imperceptible and almost imponderable victim; while, at the same time, being slightly viscous in substance, it retains the prey, or delays and entangles a dangerous enemy.

In windy weather, the continual agitation of the web prevents it from giving an account of what transpires, and the spider then remains at the centre. But usually it keeps near its machinery, hidden under a leaf, that it may not terrify its victims, or fall a prey to any of its numerous foes.

Prudence and patience, rather than courage, are its characteristics. Its experience is too great, it has undergone too many accidents and misadventures, it is too much accustomed to the severities of fate, to indulge in any surpassing audacity. It is afraid even of an ant. The latter, often a mischievous individual, a restless and rugged rodent, and afraid of nothing, frequently persists in exploring the strange woof, of which it can make nothing. The spider accordingly gives way to it,—whether it fears the acid of the ant, which burns like aquafortis, or whether, like a good artisan, it calculates that a long and obstinate struggle will cost it more time than will the manufacture of another web. Therefore, without yielding to the slightest susceptibility of self-love, it allows the ant to strut about, and takes up its post a little further off.

Every animal lives by depredation. Nature is ever devouring itself; but the prey is not always sought and merited by a patient industry deserving of respect. No being, however, is so much the plaything of fate as the spider. Like every good workman, it has a twofold value: in its work and its person. An infinity of insects—the murderous carabus, or the *libellula*, an elegant and splendid assassin—have only their bodies and their weapons, and spend their lives joyously in killing. Others possess secure and easily defended asylums, where they have cause to fear few dangers. The field-spider has neither the one nor the other advantage. It is in the position of the respectable operative, who, through his small and ill-guaranteed fortune, attracts or tempts cupidity or insolence. The lizard from below, the squirrel from above, hunt the feeble hunter. The inert frog darts at it the viscous tongue, which glues it and renders it immovable. It is the felicity of the swallow, in her graceful circle, to carry off, without injuring, the spider and his web; and all birds look upon it as a great dainty or an excellent medicine. The nightingale, faithful, like all great singers, to a certain hygiene, prescribes for herself, as an occasional purgative, a spider.

Even if she be not swallowed up herself, if the instrument of her trade is destroyed, the consequences are the same. Should the web be undone blow upon blow, a somewhat protracted fast renders it unable to secrete a fresh supply of thread, and it soon perishes of hunger. It is constantly confined in this vicious circle:—

To spin, it requires food;

To feed, it must spin.

Its thread, for the spider as for the Parceæ, is that of destiny.

We once made the experiment of removing three times running a spider's web. Three times, in six hours, it replaced it, with admirable patience, and without abating one jot of hope. The experiment was a cruel one, and we now reproach ourselves for it. We meet with too many poor unfortunates, whom accidents of this kind have thrown out of work, and who are thenceforth too exhausted to resume their industry. One sees them, like living skeletons, attempting fruitlessly a different trade, in which they succeed but poorly, and mournfully envying the long legs of the field-spiders, which gain their living by incessant travelling.

When people speak of the eager gluttony of the spider, they forget that it must either eat a double quantity, or soon perish: eat to recruit its body, and eat to renew its thread.

Three circumstances contribute to wear it out: the ardor of incessant work, its nervous susceptibility—which is carried to an extreme—and its twofold respiratory system.

For it has not only the passive respiration of the insect, which receives, or submits to, the air introduced through its stigmata; it has also a kind of active respiration, analogous to the play of the lungs in the higher animals. It takes the air and masters it, transforms and decomposes it, and incessantly renews it. If you do but examine its movements, you feel that it is something more than an insect; the vital glow traverses its frame in a rapid circulation; the heart beats very differently from what it does in the fly or butterfly.

But its superiority is its peril. The insect braves with impunity the strongest odors and mephitic miasmas. The spider cannot endure them. Instantly affected by them, it falls into convulsions, struggles, and expires. I saw this incident one day at Lucerne. Chloroform, whose action the stag-beetle had endured for fourteen days without succumbing, immediately—at the first contact— overpowered the spider. Yet the victim was a large one, and I found it engaged in eating a gnat. I wished to experiment, and poured on it a single drop. The effect was terrible. Nothing more pitiful could be seen in a case of human asphyxia. It tumbled over, raised itself, and then swooned; all its supports failed it, and its limbs appeared disjointed. One thing was very pathetic—that in this supreme moment the fecundity of its bosom became apparent; in its agony, its tubercles sent forth their little cloudy woof, so that you might have believed it to be working even in death.

I felt oppressed, and in the hope that the fresh air would perhaps revive it, I placed it on my window-sill; but it was no longer *itself*. I know not how the effect was produced; but it seemed to have melted away, and nothing of it remained but its skeleton. The vanished substance had left but its shadow, which the wind bore away to the neighboring lake.

Chapter X. The Home and Loves of the Spider

The spider greatly surpasses all other solitary-living insects. It not only possesses its nest, its ambush, its temporary hunting-station; it has (or, at least, certain species have) a regular house, a house of a very complex description: a vestibule, and a sleeping-chamber, and a mode of egress in the rear; and, finally, a door which is a very triumph of art, for it closes of itself, falling back by its own weight.

The door! It is this which is wanting even in the grand cities of the bees and the ants; these industrial republics have never hitherto attained to so lofty a climax.

The ants have just reached the point at which most of our African tribes have halted. Every evening they shut up their dwelling-places with immense labor—renewed daily—and by a little, unsubstantial lattice-work, which does not relieve them from the necessity of planting sentinels. It is true, however, that these great, valiant, and well-armed peoples have no fear of invasion, and, like Lacedæmon, need neither walls nor ditches. Their proud intrepidity has set limits to their industry.

On the other hand, the poor artisan which lives by itself, and is always exhausted by the incessant toil of spinning and weaving, cannot rely upon its valour. It has need, in certain countries and under certain alarming conditions, of profound ingenuity, and has discovered this little miracle of prudence and combination, which eclipses both the savage and the insect. I do not refer to the great animals, none of which, except the beaver, are very industrious.

In the neighborhood of Lucerne we for the first time saw the house of the spider (the *Agelena*). It was a kind of sheath, and very well made, with a vestibule facing the south, which expanded outward like a funnel. This exterior portion, forming a little sunny retreat, was the snare and the citadel. The lady of the house stationed herself quite at the bottom of the funnel; but behind this very bottom, at the lower extremity of the case or sheath, was constructed a back apartment, small and very secure, in a white substantial cocoon. In this she trusted so completely, that while we detached the silken cables which moored the entire edifice to the bush, she made no attempt to escape. We had neither destroyed nor damaged, but simply detached the dwelling, and on the day following we found it repaired and moored to the bush on every side. The exposure was no longer so favorable; but, undoubtedly, the workman, in an advanced season of the year (in September, and under the Alps), did not possess the resources for recommencing this grand summer-work.

In the Brazilian forests a little spider has its case suspended exactly in the centre of its web; and thither it hurries at the slightest approach of danger, and has no sooner entered, says Swainson, than the door suddenly closes behind it by a spring.

But the masterpiece of the genus is seen, especially in Corsica, in the laborious *Mygale*. Its residence is a kind of well, industriously walled round, with smooth and polished sides, and a double tapestry,—a coarse strong hanging on the earthward front, and a fine satiny hanging in the interior. The orifice of the well is closed by a door. This door is a disc, much larger at the top than at the bottom, and let into a groove in such a manner as to shut hermetically. The disc, which is not more than three lines thick, contains, nevertheless, thirty double woofs, and between the woofs intervene the same number of coats or layers of earth,—so that the entire door is really composed of sixty doors. Here, in truth, is a miracle of patience; but observe, too, the ingenuity,—all these doors of network and earth clamp into one another. The thread-doors at one point are prolonged to the wall, fastening the door to the wall as by a hinge. This door opens outwardly when the spider raises it to go forth, and closes by its own weight. But the enemy might eventually succeed in opening it. This has been anticipated. On the side opposite the hinge some small holes are worked in the door; to these the spider clings, and becomes a living bolt.[15]

---

[15] See the works of Audouin and Walckenaër.

The Insect

What would happen if this astonishing artisan, placed in peculiar and trying circumstances (like the bees under Huber's experiments), were called upon to vary its art and devise a novelty? Could it do so? Has it the intelligence, the resource, and, at need, the power of innovation which the superior insects display under certain conditions? It would be worth while to make the experiment. This, at all events, is certain, that the simple *Epeiras* (our garden-spiders) know very well, when deprived of the necessary space for extending their geometrical curtain, how to construct one of irregular design, decreasing in proportion to the restrictions of their area.

Experiments, moreover, are difficult. The spider is so nervous, that the fear which makes it an artist can also paralyze and utterly confound it. Its web alone gives it courage. Out of its web, everything makes it tremble. In captivity, having no web, it actually flees before its prey, and has not the resolution to confront a fly.

Its miserable condition of passive expectancy fully explains its character. To wait, while acting, running, fighting, is to cheat both time and hunger; but to remain there immovable, to be unable to stir from fear of alarming your prey, to watch it coming nearer and nearer but eventually escaping, and to suffer from an empty stomach! To be a witness of the endless, heedless dances of the fly, which, in the sunbeam, amuses and balances itself for hours without responding to the avid prayers of the tempter which whispers, "Come, little one! Come, my darling!" is a terrible punishment, a series of hopes and disappointments.

It pursues its gay measure, and thinks nothing of the sufferer.

The fatal inquiry, "Shall I dine?" returns, and lacerates its bowels. Then comes the more ominous reflection: "If I do not dine to-day, no more thread! And far less, then, may I hope to dine to-morrow!"

From all this results a suffering, restless, but prodigiously wary and attentive being, which detects not only the slightest contact, but the slightest noise. The spider is only too sensitive. A very little disturbance seems to overthrow its self-control. It apparently faints; you see it suddenly fall from its position, struck down by fear.

Jules Michelet

This sensitiveness, as you will readily believe, is especially displayed in the spider's maternal condition. However miserable and avaricious in its nature, it is tender, liberal, and generous towards its young. While the birds of prey— the winged hunters which have so many resources—drive away their young at a very early age, look upon them as greedy competitors, and force them by blows of their beaks to dwell afar from the domain which they reserve as their own, the spider is not contented with carrying its eggs in the cocoon, but, in certain species, nourishes them when living and greedy, guards them, bears them on its back; or else she makes them walk, holding them by a thread; if danger threatens, she draws in the thread, they leap upon her, and she saves them. If she cannot do so, she will perish. Some there are which, rather than abandon their offspring, will suffer themselves to be swallowed up in the gulf of the ant-lion. Others, of a slow species, which, when unable to save them, make no effort to escape, but allow themselves to be captured also.

Their nests are frequently masterpieces. At Interlaken, in Switzerland, I have admired their long soft tubes, warm in the interior, and well-lined,— externally, disguised with much skill by an artistic pell-mell of small bits of leaf, tiny twigs, and fragments of gray plaster, so as to melt perfectly into the color of the wall supporting them. But this was nothing in comparison with a work of art which I have here at Fontainebleau.

On the 22nd of July 1857, I discovered in an outhouse a very pretty round basket, about an inch across, made of all kinds of materials, and, as it had nothing to fear from rain, without any cover. It was very gracefully suspended to a beam by some elegant silken threads, which I should call little hands, such as are possessed by the climbing plants. Within, brooding on its eggs with a constant incubation, might be seen a spider. It never stirred, except, perhaps, for a moment at night, in quest of food. Never was there any animal so timid. At the gentlest approaches fear made it fly, and almost fall. Once when we disturbed it a little abruptly, it was seized with such an excess of terror that it did not recover for an entire day. It sat for six weeks, and, but for these perturbations, would perhaps have remained much longer.

An admirable mother,—an ingenious and delicate artist,—before all things a female,—a female nervous and timid to the highest degree, this strange sensitive creature explained to me perfectly the very opposite sentiments with which the spider inspires us,—those of repulsion and attraction. We start away from it, and yet we draw near to it. It is so coarse, and yet, at the same time, so prodigiously sensitive! It breathes as we do. And the delicate tubercle which secretes its silk, like a milky cloud (as the microscope shows us), is the most feminine organ which exists, perhaps, in nature.

Alas, it is alone! Except a few species (mygales) in which the father renders some assistance to the mother, it expects no help. The male, after its moment of love, becomes, indeed, an enemy. Cruel consequences of misery! It perceives that its children are capable of furnishing it with food. But the mother, who is bigger than he, makes a similar reflection,—thinks that the eater is eatable,—and frequently crunches her spouse.

The Insect

These atrocious events never happen, I am confident, in climates where ease and abundance do not deprave their natural disposition. But in our well-peopled countries, with game very rare, and competition of extreme violence, these unfortunates act towards one another like the wretched castaways on the raft of the *Medusa*.

A cruel tyrant, the stomach, dominates over all nature, and vanquishes even love. Passion, in an anxious and restless being like the spider, is very mistrustful. At the height of his devotion, the lean and feeble male dares only approach the majestic lady with a timid reverence and the utmost reserve. He advances, he retires, he watches; he seems to ask himself if he has at all succeeded in subduing the haughty creature. He resorts to the timid methods of a slow magnetism, and especially to an extreme patience. He puts little faith in the first signs, and does not willingly yield his confidence. And, finally, when the adored object shows herself sensible of his sincerity, and grows ardent in her expansion of soul, he does not so wholly trust in her but what he will escape, and fly with all his speed, at some sudden impulse, and under the influence of an indescribable panic.

Such is the terrible idyl of the dusky lovers of our ceilings. Among our garden-spiders less suspicion seems to exist. Nature softens hearts, and rugged industrialism itself grows smoother in rustic life. We see some upon our trees which behave tolerably well to their husbands, and do not too often remember that they are competitors in the chase. They permit them to reside in the same locality, although a little apart, and keeping them at a distance. A light partition separates them. The princess consents that he may live under her roof, and on the ground-floor, while she lives on the first story,—keeping him below and in subjection, so that he may not presume to think himself the king, but only the *prince consort*, and the *husband of the queen*.

Have they any sympathies beyond their own race? So some authorities have asserted, and I believe it. They are isolated from us far less than the true insects. They live in our houses, have an interest in knowing us, and seem to observe us. They pay great attention to voices and sounds, and have a marvelous perception of them. If they have not the insect-organs of hearing (which would seem to be the antennæ), it is because they are *all antennæ*. Their excessive vigilance, and the nervous irradiation which makes itself felt everywhere among them, endow them with the keenest receptivity.

Much has been said about the musical spider of Pellisson. Another and less-known anecdote is not less striking. One of those little victims which are trained into virtuosi before they are ripe of age,—Berthome, illustrious in 1800,—owed his astonishing successes to the savage confinement in which he was forced to work. At eight he astounded and stupefied his hearers by his mastery of the violin. In his perpetual solitude he had a comrade whom no one suspected,—a spider. It was lodged at first in a quiet corner, but it gave itself license to advance from the corner to the music-stand, from the music-stand to the child, even climbing upon the mobile arm which held the bow. There, a palpitating and breathless amateur, it paused and listened. It was an audience in itself. The artist needed nothing more to fill him with inspiration and double his energy.

Unfortunately the child had a stepmother, who, one day, introducing an amateur into the sanctuary, saw the sensible animal at its post. A blow from her slipper annihilated the auditory. The child fell swooning to the ground, was ill for three months, and died,—heartbroken!

Book the Third
Communities of Insects

Chapter I. The City in the Shadows: The Termites, or White Ants

M. de Prefontaine (cited by Huber, in his work on "The Ants") relates that, when travelling in Guiana, he saw a party of negroes besieging certain fantastic edifices which he calls ant-hills. They did not venture to attack them except from a distance, and with firearms; having first taken the precaution, moreover, to dig a little trench and fill it with water, to check the progress of the beleaguered army and drown its battalions, if they adventured a sortie.

These edifices are not the habitations of Ants, but of Termites,—quite a different species of insect; which are found not only in Guiana, but in Africa, New Holland, and in the prairies of North America.

A host of travelers have described them. But the standard and most instructive authority is that of Smeathman, which now lies before us, enriched with excellent plates. The drawings are taken from the termite-hills of Africa.

Figure to yourself a mound of earth, about twelve feet high (some have been discovered measuring twenty), which, from a distance, might easily be mistaken for a negro's hut. Approach it, and you will at once detect that it is the product of a higher art. Its curious form is that of a pointed dome; or, if you like, of an obtuse and preponderating obelisk. For support, the dome or obelisk has four, five, or six cupolas from five to six feet high; and against these are propped up below some small bell-like structures, nearly two feet in elevation. The whole might well be taken for a kind of Oriental cathedral, the principal spire of which had a double cincture of minarets, decreasing in height; the said whole being of extreme solidity, and composed of a compact clay, which, when burnt, makes the best bricks. Not only may several men stand upon it without injury, but even the wild bull's station themselves on its summit as sentinels to watch, through the high grasses of the plain, that the lion or panther does not surprise the herd.

Nevertheless, this dome is hollow, and the inferior platform which supports it is itself supported by a semi-hollow construction formed by the junction of four arches (two to three feet in span),—arches of a very substantial design, being pointed, ogival, and in a kind of Gothic style. Lower still extends a number of passages or corridors, plastered spaces which one might call saloons, and finally, convenient, spacious, and healthy lodgings, capable of receiving a large population; in brief, quite a subterranean city.

A broad spiral passage winds and rises gradually in the thickness of the edifice, which has no opening, no door, no window; the vomitories are disguised and at a distance, terminating afar in the plain.

It is the most considerable and important work which displays the genius of insects; a labor of infinite patience and of daring art. We must not forget that these walls, which time has hardened, were very friable at first, and always crumbling. To raise this Titanic edifice to such a height, a continuity of effort was absolutely requisite, and a succession of provisional constructions, demolished one after the other when they had served their purpose. The masons commenced with the exterior pyramids, a foot and a foot and a half in height; then with those of the second rank. But the latter being solid and indurated, they intrepidly undermined their base to make room for the passages, the windows, and the spiral staircase. The same operation was carried out beneath the dome, which was excavated with great labor, and in such a manner that the great hollow vault, in conjunction with its lower platform, rested on the narrow vaults of the four arches forming the centre and foundation of the edifice.

Observe that this dome is self-sustaining, and that its substructions, strictly speaking, would amply suffice for its support; the lateral pyramids being only its not indispensable auxiliaries. Here, then, we find the principle of a true, honest, and courageous art, which, relying on itself and its calculations, requires no assistance from external supports, and needs neither props nor buttresses. It is exactly the system of Brunelleschi.

Who has carried the art to such a climax? We must own that it is the supreme of usefulness. The sharpened dome, the belfries or needles, are admirably arranged so as to resist the terrible rain-storms of the tropics. The dome keeps off the water, and assists it to flow away rapidly. If it cracked, the platform on which it leans would throw the water, as from a roof, on to the exterior *enceinte*, which would carry it to the ground. Hollow like a kiln, it quickly gets warmed, and absorbs the heat; duly communicating it to the subterranean passages to hatch the eggs, and promote the comfort of a race which, being wholly naked, prefers an elevated temperature.

It is a masterpiece of art, precisely because it is a masterpiece of utility. The beautiful and the useful admirably harmonize. Now one would wish to know who *are* these astonishing artists: we hardly dare to confess that they are the objects of our entire contempt.

Various names have been bestowed upon them; among others, that of termites: and again, that of wood-ants,—a designation not very accurate, for the ants are their enemies, and their body, being exceedingly soft, is exactly the opposite of the dry hard body of the ant.

They have been also called wood-lice; and they seem, in truth, a soft and feeble kind of vermin, which are crushed without resistance. Magnificent jest of God, who loves to exalt his humblest creatures! The Memphis, the Babylon, the true Capitol of the insects, is built—by whom? By lice! Though their luxury of jaws, and their four stages of teeth, make them admirable rodents, nevertheless, if we except their *élite*, the soldiers, they have no important weapons. Their teeth, made to gnaw, are powerless in combat. The destiny of the termites is plain; spite of the formidable names which have been given to their species (*bellicosus, mordax, atrox*), they are simply *workers*.

Every other insect is stronger than they are; or at least harder, better protected, and more completely armed. All, especially the ants, hunt them, and devour them by myriads. Birds greedily pursue them; the poultry-yards absorb them in frightful quantities. All (even man, who cooks them) find them of an agreeable taste; and the negro can never be satiated with them.

They work without seeing their work. They have no eyes, at least none which are visible. Very probably, the darkness in which they live destroys their ocular organs, as is the case with a species of duck found in the subterranean lakes of Carinthia. The rare species of termites which venture forth into the daylight have very conspicuous and perfectly formed eyes.

The darkness and the persecution to which they are exposed under the light, seem to have developed their singular industry. Against that world of day which shows them so bitter a hostility, they have built, as they have been able, this little world of the shadows, in which they exercise their arts. They issue forth only in search of food, and the gum and other substances of which they make their magazines.

Their attachment is extreme for these cities of darkness. They defend them obstinately. The first blow that is given each resists in his own fashion; the workmen plastering the interior with a kind of mortar which closes up the holes, the soldiers attacking the assailants and drawing blood with their sharp pincers, clinging to the wound, and suffering themselves to be crushed rather than let go. A naked man (like the negro) shrinks under these bites, grows discouraged, and is conquered.

If you still persist, if you penetrate, you admire the palace, its circuits, its corridors, its aërial bridges, the halls or saloons where the population lodge, the nurseries for the eggs, the caves, cellars, or magazines. But, above all, search to the centre. There lurks the mystery of this little world; there is its palladium, its idol, incessantly surrounded by the cares of an enthusiastic crowd. A strange and shocking object, which is not the less obeyed, and visibly adored!

It is the queen, or common mother, frightfully fecund, from whose body issues an uninterrupted flood of about sixty eggs per minute, or eighty thousand eggs per day!

You can conceive of nothing more fantastic. These strange creatures, which we compare to vermin, have nevertheless their moment of supreme poesy, their hour of love; for a moment their wings uplift them, and almost immediately they sink. The couples thus bereft, having neither refuge nor strength, and no means of resistance, are a prey for all the insects,—a manna upon which they straightway throw themselves. The working termites, which have neither love nor wings, endeavor to save a couple of the victims, welcome them,—weak, and fallen, and wretched as they are,—and make them monarchs.

They remove them to the centre of the city, and establish them in the saloon on which all the apartments and corridors abut. There they are revived, recruited, and nourished day and night; and the female gradually assumes an enormous size, until in body and stomach she is two thousand times larger than her natural condition,—though, by a hideous contrast, the head does not increase. For the rest, immovable, and therefore captive, the doors through which she entered have become infinitely too narrow to admit of the egress of such a monster. Accordingly, there she will remain, pouring out, until she splits asunder, that torrent of living matter which the termites day and night collect, and which, to-morrow, will be the People.

This soft and whitish-looking creature, a stomach rather than a being, is at least of the size of the human thumb: a traveler pretends to have seen one as large as a crab.

The bigger she is, the more fertile, the more inexhaustible, this terrible mother of lice seems the more enthusiastically worshipped by her fanatical vermin. She appears to be their ideal, their poetry, their ecstasy If you carry them off, with a fragment, a ruin of the city, you may see them, under a glass shade, instantly set to work to build an arch for the protection of the mother's venerated head, to reconstruct her royal hall, which will become, if the materials be sufficient, the centre and basis of the resuscitated community.

I am not astonished, let me add, at the extravagant love which they show towards this instrument of fecundity. If every other race did not jointly labor to destroy them, this truly prodigious mother would make them masters of the world,—nay, what do I say?—its only inhabitants. The fish alone would survive; but the insect world would perish. It suffices to remember that the queen-bee takes a year to accomplish what the termite mother accomplishes in a day. Through her means they would swallow up Everybody; but they are feeble and savory, and it is Everybody which swallows up them.

When the species of termites which live and dwell in the woods unfortunately approach near our habitations, there is no means of arresting their ravages. They work with a truly incredible vigor and rapidity. They have been known in one night to eat their way through the leg of a table, then through the thickness of the table itself, descending through the leg on the opposite side.

The reader can easily imagine the effect produced by such toil as this on the joists and framework of a house. The worst of it is, that a long time may elapse before their ravages are detected. We continue to rely upon supports which suddenly, one fine morning, crumble away; we sleep peacefully under roofs which to-morrow will cease to exist.

The town of Valencia, in New Grenada, undermined by the subterranean galleries these insects have excavated in the earth, is now literally suspended upon their dangerous catacombs.

We have ourselves seen, at Rochelle, the formidable beginnings of the ravages they executed in the timber-work of a quarter of the town where they were introduced by foreign ships. Whole buildings are found eaten up, though apparently sound,—all the wood hollowed and tunneled, even to the banisters of the staircase: do not rest upon them, or they will yield and give way under your hand. These terrible nibblers seem willing, however, to confine themselves to one district of the town, and not to invade the remainder. Otherwise, this historical city, important still through its marine and its commerce, would be reduced to the condition of Herculaneum and Pompeii.

Chapter II. The Ants:—Their Domestic Economy—Their Nuptials

The ants enjoy a superiority over all other insects, inasmuch as they are less specialized by their mode of life, their nourishment, and the instruments of their industry. Generally, they adapt themselves to all conditions, and work in all climates; nor in all Nature do more energetic agents in purification and cleansing exist. They are, so to say, the factotums of Nature.

The termites, at least the majority of them, work in the darkness, under the earth; the ants both above and below.

Like the termites, they build, at least in tropical countries, the most remarkable edifices,—domes under which their chrysalides enjoy the warmth of the sun without being injured by its scorching rays. But these are not fortresses; the ants have no need of them; for in the tropical regions they are the sovereigns and tyrants of all other beings. The exterminating *carabi*, the invading *necrophori*, which play among us, as insects, the *rôle* of the eagle and the vulture, scarcely venture to make their appearance in the burning latitudes where the ants hold sway. Everything which lies on the earth's surface they immediately devour. Lund, in his *Mémoire sur les Fourmis*, says that he had scarcely time to pick up a bird which he had seen drop. The ants were already on the spot, and had seized upon it. The sanitary police is performed by them with an implacable and energetic exactitude.

The great ants of the South are much more savage than our European species; and feeling themselves sovereigns and mistresses, feared by all, dreading none, they march forward imperturbably, without suffering any obstacle to divert their course. If a house stand in their way, they enter, and all that is alive within it—even the enormous, venomous, and formidable spiders, ay, and small mammiferous animals also—is devoured. Men give place to them. And if you cannot quit your house, you have reason to fear their invasion. Once, at Barbadoes, a long column was seen defiling for several days in formidable numbers. All the earth was black with them, and the torrent poured forward straight in the direction of the houses. They were crushed by hundreds, without heeding their losses; myriads were destroyed, but they continued to advance. No wall, no ditch, was of any service; water even could not arrest their progress: for it is known that they construct living bridges, by fastening on to one another in clusters and garlands. Fortunately, the plan was adopted of sowing the ground in advance of them with numerous tiny volcanoes, small heaps of gunpowder, which were fired at intervals beneath them, and exploding, swept away whole files, and dispersed the rest,—covering them with fire and smoke, and blinding them with dust. This scheme proved successful. At least, the ants turned aside a little, and moved in a different direction.

Linnæus calls the termites the scourge of the two Indies; and we might equally well bestow this appellation on the ants, if we considered only the havoc they commit among the labors and cultivation of man. In a few hours they strip a large orangery, denuding it of every leaf. In a single night they devastate a field of cotton, manioc, or sugar-cane. Behold their crimes! Their virtues? they destroy to a still greater extent all things that might prove hurtful to man, and but for them certain countries would be uninhabitable.

As for our European species, I cannot see that they do the slightest harm, either to man, or to the plants he cultivates. Far from it, they deliver him from an infinity of little insects. I have frequently seen long files of them, with each carrying in his mouth a very small grub as a contribution to the food stores of the republic. Such a picture should ensure them the benedictions of every honorable agriculturist.

The mason-ants, which work in and entirely under the earth, are difficult to observe. But the "carpenters" may be easily followed, at least in the upper part of their constructions. The cupola of their edifice being subject to dilapidation, they are constantly under a necessity of repairing and re-excavating it. With the small amount of soil which they make use of, they mix the leaves and spines of the fir, and the catkins of the pine. If they meet with a bent; twisted, and knotty twig, it is a treasure; they employ it as an arcade, or, better still, as an ogive; for the pointed arch is the most solid. The numerous avenues which lead to the surface spread out in radii like a fan; they start from a concentric point, and extend to the circumference. The mass of the edifice is divided into low but spacious apartments. The largest is in the centre and under the dome; it is also the most elevated, and destined, apparently, for public communications. There, at all hours, you will find a knot of busy citizens, who, by the rapid contact of their antennæ (a kind of electric telegraph) seem to relate to one another the news, and exchange opinions or mutual directions. It is a kind of forum.

There is nothing more curious than to observe the various occupations and movements of this great people. While some, as purveyors, go in search of grubs, hunt insects, or collect materials, others, sedentary in their habits, attend entirely to domestic cares and the education of the young. An immense and an incessant occupation, if we may judge from the continual movement of the nurses round the cradles. Let but a raindrop fall, or a single sunbeam penetrate, and a general stir takes place, a general removal of all the children of the colony, and this with an ardor which never wearies. You may see them tenderly taking up the big children—which weigh as much as themselves—and transferring them from stage to stage, to rest them in a convenient position.

This scale of heat, extending over forty degrees, what is it but a thermometer?

But more remains. The cares of alimentation, of what one might call "suckling," are much more complicated than among the bees. The eggs must receive a nourishing humidity from the mouth of the nurses. The larvæ take the beakful. And the young one which has worn through its husk and become a nymph, would not have strength enough to emerge from it if the attentive guardians were not at hand to open the husk, release the little tenant, and initiate it into the light. In the artificial ant-hills, which we have procured for the sake of closer examination, we have even succeeded in observing a circumstance which Huber regrets he had been unable to discover.

Some light movements which the infant communicates to its swaddling-clothes give warning that its hour is come. We took great pleasure in watching the nurses seated upon their hind limbs like little motionless, upright fairies, plainly discerning under the silent veil the first yearning for liberty.

As in every superior race, the young comes into the world weak, and frail, and incapable of effort. Its first steps are so infirm that at every movement it falls upon its knees. It requires, as it were, to be kept in leading-strings. Its great vitality is only shown by an incessant demand for food. Therefore, when the heat is great, and numerous swaddling-husks must be opened daily, the new-born are all lodged in the same part of the city.

NEST OF RUSSET ANTS.

One day, however, I saw a young ant thrust forth its head, still somewhat pale, at a gate of the city, then step across the threshold, and march along the summit of the ant-hill. The escapade, however, was not long permitted. A nurse encountering the fugitive, seized it by the top of its head, and conducted it gently towards a neighboring entrance.

The child resisted; it suffered itself to be dragged along, and on the way coming in contact with a small piece of wood, profited by it to stiffen itself, and exhaust its conductor's strength. The latter, always keeping its temper, let go for a moment, executed a flank movement, and then returned to the charge, until its nursling, tired out, was compelled to yield obedience.

As soon as the young are strong enough, they have to be brought acquainted with the interior labyrinth of the city, the suburbs, the avenues which lead to the outer world, and the neighboring roads. Then they are trained to hunt, are accustomed to provide for themselves, to live hap-hazard and upon little or any kind of food. Temperance is the basis of the whole commonwealth.

The ant, not being fastidious, but accepting all descriptions of food, is from this very cause the less anxious, restless, and selfish. It is very wrong to call it a *miser*. Far from being so, it seems solely intent upon multiplying in its city the number of its co-partners. In its generous maternal care of those whom it has not begotten, in its solicitude for those little ones of yesterday which to-day become young citizens, originates a feeling quite novel and very rare among insects,— that of fraternity. (See the works of Latreille and Huber.)

The obscurest and most curious point of their education is, undoubtedly, the communication of language, which reminds the observer of the forms of freemasonry. It enables them to transmit really complicated directions to their legions, and to change in a moment the march of a whole column, the action of an entire populace.

This language principally consists in the touch of the antennæ, or in a light collision of the mandibles. They urge (or perhaps persuade) by blows of the head against the thorax. Finally, they sometimes carry off the auditor, who makes no resistance, and transport him to some designated place or object. In this case, which undoubtedly is both difficult to believe and explain, the convinced auditor unites with the other, and both together carry off other witnesses, which in their turn perform upon others—the number continually increasing—the same operation. Our parliamentary phrases, "to carry away the crowd," "to transport the hearer," are by no means mere metaphors among the ants!

To this lively gesticulation they join many other scarcely explicable movements,—such as cavalcades, in which they march mounted one upon another, exchanging gay defiances and light blows upon the cheeks. Then they rear themselves upright, and contend by couples, seizing upon a leg, a mandible, or an antenna. Naturalists have spoken of these as their pastimes, but I know not what to think. Among so busy, and obviously serious a family, this gymnastic exercise has perhaps a hygienic object which we do not understand.

We had so well managed our prisoners that they had become habituated to their new domicile, and toiled under our eyes as they would have done in their own city. They rebuilt for themselves a small town in miniature, with gates whose number they carefully augmented, especially on very hot days, for the purpose of giving air to their little ones, whom they took care to place near the openings.

In the evening they conscientiously proceeded, according to their invariable custom, to shut up the gates, as if always afraid of some nocturnal invasion of idle vagabonds. A spectacle of deep interest, which we frequently took occasion to enjoy in front of the great swarming ant-hills.

Nor could there be a more varied picture; on all sides, and at great distances, you might see them coming in long files, each bearing some little article,—one a long straw, another a pretty pine nut-cup, or (according to the country) a black needle-like leaf of the fir-tree. These, like little woodcutters returning at close of day, brought back imperceptible bundles of twigs; others, which seemed empty-handed, were but the more heavily loaded, having just taken prisoners some wood-lice, which they carried home for the evening meal of the little ones.

At the approaches of the City, the points where the ascent commenced, it was a pleasure to see the vigor, the zeal, and the ardor with which they dragged up such heavy materials. If one let go, exhausted, two or three others succeeded. And the joist or beam, full of animation, and apparently alive, gradually ascended. Skill and foresight supplied the want of strength. If checked at any particular point, they turned and advanced in a somewhat different direction, ascending a little higher than was necessary; then they let down the weight exactly over the opening which they wished to conceal; a quick light movement made the mass pirouette, and it fell into its place.

Numerous problems in statics and mechanics were solved by a felicitous audacity and with a great economy of effort. By degrees all was secured. The vast dome, embracing with a soft and delicate curve a great nation of workers in its lawful repose, offered nothing to the sight, neither door nor window, and appeared to be a simple heap of tiny fragments of fir. Do I mean that all slumbered in full confidence? It would be wrong to think so. A few sentinels wandered to and fro; at the lightest touch of a switch, or the rustle of a leaf, the guards would issue forth, perambulate the exterior of their city, and when reassured would re-enter, but, undoubtedly, to continue their watch, and remain upon duty.

The most surprising scene at which any one can be present is a marriage of ants.

Of all follies, as everybody knows, the worst are those of the wise. The honorable, economical, and respectable republic accordingly presents (one single day yearly, it is true) a prodigious spectacle—of love? of madness?—we do not know, but certainly of vertigo, and to speak plainly, of terror. M. Huber saw in it the appearance of a national holiday. What a holiday! And what a scene of intoxication! But no; nothing human can give an idea of this boiling effervescence.

I watched it on one occasion, between six and seven o'clock in the evening. The day had been one of heavy showers and warm gleams of light. The horizon was lowering, and yet the air calm. It was Nature's pause before resuming her storms of rain.

Upon a low sloping roof I saw descend quite a deluge of winged insects, which seemed stunned, confused, delirious. To describe their agitation, their disorderly movements, their somersaults and shocks to arrive more quickly at the goal, would be impossible. Many rested, and loved. The greater number whirled round and round without stopping. All were so eager to live, that their very eagerness proved an obstacle. This feverish desire produced a feeling of alarm.

A terrible idyllic poem!

It was impossible to make out what they wished. Were they enjoying a festival of love? Were they devouring one another? Right through this distraught multitude of *fiancés* who had lost their senses passed other and wingless ants, which threw themselves without mercy on the most embarrassed individuals, bit them, and treated them so severely, that we thought we could see them crunching the lovers. But no! They wanted nothing more than to force them to obey, and to recall them to their senses. Their vivid pantomime was the counsel of prudence translated into action. The wingless ants were the wise and irreproachable nurses, who, having no children, bring up those of the others, and bear all the burden of the toil and management of the city.

These virgins maintained a surveillance over the amorous and slothful, and rigidly inspected the marriage-festival as a public act, which, every year, renews the nation. Their natural fear was lest the winged fools should be wooed and won elsewhere, and create other tribes, without any thought of the parent community.

Numbers of the winged ones submitted, and allowed themselves to be carried below towards their country and virtue. But many tore themselves away, and flew afar, obedient only to the dictates of love and caprice.

It was an astonishing vision, a fantastic dream, which can never be forgotten.

In the morning nothing remained as a memorial of the excesses of the preceding evening, except the fragments of some severed wings, in which no one could have divined the trace of a unique *soirée d'amour*.

Chapter III. The Ants:— Their Flocks and Their Slaves

When I learned for the first time, from the pages of Huber, the strange and prodigious fact that certain ants keep slaves, I was greatly astonished—as everybody has been by this singular revelation—but I was especially saddened and wounded.

What! I turn aside from the history of man in search of innocence. I hope at least to discover among the brute creation the even-handed justice of nature, the primitive rectitude of the plan of creation. I seek in this people, whom I had previously loved and esteemed for their laboriousness and temperateness, the severe and touching image of republican virtues—and I find among them this thing without a name!

What a joy, what a triumph for the partisans of slavery, for all the friends of evil! Hell and tyranny, laugh ye, and make merry! A black spot is revealed in the brightness of Nature.

I had flung aside Huber, and no book had ever seemed to me more hateful. Pardon, illustrious observer! your grandfather and your father had enraptured and charmed me. The first of the clan—Huber, the great historian of the bees—

has inspired with new warmth the religion of man, and lifted up his heart. But Huber of the ants has broken mine.

It was, nevertheless, a duty to resume my perusal of his work, and examine it more attentively. An immoral, a Machiavellian, and a perverse insect is worthy of investigation.

But, in the first place, let us make a distinction. A portion of these pretended slaves may only be cattle.

It is enough to look at the ants, thin to an excess, brilliant, and varnished, to conclude that they are the driest and most parched of beings. Their singular acridity has been established by chemical researches, and science has contrived to extract the mordant formic acid from their bodies. Sometimes, when they are in peril, they hurl it at their enemies like a venom. Not a few species employ it in drying, blackening, and almost burning the trees where they establish their abodes. Is not a substance so corrosive for others equally dangerous to themselves? I should be tempted to think so, and to this extreme acridity should attribute their greediness for honey and other lubricating substances. I submit my hypothesis to the consideration of the scientific.

The ants of Mexico, in a specially favored climate, have two classes of workmen,—one charged with the duty of seeking provisions; the other, inactive and sedentary, entrusted with the work of elaborating them, and making out of them a kind of honey for the common nourishment.

The ants of our temperate climates, for the most part incapable of making honey, satisfy their imperative need of it by licking the honey-dew found upon certain grubs, which, without labor, by the mere fact of their organization, extract saccharine juices from all species of plants. The transmission of this honey to the ants is effected quietly, and, as it were, by mutual agreement.

It operates by a kind of titillation or gentle traction, such as we exercise upon the cow. These grubs, placed at the extreme limit of animal life— viviparous in summer, oviparous in autumn—are very humble creatures, and prodigiously inferior in intelligence to the ants. The magnifying-glass reveals them to the observer as always bent, and always engaged in feeding. Their attitude is that of the cattle. They are, in truth, the milch-cows of the ants; and that they may always profit by them, the latter frequently transport them to their ant-hill, where they live together on admirably good terms. The ants take great care of the grubs, superintend the incubation, and nourish the adults with their favorite vegetables.

In situations where great difficulty would be experienced in transporting and installing them, they empark them on the ground by throwing up around their field of pasture a fence of twigs and cylinders of earth. This may justly be termed the grazing-field, the *chalet* of the ants; which repair to it at certain hours to milk their herds, and sometimes carry their young thither for the easier distribution of the food. I am frequently present, especially in the evening, at these Dutch-like scenes, which have hitherto found no Paul Potter among the ants to depict them.

Observe that these grubs, whether transported to the ant-hill or emparked on their favorite feeding-ground, possess the inestimable advantage of having their safety guaranteed by the redoubtable republic. The "lion of the grubs" (as a small worm is called), and other wild beasts, if they dared approach the herd, would feel very cruelly their strong mandibles and burning formic acid.

So far, then, we have no reproach to make; the grubs are cattle, and not slaves. The ants do exactly what we do; they make use of the privilege of superior beings, but exercise it with more gentleness and management than does man.

But we now come to a more delicate consideration. There are two kinds of ants, of a tolerable size, but otherwise of no peculiar distinction, which employ as servants, nurses, and cooks, certain small ants endowed with more skill and ingenuity.

This strange fact, which ought apparently to change our ideas of animal morality, was discovered early in the present century. Pierre Huber, the son of the celebrated observer of the manners and habits of bees, walking one day in a field near Geneva, saw on the ground a strong detachment of reddish-colored ants on the march, and bethought himself of following them. On the flanks of the column, as if to dress its ranks, a few speed to and fro in eager haste. After marching for about a quarter of an hour, they halt before an ant-hill belonging to the small black ant, and a desperate struggle takes place at its gates.

A small number of the blacks offer a brave resistance; but the great majority of the people thus assailed flee through the gates remotest from the scene of combat, carrying away their young. It was just these which were the cause of the strife; what the blacks most justly feared was the theft of their offspring. And soon the assailants, who had succeeded in penetrating into, the city, might be seen emerging from it loaded with the young black progeny. It was an exact resemblance of a descent of slave-dealers on the coast of Africa.

The red ants, encumbered with their living booty, left the unfortunate city in the desolation of its great loss, and resumed the road to their own habitation, whither their astonished and almost breathless observer followed them. But how was his astonishment augmented when, at the-threshold of the red ants' community, a small population of black ants came forward to receive the plunder, welcoming with visible joy these children of their own race, which, undoubtedly, would perpetuate it in the foreign land.

This, then, is a mixed city, where the strong warrior-ants live in a perfectly good understanding with the little blacks. But what do the latter? Huber speedily discovered that, in effect, they do everything. They alone build; they alone bring up the young red ants and the captives of their own species; they alone administer the affairs of the community, provide its supplies of food, wait upon and nourish their red masters, who, like great infant giants, indolently allow their little attendants to feed them at the mouth. No other occupations are theirs but war, theft, and kidnapping. No other movements in the intervals than to wander about lazily, and bask in the sunshine at the door of their barracks.

The most curious circumstance is, that these civilized helots really love their great barbarous warriors, and carefully tend their children, gladly and cheerfully perform their tasks of servitude, and, more, encourage the extension of their slavery and the abduction of the little blacks. Does not all this wear the appearance of a free adhesion to the established order of things?

And who knows but that the joy and pride of governing the strong and tyrannizing over their tyrants, may be for the little blacks an inner liberty—an exquisite and sovereign freedom—far superior to any pleasure they could have derived from the equality of their native country?

Huber made an experiment. He was desirous of observing what would be the result if the great red ants found themselves without servants, and if they would know how to supply their own wants. He thought, perhaps, that the degenerate creatures might be inspired and uplifted by the maternal love which is so strong among the ants.

He put a few into a glass case, and with them some *nymphs*. Instinctively they began to move them about and to cradle them after their fashion; but soon discovered (big and robust as they, nevertheless, were) that the weight was too much for them; they accordingly left them on the ground, and coolly abandoned them. In truth, they abandoned themselves. Huber put some honey for them in a corner, so that they had nothing to do but to take it. Miserable the degradation, cruel the punishment with which slavery afflicts the enslavers! They did not touch it; they seemed to know nothing; they had become so grossly ignorant and indolent that they could no longer feed themselves. Some of them died from starvation, with food before them!

Huber, to complete the experiment, then introduced into the case one black ant. The presence of this sagacious helot changed the face of things, and re-established life and order. He went straight to the honey; he fed the great dying simpletons; he dug a hole in the ground, placed in it the eggs, prepared the incubation, watched over the nymphs (or *maillots*), and restored to life and happiness the little people, who, becoming industrious in their turn, seconded the efforts of their nurse. Felicitous influence of genius! A single individual had re-created the city.

The observer then understood that with such a superiority of intelligence these helots might, in reality, wear the chains of servitude very lightly, and perhaps govern their masters. A persevering study proved to him that such was, indeed, the case. The little blacks in many things carry a moral authority whose signs are very visible; they do not, for example, permit the great red ants to go out alone on useless expeditions, and compel them to return into the city. Nor are they even at liberty to go out in a body, if their wise little helots do not think the weather favorable, if they fear a storm, or if the day is far advanced. When an excursion proves unsuccessful, and they return without children, the little blacks are stationed at the gates of the city to forbid their ingress, and send them back to the combat; nay more, you may see them take the cowards by the collar, and force them to retrace their route.

These are astounding facts; but such as they are, they were seen by our illustrious observer. He could not trust his eyes, and summoned one of the greatest naturalists of Sweden—M. Jurine—to his side, to make new investigations, and decide whether he had been deceived. This witness, and others who afterwards pursued the same course of experiments, found that his discoveries were entirely accurate.

Yet—shall I dare to confess it?—after all these weighty testimonies I still doubted. Let me say, I *hoped* that the fact, without being absolutely false, had not been correctly observed. But on a certain occasion I saw it—with my own eyes saw it—in the park of Fontainebleau. I was accompanied by an illustrious philosopher, an excellent observer, and he too saw exactly what I saw.

It was half-past four in the afternoon of a very warm day. From a pile of stones emerged a column of from four to five hundred red or reddish ants, precisely the same color as the wing-cases of the gnat. They marched rapidly towards a piece of turf, kept in order by their sergeants or "pivot-men," whom we saw on the flanks, and who would not permit any one to straggle. (This is a circumstance known to everybody who has seen a file of ants on the march.) But the novel and astonishing thing to me was, that gradually those who were at the head drew near to each other, and advanced only by turning; they passed and repassed the whirling crowd, describing concentric circles; a manœuvre evidently fit to produce enthusiasm, and to augment energy,—each, by contact, electrifying himself with the ardor of all.

Suddenly the revolving mass seemed to sink and disappear. There was no sign of ant-hills in the turf; but after a while we detected an almost imperceptible orifice, through which we saw them vanish in less time than it takes me to write these words. We asked ourselves if it was an entrance to their domicile; if they had re-entered their city. In a minute at the utmost they gave us a reply, and showed us our mistake. They issued in a throng, each carrying a nymph on its mandibles.

From the short time they had taken, it was evident that they had a previous knowledge of the localities, the place where the eggs were deposited, the time when they were to assemble, and the degree of resistance they had to expect. Perhaps it was not their first journey.

The little blacks on whom the red ants made this *razzia* sallied out in considerable numbers; and I truly pitied them. They did not attempt to fight. They seemed frightened and stunned. They only endeavored to delay the ravishers by clinging to them. A red ant was thus arrested; but another red one, who was free, relieved him of his burden, and thereupon the black ant relaxed his grasp. In fine, it was a pitiful scene for the blacks. They offered no serious resistance. The five hundred red ants succeeded in carrying off nearly three hundred children. At two or three feet from the hole, the blacks ceased to pursue them, abandoned all hope, and resigned themselves to their fate. All this did not occupy ten minutes between the departure and the return. The two parties were very unequal. It was evidently a facile abuse of strength,—very probably an outrage often repeated,—a tyranny of the great, who levied a tribute of children from their poor little neighbors.

Jules Michelet

Let us now endeavor to understand this shocking and hideous fact. It is peculiar to certain species; it is a particular incident, an exceptional case, yet related on the whole to a general law of the life of the ants. Their societies are founded on the principle of the *division of labor*, and the *speciality of functions*. The ant-hill, in its normal state, comprehends, as we know, three classes:—

1st. The great multitude, composed of laborious virgins, who confine themselves to the love of the children of the commonwealth, and perform all the work of the community;

2nd. The fecund females, feeble, soft, and, unintelligent; and,

3rd. Some little shriveled males, who are born only to die.

The first class is, in truth and reality, the people. But in this people you find two industrial divisions, two great bodies of workmen. The one executes all the more arduous tasks, such as the transportation of heavy burdens, and the far and perilous hunt after provisions,—and, at need, carry on war. The other, nearly always at home, receives the materials, superintends the domestic economy, and undertakes the principal duty of the republic,—the education of the young.

The two corporations, that of the purveyors and warriors,—that of the nurses and tutors,—are, in every tribe, of unequal size, but identical in species, color, and organization.

Between the big warriors and the little industrials the moral equality seems perfect. If there were any difference, we should say that the class of the little ants, who build up the city and train up the people, is the more important, the life, genius, and soul of the state; the one which of itself could, at need, constitute the republic.

M. Huber has discovered two species (the red-brown and red) who do not possess this essential class, this fundamental element of the ant communities. It would not surprise us if the accessory or warrior class were wanting. But here, in reality, it is the basis which we find deficient,—the vital foundation,—the *raison d'étre*. We are, therefore, not so much astonished at the depraved resource by which these red ants subsist, as at the monstrous lacuna which compels them to adopt it.

The Insect

There is a mystery in the matter which we cannot at present explain, but which would probably be cleared up if we could arrive at a knowledge of the general history of the species, its changes, and migrations. Who does not know the modification effected in animals, both externally and internally, in their forms and their manners, by the displacements they undergo? Who, for example, would recognize the brother of our bull-dog—of the St. Bernard—of the giant dog of Persia, which could strangle lions—in that abortion, the Havannah dog, so weak and frail, that even in a torrid climate Nature has clothed it with a thick fleece, which conceals it, and converts it into an enigma?

The animal, when transplanted, may become a monster.

The ants also may have had their revolutions, their moral and physical changes, in proportion, as the globe, everywhere becoming inhabitable, has favored their migrations. Several species, in the beautiful American climates, have preserved the honey-making industry; our own are ignorant of it, and are compelled to have recourse to the grubs; thence arises an art and a progress,—the art of breeding, preserving, and pasturing cattle.

Some species may have advanced, others retrograded. And it is thus I should explain the kidnapping habits of the red ants. Probably they belong to expatriated and demoralized classes—fragments of decayed communities which have lost their arts,—and which could not live but for this barbarous and desperate method of slavery. They no longer possess the artistic and teaching class, without which all peoples perish. Reduced to a military career, they could not live two days if they did not take unto themselves *souls*. Therefore, that they may not perish, they carry off the little black souls, which tend them, it is true, but also govern them. And this not only in the city itself, but in its external relations,—deciding or adjourning their expeditions, and regulating their campaigns; while the red, far from regulating the affairs of peace, do not seem even to comprehend them.

Singular triumph of intelligence! Invincible power of genius!

Chapter IV. The Ants:—Civil War—Extermination of the Community

It is the tyrant's punishment that he could not, even if he would, easily deliver his captive. So long as my nightingale sings, I know that he cares little for his cage, and I bear his captivity lightly; but when the time of song has gone by, I share his melancholy, and the question again and again recurs to my mind, "How can I release him?" He no longer knows how to fly; in truth, is almost without wings. If I set him free, he would perish before he had gone two steps. The liberties which he takes at Paris in a large chamber, and here, at Fontainebleau, in a small garden, are, really, of but little importance. He does not profit by them; almost always remains concealed in a gooseberry-bush, dreaming and listening.

The strains he hears,—the lively songs of the warblers, the voices of love and, maternity,—augment, I believe, his sadness; so much so, that here, in the open air, under the blue sky, enjoying a relative degree of freedom, he loses his appetite, and will eat no longer.

The Insect

We bethought ourselves of giving him his natural diet, and of feeding him with the insects on which he lives in the woods. But here is another difficulty. Who would not shrink from hunting after and carrying living victims to be devoured? We preferred to give him insects *in futuro*, the eggs of insects, and inert sleeping nymphæ. We carried on a traffic in them at Fontainebleau, where our aristocratic pheasants, a feudal race, do not deign to eat anything but ants' eggs.

On the evening of the 8th of June, there was brought to me from the forest a great clod of earth, mixed with dry twigs, and especially with tiny débris of the Northern trees, such as the needles of the firs, or little prickly leaves resembling thorns.

In the midst, the inhabitants pell-mell, of every size and grade, eggs, larvæ, nymphæ, diminutive artisans, great ants, which seemed to be warriors and defenders; finally, a few females which had just assumed their wedding garments, the wings which they wear for the moment of love. Thus it turned out to be a very complete specimen of the republic, varied, but well distinguished by one identical sign,—all this brownish-colored populace having on their corselets a dull red spot. As for the classes and professions of the ants, they were easily characterized by their very habitations, notwithstanding the general confusion. They were carpenter-ants, of the species which prop the upper stories of their buildings with timber framework.

Though their situation was so completely altered, my ants were in no wise prostrated. They continued their different tasks, of which the principal was, to protect the eggs and nymphæ from the action of a too powerful sun.

The general commotion had flung them out of their subterranean cradles, and exposed them on the surface. The little ants busied themselves actively in rectifying the disorder. The great ones went and came, and circled about a great earthen vase which contained the dismembered fragment of the republic. They marched with a firm step, and recoiled before no obstacles. We could not frighten them. If we placed in their way any impediment,—a bit of twig or our finger,—they crouched upon their loins, manœuvred with great address their tiny arms, and patted us like a young kitten.

In their revolutions around our vase, they encountered upon the sand some ashy-black ants which had taken possession of our garden, and constructed underneath its soil a large establishment. The latter do not have recourse to timber, but build in masonry,—cementing the earth with their saliva, and drying and seasoning it with their formic acid.

The spot was rendered peculiarly agreeable to them by its rose trees, apple and peach trees, which furnished them with abundant herds of gnats, that they might extract honey-dew for themselves and their little ones.

The rencontre was not very friendly. Though among the big carpenters were some ants of a sufficiently diminutive stature, they wholly differed from the black through their long legs and the red-spotted corselet. They were pitiless. Perhaps they suspected the blacks had been sent out as spies, to explore the ground, and lay snares for the emigrant colony which had just been disembarked. At all events, the big carpenters slew the little masons.

Jules Michelet

The act was followed by terrible and wholly unexpected results. Our vase was unfortunately placed near an apple-tree covered with those woolly grubs which are the despair of the gardener and the joy of the ants. Our masons had just taken possession of the precious sugary herd, and encamped themselves in the very roots of the tree, within reach of the invaluable booty. There they were, under the ground, a complete nation, an infinite number.

The massacre took place about twelve o'clock. At a quarter past eleven, or a little later, all the black legions were warned, aroused, erect, and ascending from their subterraneous habitations, poured out through every gate. The sand was hidden beneath the long black columns; our paths were all alive. The sun, shining full upon the little garden, stimulated and burned up the multitude, which only quickened their pace. Living always underground, they have necessarily a very susceptible brain. The furious heat, and especially their fear lest the invading giants should pounce upon their families, impelled them to confront death unflinchingly.

And a death which seemed certain; for each of the big carpenters, as far as size and thews were concerned, was well worth eight or ten of the little masons. At the first collision we saw a big ant fall upon a brown dwarf, and annihilate it at one blow.

The masons, however, had the advantage of numbers. But what of that? Suppose the front ranks were checked in the assault, and perished,—then the second, then the third,—if the army, still advancing, did but furnish the enemy with new victims? Such was our apprehension. All our fear was for the little aborigines of our garden, disturbed by that invasion of a foreign people which we had brought upon them,—a people ill-bred and brutal, which, without any provocation, had marked their first arrival by slaughtering the inhabitants of the country.

But it must be acknowledged that we had compared only the material forces of the two armies, and had not taken into account their moral strength.

We recognized at the first onset an astonishing amount of skill and intelligence on the part of the little blacks. By sixes, they seized upon one of their gigantic opponents, each holding and neutralizing a claw; then two leaped on its back, and firmly grasped its antennæ, until the giant, bound in every limb, was reduced to an inert body. It seemed to lose its senses; to grow dull and stupid; no longer to be conscious of its enormous superiority of strength. Others then rushed to the attack, and, without incurring any danger, stabbed him above and below.

The scene, regarded from a near point of view, was frightful. Whatever admiration the little ones merited for their heroic courage, their fury made one shudder. It was impossible to see without a feeling of pity these poor garotted giants, dragged miserably to and fro,—fired at from right and left,—floating as in an open sea on these billows of rage and impetuosity,—blind, powerless, and incapable of resistance,—like lambs beneath the butcher's knife.

We longed to separate them. But how was it to be done? We were in the presence of infinity. A man's strength was nothing when tested against such multitudes. We might have proceeded to the extremity of a universal deluge,—a moment's *noyade*[16]—but even this would have proved insufficient. They would not have let go their death-grasp; and when the torrent had flowed by, the massacre would have continued. The sole remedy, and an atrocious one—worse even than the evil—would have been to have burned alive, with a wisp of flaming straw, the two contending hosts, the conquerors and the conquered.

We were particularly struck by the fact that, after all, it was only a very few of the big ants that were garotted and captured; and that if those which remained free had fallen upon the assailants, they might easily have wrought a frightful carnage, their action being so rapid, and one blow inflicting death. But no such idea occurred to them. They ran hither and thither in a panic of fear, and rushed into the very throes of danger, into the thickest press of the hostile masses. Alas, they were not only vanquished, but seemed to have lost their senses! While the little ants, feeling themselves at home, on their native soil, showed so firm a front, the gigantic foreigners,—without any stake in the ground,—a desperate fragment of an annihilated city,—wholly ignorant of the country whither they had been transplanted,—recognized that everything was antagonistic to them, that a snare was hidden at every step, that no refuge was open to their scattered forces. Ah, woful condition of a people whose fatherland has perished, and who have lost their gods!

Yes, I excuse them. We ourselves were almost terrified at the sight of those legions of death,—that formidable army of little black skeletons which had all escaladed the earthen vase, and in that confined region, choked and burning, crowded and furious, mounted one upon another. As the discomfiture of the giants became a thing assured, horrible appetites were revealed among the blacks. An opportune moment arrived. It was a dramatic stroke! In their mute but terribly eloquent pantomime, we heard this cry: "Their young ones are fat!"

The gluttonous army of the lean threw themselves on the children. The latter, belonging to a superior race, were sufficiently heavy; and more, their oblong nymph-like envelope, round and smooth, offered no points of vantage. Two, three, four little blacks, by combining their efforts, succeeded, though not without difficulty, in carrying a single one of these up the smooth sides of the earthen vase. Then they came abruptly to a terrible resolve,—to seize upon the *maillots*, to bear off the naked children. It was no easy matter, for the little one clung stoutly, and its interwoven limbs were, so to speak, soldered together; in such wise that this violent and sudden development could only be effected by severe wounds,—in fact, by quartering them. The black ants then carried them off, torn and palpitating.

At the commencement of this kidnapping of children, we had expected to see some such spectacle as a *razzia* of slaves, which is only too common among both men and ants. But we now understood that something more was meditated. In drawing them cruelly from their outer coat, which is to them the very necessity of life, it became too evident that their captors cared very little whether

---

[16] The wholesale drownings which took place at Lyons during the Reign of Terror were known as *noyades*.—Translator.

they lived or did not live. It was for their flesh they seized them; as a tender prey for the young ones they had left at home, the fat children being delivered up alive to the furious appetites of the lean!

To understand the horror of the scene, you must know the true nature of the large eggs of the ants,—improperly called eggs, but in reality their nymphs or chrysalides,—diminutive organized ants which, under a thin veil, strengthen their tender, delicate, and still soft existence. They remain in this envelope for the purpose of accomplishing a progress of successive solidification and coloring.

The very fine and wonderfully soft web which they weave for themselves is, as we know, of a dull white, lightly shaded with a delicate yellow, which, when stronger, turns into a nankeen tint. Open it shortly before the emergence of the perfect insect, and you find a being of exactly the same color, all folded and rolled up in itself like the human embryo in its mother's womb. When stretched out, the aspect of the future ant is easily recognized, but it singularly differs from it in character: the head is quite innocent; lift up the antennæ, which, in this condition, resemble ears, and the young white head reminds you of that of a little white rabbit. The eyes alone,—two black points,—marked with sufficient prominency, indicate the next stage of coloring. For the rest, there is nothing to forewarn you that this little, weak, and denuded animal, so touching and so interesting, will become in a few days the black being so full of energy, so keen with life, so fierce in blood, which will traverse the earth in a fury of labor and burning activity.

One comprehends that in this stage of existence the milky and succulent nymphs of the ants will prove a very appetizing dish for the bird, and for the infinite number of creatures which hunt them greedily.

I have dissected only one nymph in the last days of its nymph-period, and when near its time of hatching. But that one was sufficient. The sight (seen through a lens of twelve times magnifying power) was very painful. The being was completely formed, and already black on the belly, yellow on the corselet. The head was intelligent, like that of an old ant, but pale, and changing from yellow to black. Still weak and heavy, and seized, as it were, with vertigo, it rolled from right to left, and from left to right, with a singular effect of somnolence and pain. You might have supposed it to be saying: "Ah me! so soon! Why hast thou called me so cruelly, before the proper hour, from my soft cradle to the harsh drudgery of life? But it is all at end for me!" It struggled nevertheless to confront the unknown chances of its novel situation, and to disengage its trammelled limbs. The antennæ were already perfectly free, and stirred about in their anxiety to discern the new world; this cerebral organ revealed very plainly the disquietude and agitation of the brain. Its greatest perplexity arose from its failure to release its two arms (or anterior limbs). It labored violently to do so. They were glued to the body by an indescribable something which might be called a pale blood, and one sweated to see the poor little creature, already prudent and timid, unable to complete its offensive arrangements, and to extricate (apparently to snatch or pluck away) its two bleeding arms.

The Insect

I have explained this at some length, in order to make the reader understand the passionate interest felt by the ants in the little balls which, to our eyes, seem so insignificant. Beneath its soft and transparent tissue they feel the infant palpitating under its two touching forms,—the creature, denuded and innocent, which dreameth still—the creature already formed and intelligent, perceiving everything, but incapable of self-defense, and, before it sees the light, disturbed by all the fears and agitations of existence.

The most painful shock for the young of the insects is the sudden cold; at least, the nudity, the exposure to the air and light. This is so antipathetic and painful to them, that in certain species it is the source of their arts and their most ingenious devices. The eggs and nymphs of the ants in their tiny transparent swaddling-robe,—and still more the larvæ which are deprived of it,—feel with an excessive sensibility every atmospheric variation. Hence the delicate and continual attentions of their nurses in carrying them from place to place, in translating them from one to another of the well-contrived steps of their thirty or forty stories, in protecting their dear little chilly charge from cold, damp, or excessive heat. A degree more or less means for it life or death.

It is a cruel and tragical change for these children of love, spoiled hitherto with excessive indulgence, and tended with greater care than any princess, when they are abruptly deprived of their garments,—stripped, with blows from pincers, teeth, and claws,—and despoiled by the hands of the executioner. Suddenly exposed to the burning sun, dragged hither, pushed thither, rolled over all the roughnesses of a coarse sandy soil,—sensible, infinitely sensible, in their new condition of nakedness, to the shocks, blows, and rude somersaults which their violent enemies do not spare them!

In towns captured by a furious enemy, it has happened that the tombs of the dead have been desecrated. But here, we behold the exhumation of the living,—the despoiling of innocent and all vulnerable creatures, poor bits of skinless flesh, to whom the very lightest touch had been a sufficient agony!

This immense execution upon the population and their young was hurried over so rapidly, that at three o'clock in the afternoon nearly all was ended; the city was sacked and depopulated in every corner, and its future beyond all hope of a resurrection.

We thought that some fugitive might still be lurking in concealment; that perhaps the conquerors would abandon the desert if we transported them, with the destroyed city, into a paved coach-yard outside the garden; that then would awake in them the remembrance of their family, to whom, moreover, they could carry nothing more to be devoured. Our expectation was realized.

On the morning of the 10th of June we saw them scattered along all the roads which led towards their dwelling-place, at the other end of the garden. But the destiny of the vanquished seemed accomplished. The dead and silent city was nothing but a cemetery, where, with the exception of a few scattered bodies, could only be seen some dead wood, some old pods of Northern trees, and their gloomy *aiguilles* (pines and once-green firs), not less dead than the city itself.

I confess that such a vengeance, so disproportionate to the act which was its cause or pretext, excited in me a strong feeling of indignation, and my heart, changing sides, was completely alienated from those little black barbarians.

So, observing that some of them, still implacable, were promenading among the ruins, I sent them rudely flying over its walls (that is, the edges of the vase). In vain it was gently pointed out to me that these blacks had been provoked, that they had shown the greatest courage, having braved so great a peril that their destruction might almost have been predicted. They were cruel and savage but heroic tribes, like the Iroquois, the Hurons, the revengeful heroes who formerly peopled the forests of the Mississippi and Canada. These reasons were good, but did not calm me. I felt too keenly the enormity of the crime. Without wishing to annihilate them, I confess that if these ferocious blacks had chanced to come under my foot I should not have turned aside.

The unfortunate empty vase continually reminded me of what had occurred, and held me as by a spell. On the evening of the 11th we were still seated on the ground before it, with our chin in our hand, completely absorbed in thought. Our gaze plunged into its depths. We persisted in longing for a sign of life to appear upon its perfect immobility, a something which might still say that all was not finished. This firm resolve seemed to have the potency of an evocation, and as if our desires had recalled to daylight some miserable spirit of the widowed city, one of the victims which had escaped made its appearance, and hurried headlong away from the field of death. And we perceived that it carried a cradle.

Night came, and it was in a completely strange locality, surrounded by enemies. A few holes, which one might mistake for places of refuge, were precisely the mouths opening into the Inferno of the blacks. The unhappy fugitive, with its misfortune increased by the burden of its infant, ran distractedly, and without knowing whither. I followed it with my eyes and heart, until the darkness concealed it from me.

Chapter V. The Wasps: Their Fury of Improvisation

When the wasp on a summer's day enters at the window, with its loud, aggressive, and menacing *zou! zou! zou!* everybody is on his guard. The child trembles, the mother suspends her work, even the husband lifts his eyes: "Insolent, impudent intruder!" and he arms himself with a handkerchief.

Meanwhile, the superb insect, having flown into every corner, and cast around the room a rapid and scornful glance, departs with a loud noise, not condescending to notice the unfriendly welcome accorded to him. His only reflection has been this: "A paltry house! Not a fruit, not a spider, not a fly, not the smallest bit of meat!"

Then he makes a descent on the shop of the country butcher: "Butcher, my custom is yours. I am desirous of dealing with you. Do not hesitate, foolish miser. Cut me a good slice of meat, and I will pay you for it; I will kill all your flesh-flies. Let us agree to be friends. We are both born to kill."

The slow dull animals of the genus *Man* are much scandalized at the proceedings of the wasp. It acts, it does not talk. But if it deigned to speak, its apology would be simple. A word would suffice. It is the being on whom Nature imposes the terrible destiny of suppressing time. We speak of the ephemera which lives a few hours: the period is sufficient for a creature that does nothing. The true ephemera is the wasp. In a brief six months' summer (not more than four months of full activity) it has to accomplish, not only the cycle of the individual life—to be born, to eat, to love, to die—but, what is far more onerous, the cycle of a prolonged social life, the most complicated which any insect is required to perform. What the bee leisurely elaborates in several years, the wasp must realize immediately. Much more than the bee! For the latter makes its honeycombs in a completed house (the hive, the hollow of the rock, the trunk of a tree); but the wasp must improvise without as within, the ramparts of the city no less than the city itself.

Four months to create everything, to make and unmake a people, and a people of lofty organization!

Learn, ye idle races which mutter that in fourscore years ye have no time, learn to despise it. It is a purely relative affair. There is never any time for the flat-bellied snail, were it to crawl through centuries. There is always time for heroic activity, firm will, and resolute energy.

The wasp dies. Its city of thirty thousand souls, improvised by a revolution, as by a thundering stroke of genius and courage, subsists as a testimony to its labors. Solid, eminently substantial, conscientiously wrought, and seemingly intended for eternity!

Let us note the starting-point.

A miserable fly, which in winter has survived the destruction of its race, issues all a-dust from its hiding-place. Thank Heaven, it is the spring-time! Does it seek to enjoy the sun? No, it will not allow itself a day's repose. What is its first duty? To love with a rapid and burning love, to go straight to its goal, to seize and take up as it passes that vital force which will create an entire people. Love on the wing,—no delay,—everything made to bear on the great social aim!

Savage and alone, with its idea and its hope, this mother of the future commonwealth creates in the first place its citizens, some thousands upon thousands of laborers. You have already learned that among insects every worker is a female. These too are workers, but the harsh necessities of toil suppress in them their sex. They love with a lofty devotion. The austere virgin looks for no other spouse than the community.

The chain of ardent labor is continued from the mother to her daughters. Her task was to beget: it is theirs to build. The fury of improvisation is the same in them, however, as it was in her. According to the region and the climate, the tribe, the species, and the work vary. Here they will excavate underground the cave in which they construct their edifice, isolating it from the soil, and preserving it from damp. There they suspend it in the air, and build it of strong coarse pasteboard to defy the heaviest rains. To make this paper or pasteboard, they hasten to the forest, where they select some thoroughly prepared wood, which has been long soaking, and has been already steeped by Nature just as we steep flax. Then within, with a strong sharp tooth (for theirs are not the graceful probosces of bees intended to kiss flowers), they gnaw, and tear, and loosen, and

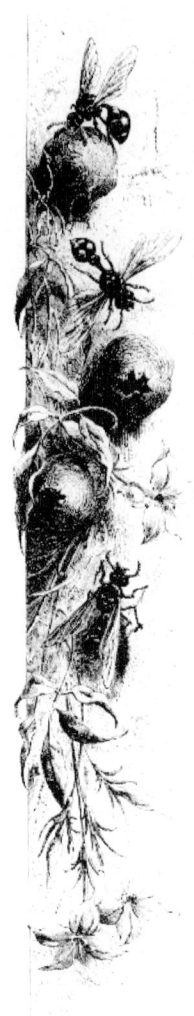

sever the rebellious filaments, pound them into pulp as we do the linen rags, and knead them with a heavy tongue. After the paste has been mixed with a viscous and adhesive saliva, it is spread out into thin layers. With teeth closed like a press, the work is completed. The elementary substance of the pasteboard is prepared.

A second industry now commences. The paper manufacturer is transformed into a mason. It has not the beaver's tail to serve as a trowel, but with the American wasp a sort of palette on the leg serves the same purpose. The operation is not the same here as in Guiana. The mason of Cayenne, having built up the walls, has only to suspend to them a succession of floors or platforms, following in that dry hot land the type of our human habitations. But the European mason, working with pasteboard, in a damp climate, where even in the summer heavy rains are frequent, adopts a different plan: *a house within a house*, a hive completely isolated from the envelope which encloses it. This is the most successful device for an ardent and chilly people, whose life-flame needs careful guarding.

As it is without, so it is within. As the house, so too the inhabitant. We men are not yet sufficiently acquainted with the influence exercised upon our moral dispositions by our habitations. This duplication of walls, this potent envelopment of a people so completely shut up under its strong twofold enclosure, largely contributes to the unity of the commonwealth.

Observe another singularity: shall we call it a trivial one? No; to the serious observer it is of importance. The city has two gates; its people enter by the one, and pass out by the other, so that no confusion can take place, and no collision between the ingressing and egressing crowds. This plan is adopted by all people who economize time, and wish to transact their business expeditiously. In London, the rule is the same as with the wasps: on the one side those who are coming, on the other those who are going; each person keeps to the right; these take one footpath, those another. No such impediment is met with in the Strand as the idlers of our Rue Vivienne, who incessantly convert themselves into a serious obstacle, and swim laboriously in the confusion they create.

But to return to our subject.

What is the object of these constructions? Is this robust being, endowed with such an intensity of vital force, more afraid of the air than numbers of delicate insects,—than the nervous spider, which has only a house of thread, or even lives under a leaf? Therein lies the lofty mystery of life for the higher insect. It is this which stimulates the universal genius of the ant either above ground or under ground. It is this which inspires the activity, the persevering toil and economy of the bee. What, then, is it? The *love of the future*,—the yearning to perpetuate and eternize that which one loves. All their love centres in their offspring.

To love the child and the future; to toil in view of time and of that which as yet is not; to exhaust their vitality and die of work, that posterity may have less cause to labor,—a noble ideal, assuredly, of society, wherever it may be. One can well understand it in those who have time before them, and a life to make use of, like men and bees. But that this insect which has no time, which perishes in the evening, should love the time that will never be its own, should immolate its little life for the sake of the life that is to come, should devote to the child of to-morrow its solitary day, is a sacrifice peculiar to the wasp: it is original and sublime!

There is not a minute to lose; and the mother incessantly increases the burden. Besides the female workers, she produces some few males who do not work, whose little and very brief function scarcely prevails as an excuse for their inactivity. Among those tragical and serious insect-races, Nature, as if to divert herself a moment by a comical distraction, has made the poor little males ordinarily squat and obese, innocent little Falstaffs, who are guarded like a seraglio of unimportant servants. The caricature is complete in the case of the male bee, which, alleging that it neither knows how to glean abroad nor to build at home, passes the time in humming before its bee-hive (like our young cigar-smoking idlers).

Among the wasps life is so tense, burning, and keen, that the very males, slothful as they may be, dare not abandon themselves to complete indolence. Yonder ladies, who do not jest, and who have stings of which the males are deprived, might look upon their idleness sourly, and stir them up with dagger-thrusts. So they have conceived the idea of working without work; they have the air of doing something,—a small part of the domestic labor, cleaning, and sweeping. If any one dies, the ceremony of interment provides them with a pretence; with the effort of carrying a slight weight they sweat and groan, and several put their shoulders together. In a word, they are very ridiculous. And I am confident that their terrible companions laugh at them.

Theirs truly is an onerous undertaking. Twenty or thirty thousand mouths to feed, is a very extensive household. If they were only gifted with the prudent activity of bees, their community would perish of famine. What they need is a violent, furious, murderous rapidity,—all the appearances of an immense gluttony,—all the love and devotion which Sparta had for the art of thieving. But the secret of their power, which is plainly discernible in them if we observe them but a moment, is their magnificent insolence, their superb contempt for all other beings, and their firm conviction that the whole world is their inheritance. If we consider, it is true, their wonderful energy, compared with which lions and tigers are mere races of sheep,—and their prodigious yearly effort of improvisation,—and, finally, their absolute devotion to the public welfare,—we shall not find in all nature creatures relatively of greater power, nor which possess a clearer right to value themselves highly.

Our modern minds, however, find a difficulty in admiring the violence of the antique virtues. Their boundless love of the commonwealth is pushed to an almost criminal excess. Who has not marked with how ferocious an ardor they hunt the bees! Yet certain species of wasps can make honey; but only in fine climates, which, knowing no winter, allow the wasps an interval of peaceful labor. Here the case is different. Their life, cut short in six months, compels them to resort to measures of cruel simplicity. Honey is needed for their children. Thereupon they attack the bee, and take it prisoner; with their pliable body, whose waist is a mere thread, they so curve the extremity as to stab the prisoner underneath with their deadly sting; when thus stricken, the wasp saws it with three strokes of its teeth, and leaves the head and corselet to palpitate for some time longer, while the belly, filled with honey, the barbarian carries off as a gift for its young.

It feels no remorse. The death of others apparently does not cause a pang to this creature, which knows that it too will die to-morrow.

What do I say?

Our virgins of Tauris do not wait until Nature lays upon them her heavy hand and the ignoble leaden shroud of winter. They have borne the sword; they will die by the sword. The republic ends in a general massacre. The children, recently, ay, and still, so dear, are slain; dilatory children whom cold and want would kill to-morrow; their sisters, aunts, and affectionate nurses securing them at least the advantage of dying by the hands of those who love them. This latter gift, a speedy death, is freely bestowed on numerous unfortunates who had no thought of soliciting it,—on little useless males, even on young workers who were born late, and cannot boast of a constitution sufficiently strong to resist the winter.

Let it not be said that the heroic race of wasps is ever seen to request the humiliating hospitality of the smoky roofs of man, and, for the sake of living a little longer, to expose its melancholy remains in the shambles of a spider's web! No, children! No, sisters! Die! The republic is immortal. Some one of us, favored by the yearly miracle and great lottery of Nature, will be called upon to recommence the entire work. And if but one remains, it is enough. Should the world perish, a single true heart would suffice to re-create it.

Chapter VI. "The Bees" Of Virgil

All modern writers have triumphed over the ignorance displayed by the poet Virgil in his fable of Aristæus, who draws life out of the womb of death, and causes his bees to spring from the entrails of immolated bulls.[17] But, for

---

[17] The passage to which Michelet refers is found in the fourth book of the *Georgics*, and is thus translated by Dryden:—

"The secret in an easy method lies:
Select four brawny bulls for sacrifice,
Which on Lycæus graze, without a guide;
Add four fair heifers yet in yoke untried:
For these, four altars in their temple rear,
And then adore the woodland powers with prayer.
From the slain victims pour the streaming blood,
And leave their bodies in the shady wood:
Nine mornings thence, Lethean poppy bring,
T' appease the manes of the poet's king:
And, to propitiate his offended pride,
A fatted calf and a black ewe provide:

myself, I have never laughed at it. I know, I feel, that every word of this great sacred poet has a weighty value, an authority which I would designate as that of an augur and a pontiff. And the fourth book of the *Georgics*, particularly, was a holy work, issuing from the inmost recesses of the heart. It was a pious homage rendered to sorrow and to friendship; an eulogium on the proscribed Gallus, Virgil's dearest friend. This eulogium, undoubtedly, was struck out by the prudent Mæcenas; and Virgil then substituted his Resurrection of the Bees: a song full of immortality, which, in the mystery of Nature's transformations, embodies our highest hope, that death is not a death, but the beginning of a new life.

Would he have descended to the empty pleasure of inserting a popular fable in that consecrated portion of his poem which had been occupied by his friend's name? I will never believe it. The fable, if it be one, must necessarily possess some serious foundation, and a truthful side. We are not dealing here with the worldly poet, the urbane singer, like Horace, the elegant favorite of Rome. It is not the charming improvisatore of the court of Augustus, the gay and indiscreet Ovid, who betrays the loves of the gods. Virgil is the child of Earth, the pure and noble figure of the old Italian peasant, the religious interrogator, the reverently simple interpreter of the secrets of Nature. But he may be mistaken in his words,—that he may have ill-applied the names,—this is not impossible; but so far as the facts are concerned, it is an entirely different matter: whatever he describes, I firmly believe he saw.

An accident threw me into the way of understanding the poet's intention. On a certain memorable day, my wife and I repaired to the cemetery of Pére-Lachaise, to visit before winter the burial-places of my family, the tomb which reunites my father and his grandson. This latter had been born to me in the very year which terminated the first half of the present century, and I had named him Lazarus in my devout hope of the Awakening of the Nations. I had imagined that I saw upon his countenance a gleam, as it were, of the strong and tender thoughts which throbbed in my heart at that last moment of my teaching. Oh, vanity of human hopes! This flower of my autumn, which I yearned to animate with the potent vitality that had been of too tardy development in myself,

---

This finished, to the former woods repair.
His mother's precepts he performs with care;
The temple visits, and adores with prayer.
Four altars raises, from his herds he calls,
For slaughter, four the fairest of his bulls;
Four heifers from his female store he took,
All fair, and all unknowing of the yoke.
Nine mornings thence, with sacrifice and prayers,
The powers atoned, he to the grove repairs.
Behold a prodigy! for, from within
The broken bowels, and the bloated skin,
A buzzing noise of bees his ears alarms,
Straight issue through the sides assaulting swarms;
Dark as a cloud they make a wheeling flight,
Then on a neighbouring tree, descending light:
Like a large cluster of black grapes they show,
And make a large dependence from the bough."

disappeared almost in the act of birth. And there was no help but to deposit my child at the feet of my father, who had already been four years dead. Two cypresses which I then planted in that ill-omened nook of clay have acquired in the brief interval an extraordinary growth. Two, nay, three times taller than myself, they clothe their vigorous branches with a young, rich foliage which ever points towards heaven. If, with an effort, you lower them, they rear themselves again, in all their pride and strength, flourishing with a marvelous pith, as if they had drank from the earth where I planted them the precious treasure of my past and my unconquerable aspiration.

While revolving these thoughts I ascended the hill, and before arriving at the tomb, which is situated in the upper alley, I made this observation,—that though I had on so many occasions frequented this melancholy and beautiful spot, having been in earlier life the most assiduous visitor of the dead, I had scarcely ever seen any insects in the Pére-Lachaise. Hardly even at the great epoch of the flowers, when everything is covered with bloom, and numbers of the old deserted sepulchres are embowered in roses, I had not remarked that animal life abounded there as it abounds elsewhere. Very few birds, and very few insects. Why? I could not say.

While making this reflection, we had finished climbing the hill; we stood in front of the tomb. And there, with admiration, with a species of astonishment, I found a surprising contradiction of what I had just been saying.

About a score of very brilliant bees hovered above the little garden-plot,—which was narrow as a shroud, stripped of bloom and bare of flowers, and saddened by the influence of the season. In the whole cemetery remained only the last autumnal flowers,—some withering and half-leafless Bengal roses. The spot where we stood, full of new buildings, masonry, and plaster, was an Arabia Deserta. Finally, on the tomb, towards the head of the grandfather, flourished only a few sickly white asters, and over my child the cypresses. It must needs have been that these asters, in their cold clayey soil, nourished either by the whispers of the air or the spirits of the earth, treasured up a modicum of honey, since the little gleaners resorted thither for their harvest.

I am not superstitious. I believe in but one miracle, the constant miracle of the Providence of Nature. I experienced nevertheless how powerfully the mind may be affected by a lively surprise of the heart. I felt an emotion of gratefulness at the sight of the mysterious little creatures animating this solitude, whither, alas! I myself came but rarely. The increasing absorption of my work, in which day pressed upon day,—the palpitating flame of the forge where one forges more and more quickly, in the doubt whether one will be living to-morrow,—all this kept us further from the tombs than in the days of our dreamy youth. I was much affected by seeing my place supplied. In my absence the bees peopled and vivified the spot, consoled, and perhaps rejoiced my dead. My father may have smiled on them in his kindly indulgence; they may have been the happiness and first delight of my child.

Selfish motives could not have led them thither; there was so little for them to take. Nevertheless, when we suspended to the cypress-boughs the garlands of *immortelles* we had brought with us, they were curious enough to ascertain if there was any treasure in the new flowers. The hard, prickly corolla soon repulsed them, and sent them back to the faded asters. I felt very sad, and said to them:—"Late, very late, my friends, you come, and to the tomb of the poor! Why am I not able to recompense you with a banquet of friendship, which should sustain and warm you during the first cold breezes, already blowing on these icy heights, so exposed to the northern wind!"

As if they had understood me, their movements afforded an exact reply. Some I saw, with their little limbs skillfully bent forward, rubbing their backs in the sun; they longed to absorb into every vein its genial radiance. They made the most of that brief hour when the sun revolves too quickly; one scarcely feels it before it has gone! Their significant gesture plainly said:—"Oh, what a cold morning we have had! Let us make haste! In less than an hour commences the equally inclement evening, the frozen night,—nay, who knows? the winter! and then our death is at hand."

They were still full of life, however; marvelously trim and bright,—I may even say radiant,—under their illuminated wings, all shot with gold. I never saw more beautiful insects; insects more clearly inspired by a higher life. One thing embarrassed me; namely, that they were too handsome, and too shining, inasmuch as they did not wear their industrial attire, their velvety coat, their pincers, and their brushes. And, finally, I discovered another circumstance: that they had not the four wings of the bee, but only two.

I perceived my mistake. It was these insects which had deceived Virgil. Like myself, he thought them bees, and so he erroneously called them. Réaumur confesses that for a moment even he was deceived by them.

But the fact related by Virgil is not inaccurate. We can understand how keenly it would impress the minds of the ancients, and how they would see in it a type of resurrection. They seem the daughters of death. Of the three ages of their existence, they spend the first in morbid and deadly waters, fatal to all other creatures, which permit the escape of the residuum of life in dissolution; with ingenious tenderness, Nature there preserves them, maintains them alive, and enables them to breathe in the very midst of death.

Their second period is passed under the earth,—in the shades,—where they sleep their chrysalis-like slumber.

But when once they have quitted the place of sepulture, they are fully compensated for their previous abasement; a light aërial life, exempt from the bee's incessant toil, and glorified by golden wings, such as the latter never boasts of, is bestowed upon them, with the gift, moreover, of gentle manners. Innocent, and without stings, they live their season of love under the sun and among the flowers. Far from blushing at their origin,—these noble Virgilian bees!—they do not disdain the flowers of the cemetery, they keep company with the dead, and for the living collect that honey of the soul,—the hope of the future!

Chapter VII. The Bee in the Fields

"When the plant attains to the flower, the climax of its existence,—when it assumes its symmetrical outlines, its perfumes, its colors, and a certain degree of animal irritability,—it emerges from its condition of isolation, and connects itself more closely with the great Whole. But it remains fixed in one place, without any reciprocation of love. The animal, on the contrary, is movement itself, and manifests its joy in living by its capricious mobility. Then the captive plant casts a glance of amicable confidence on the animal's life of freedom, offers it the abundance of its substance, and for sole reward expects that it will achieve its fecundation.

Then, too, as an elder brother might do, the animal assists the plant, and affords it in its dependent state the succor of liberty. But, for this purpose, the animal must be completely free, I would say winged, bound up with the vegetable life which was its kindly nurse. Behold the insect, love's messenger and mediator to the plants, their propagator, and the zealous instrument of their fertilization.

"With a maternal care, the plant provides a place in its own body where the insect's egg may be developed. It nourishes the young larva which as yet is incapable of action, but which, in due time, emerging from its vegetation in the egg, will move freely to and fro, and seek its own sustenance. The creative fecundity of the plant easily replaces whatever the insect has extracted from it; and thus both animal and plant harmoniously attain to the climax of existence.

"The animal, from its low sphere of nutrition, rises to a more elevated sphere, the pure need of motion, and the pursuit of love. The plant, it is true, does not soar so high; but its flower is a bright dream of a higher state of being,—a dream which, though fugitive, proceeds, by means of its fruits, to secure the conservation of the species. The blossoming plant and the winged insect reach, as if by concert, an analogous development, manifested by their colors, their beautiful symmetrical forms, and their refinement of substance. Papilionaceous flowers, for instance, might almost be called insects-become-plants.

"This harmonic existence marches forward with the same rhythm as the moments of the day. Each flower to whose juice an insect is assigned expands at the hour when its life is most intense, and shuts at the hour of its repose. Thus they feel their unity; love attracts them one towards the other. Here the plant plays the part of the female, the fixed basis of creation, absorbed in nature. The insect resembles the tiny male who frees himself from earth and curvets in the air; recalled, nevertheless, by the plant to the oneness of the terrestrial whole. It is a winged anther, which diffuses life among the flowers."[18]

What the wind accomplishes hap-hazard, flinging abroad in capricious showers the generative elements, the insect performs through love,—the direct love of its species, the *in*direct and confused love of the amiable auxiliary which welcomes and nourishes it, which will hereafter nourish also its eggs and continue its maternal work. Its action, therefore, is not external and superficial, like that of the wind; it is internal and penetrating. The ardent, curious insect will not suffer itself to be checked by the light and trivial obstacles with which vegetable modesty surrounds the threshold of its mysteries; it boldly dashes aside the veil, and enters into the inmost economy of the flower. It seizes, it pillages, and it carries away, assured that all it does will be approved. The flower, in its powerless expansion, rejoices only too keenly in the deeds of these thievish liberators, who will transport its desire whither it would fain transport itself. "Take," she says, "and take yet more!" The insect then exhausts its utmost effort; each of its hairs becomes a tiny magnetic dart, which attracts and wishes to attract. Would that it might be enveloped in these points, and over all its surface (like the lightning conductor) concentrate this treasure of vegetable electricity! Such is its aspiration. An aspiration realized in the higher insect, in the bee, which bristles everywhere with a magnetic apparatus,—the bee, predestined by the tools peculiar to it, both to its little individual industry of

---

[18] Burdach, bk. ii., c. 3.

honey-making, and to the grand, general, universal industry of the fecundation, of plants.

It is an admirable creature, and what the great physiologist has just said of the loves of the flower and the insect applies particularly to it; except with this notable distinction on the part of the bee, that it robs the flower only of that noble luxuriance of life which it lavishes upon love. The bee does not establish its cradle in the plant that the young may thence derive its sole sustenance, and gradually devour its nurse. Instead of depositing its egg, and exposing it to the hazards of the vegetable existence, as the butterfly does with its future caterpillar, the bee economizes the plant, and, without attacking it, borrows from it the precious materials which its art works up into palaces of alabaster, amber, or of gold, where its children will in due time repose.

The innocency of the bee is one of its lofty attributes, no less than its miraculous art. Its sting is simply a defensive and indispensable weapon, not against man-with whom, of its own accord, it does not wage war—but against the cruel wasps, its terrible enemies. The bee, on the other hand, injures none. It does not live by death; its inoffensive life does not demand the sacrifice of other lives. It stimulates innumerable existences; it vivifies and fecundates them. There is no uncultivated desert, no wild, bare region which it does not animate,—where it does not infuse fresh vigor into the languishing vegetation, urging the plants to bud, watching over and inspecting them. It reproaches them with their slothfulness; and as soon as they open to the influence of love-these poor dumb virgins!—it establishes between them the requisite interpreters, carries off in its murmurs their pollen and perfume, and harmonizes the aromas which are their blossoms of thought.

This process begins in the month of March. When an uncertain but already potent sun reawakes the sleeping sap, the tiny flowers of the fields, the wild violet, the Easter-daisy of the sward, the buttercup of the hedgerow, the precocious gillyflower, expanding, perfume the air. But their expansion lasts only for a moment. Barely open at noon, by three o'clock they fold themselves up again, and veil their shivering stamens. In this brief interval of gentle heat you may see a little wan-looking creature, completely clad but very chilly, which also ventures to unfurl its wings. The bee quits its city, in the knowledge that the manna is ready for it and its little ones.

A little matter then, it is true, but most cradles are empty at this epoch. The great fecundity of the mother bee still lurks concealed in her bosom. The regular and rapid incubation, which might suffice to create a world, will not commence until a much later period,—the sunny time of May.

How admirable is this agreement! Most of the shivering flowers, like the shivering bee, wait a more equable season before they bare to the sun their corolla, too delicate to endure the caprices of April.

It is pleasant to watch the intercourse between these charming creatures. The docile flower inclines and yields to the insect's unquiet movements. The shrine which it had closed against the winds, and the inquisitive glance, it opens to the beloved bee, which, impregnated by it, speeds afar on her message of love. The delicious precautions which Nature has taken to veil from profane

eyes the mysteries enacted therein, do not delay for a moment the audacious seeker, who is completely at home, so to speak, and has no fear of being considered an intruder. One flower, for example, is protected by a couple of petals which join together in the form of an arch (as, for instance, the iris on the border of the waters, which in this manner defends from the rain its delicate little lovers). Another, like the sweet-pea, dons a kind of helmet, whose vizor must be lifted by its suitor.

The bee takes its stand at the bottom of these recesses worthy of the fairies, covered with the softest tapestry, under fantastic pavilions, with walls of topaz, and roofs of sapphire. Paltry comparisons these, for they are borrowed from dead gems, while the flowers live, and feel, and desire, and wait. And if the happy conqueror of the little hidden kingdoms,—if the imperious violator of their innocent barriers, the insect, mingles and confuses everything, they readily whisper its pardon, overwhelm it with their sweetnesses, and load it with their honey.

There are favored localities, and there are happy hours, where and when the bee, while gathering its harvest, accomplishes—chaste toiler!— myriads of marriages. On the coasts, for example, and in the immediate neighborhood of the savage sea, where one would hardly expect to meet with such pacific idyls, should there be but one shadowy, secure, and warm recess, Nature never fails, in the warm and humid mildness of that maternal retreat, to create a little chosen world; and there the flower distils to the bee its sweetest nectar,—there the bee assuages the impetuous yearning of the flower.

Genial, bland, and still is the hour which precedes the evening. Caressed by the last rays of the sun, whose warmth it preserves within its bosom, besprinkled in its corolla by the light and already radiant mist, the flower becomes conscious of two lives and a twofold electricity; it is urged to love, and it loves! The stamens blaze forth, and scatter abroad their cloud of incense. Then at that charming and sacred hour let the mediatrix come; let the Samaritan bee appear! Let her collect the sweet odors dispersed by the evening breeze; let her redivide them with wise forethought, giving here and taking there! The blossoms are no longer solitary; through the agency of the bee, the meadow has been converted into a society where all understand and all love each other, initiated into the hymeneal rites by their friendly little high-priest.

It is not a less important duty for the bee to rise at an early hour and be present at the moment when the flower—which has slumbered under the penetrating dew (exhaled by its divine master, father, and lover, the sun)—awakes, and recovers its consciousness. Struck by the sympathetic beam, it no longer resists; it gives up the softened essence of its choicest sweetness; it becomes, as it were, a tiny fountain, which distils honey drop by drop. Opportunely comes the bee; its work here is very nearly completed: the sweet treasure, finely prepared in that hour of perfection, will entail but little labor. It bears it off to its children: "Eat; it is the soul of the blossom."

But in the noonday heat will she remain inactive? The burning sun and dry air have withered up the blossoms of the plain. But those of the woods, sheltered by the fresh cool shades, present their cups brimming over; those of the murmurous brooks, and silent and deep marshes, are then instinct with vitality. The forget-me-not dreams, and weeps tiny tears of nectar. Even the white water-lily, in her pale virginity, yields a rare treasure of love.

"Night does not injure the bee, but cold is extremely harmful. Such is her conscientiousness, that, in order to avoid losing a day's labor in our brief summers, she takes too little heed of the sudden returns of winter, of the sharp caprices of the north wind, which sometimes visit us on the finest days. Insects of inferior intelligence, but also less industrious, perfectly understand the secret of escaping its influence. In their prudent idleness they say to one another, 'Tomorrow! Let us keep holiday!' And they patiently wait for one, or two, or more days, until the wicked spirit of the north has abandoned its evil mood. But those who have charge of souls, and a large family to maintain,—those who know that a mild winter may chance to keep their offering awake, and, accordingly, famished, will hesitate before they take a single day's repose.

"And, therefore, on the cold mornings of a June not less bleak than March, they do not fear to rush boldly into the fields. But they are more valiant than robust; the cold catches them, and I have known them drag their limbs to my windows, faltering and half-paralyzed. They have made no attempt to escape; they have suffered themselves to be taken prisoners. They were in a scared condition; still bearing the signs of their courageous and indefatigable work, impregnated with the dust of flowers, and their little, baskets loaded and overloaded with pollen. They seemed to say:—'We are no sluggards. On the contrary, in the cold hours of morning, when many are still asleep, we have already completed a day's work. But, alas, the times are so hard, and the north wind is so keen! Behold us half-frozen. A moment's hospitality, I pray you.'

"Who would not respect the misfortune of such blameless and over-eager workers? I lent them not only a roof, and the warmth of an apartment closed to the wind and open to the sun, but immediately improvised for them a friendly repast. Where? At the bottom of a sugar-basin.

"The chilly creatures, having revived at a genial beam their lost warmth, and restored to a good condition all the little electric world of hairs with which they bristle, began the exploration of their temporary prison, and were agreeably surprised to find the crystal a dining-hall. With a good appetite, seating themselves at the table, they attacked a fragment of sugar, and sucked up with their proboscis all the sweetness they could find. When they had finished their repast, and were completely restored, were fluttering to and fro, demanding the way out, I set them free, without causing them to lose one moment of a day already far advanced. With a rapid flight, charmed by the noonday sun, they returned to their occupations, distinctly humming:—'Farewell, madam, and many thanks!'"

Chapter VIII. The Bees as Architects: The City

If the wasp's nest resemble Sparta, the bee-hive is the veritable Athens of the Insect World. There, all is art. The people—the artist-élite of the people—incessantly create two things; on the one hand, the City, the country,—on the other, the Universal Mother, whose task it is not only to perpetuate the race, but to become its idol, its *fetish*, the living god of the community.

The bees share with the wasps, the ants, and all the sociable insects, the disinterested life of aunts and sisters,—laborious virgins, who devote themselves entirely to an adoptive maternity.

But from these analogous peoples the bee differs in the necessity it is under of creating a national idol, the love of which impels it to work.

All this has been long misunderstood. It was at first supposed that this State was a monarchy, *that it possessed a king*. Not at all; the king is a female. Thereupon one is driven to say, *This female is a queen*. Another error. Not only does she not govern, or reign, or control, but in certain conjunctions she is governed, and sometimes even placed in private confinement. She is at once something more and something less than a queen. She is an object of legal and public adoration; I should say legal and constitutional, for this adoration is not so blind but that the idol, in some cases, as we shall see, may be treated very severely.

"Then, at bottom, the government will be democratic?" Yes; if we take into consideration the unanimous devotion of the people, the spontaneous labor of everybody. No one commands. But, nevertheless, you can clearly see that in every higher work an intelligent body of the *élite*, an aristocracy of artists, takes the lead. The city is not built or organized by the entire people, but by a special class, a kind of guild or corporation. While the mob of bees seeks the common nourishment abroad, certain much larger bees, the wax-makers, elaborate the wax, prepare it, shape it, and skillfully make use of it. Like the medieval freemasons, this respectable corporation of architects toils and builds on the principles of a profound geometry. Like those of the old days, they are *the masters of the living stone*. But our worthy bees are far more deserving of the title! The materials which they employ they have made, have elaborated by their vital action, and vivified with their internal juices.

Neither the honey nor the wax is a vegetable substance. Those little light bees which go in quest of the essence of the flowers bring it back already transformed and enriched by their virginal life. Sweet and pure, it passes from their mouth to the mouth of their elder sisters. These, the grave wax-makers, having received the aliment vivified and endowed with the charming sweetness which is, as it were, the soul of the race, elaborate it in their turn, and communicate to it their own peculiar life,—solidity. Wise and sedentary, they work up the liquid into a sedentary honey, a honey of the second quality, a kind of reflected honey. This is not all: the substance twice elaborated, and twice penetrated with animal juice, they incessantly moisten with their saliva, when using it so as to render it softer for working, but more tenacious afterwards.

Was I wrong, then, in saying that this construction is truly one of "the living stones"? There is not an atom of the materials which is not three times impregnated with life. Who shall say of yonder hive whether the flower or the bee has furnished the greater part? The latter has certainly contributed an important share. Here, the home of the people is the people's substance and visible soul; from themselves they have extracted their city, and their city is, in truth, themselves. Bee and hive, it is one and the same thing.

But let us observe them at work.

Alone, in the centre of the still empty and to be created hive, the learned wax-maker advances. From beneath its wings it delicately extracts a thin slab of wax, and conveys it to its mouth, where it is well kneaded and pounded, and drawn out into the shape of a ribbon. Eight strips are in this wise furnished, wrought, and absorbed; and the result is eight little blocks, which the bee lays down as the first beams of the future edifice, the foundations of the new city.

Others continue the work without moving too far from the place where it was begun. If any unintelligent laborer does not follow the prescribed plan, the mistress-bees, experienced and accomplished, are on the spot to detect any error, and immediately remedy it.

In the solid mass, well placed and skillfully squared, where such numbers have harmoniously deposited their contribution of wax, an excavation must now be made, and some degree of form attained. A single bee again detaches herself from the crowd, and with her horny tongue, teeth, and paws, she contrives to hollow out the solid matter like a reversed vault. When fatigued she retires, and others take up the work of modeling. In couples they shape off and thin the walls. The only point to be remembered is a skilful management of their thickness. But how do they appreciate this? Who or what warns them the moment a stroke too much would break an opening in the partition? They never take the trouble to make a tour of their work and examine it from the other side. Their eyes are useless to them; they judge of everything by their antennæ, which are their plumb-line and compass. They feel about, and by an infinitely delicate touch recognize the elasticity of the wax, perhaps by the sound it renders, and determine whether it is safe to excavate it, or whether they must stop short, and not push their mining operations further.

The building, as everybody knows, is destined to serve two ends. The cells are generally used in summer as cradles, in winter as magazines of pollen and honey,—a granary of abundance for the republic. Each vessel is closed and sealed with a waxen lid, a *clôture* religiously respected by all the people, who take for their subsistence only a single comb,—and when that comb is finished pass on to another, but always with extreme reserve and sobriety.

It has been said and repeated that the construction is absolutely uniform. Buffon goes so far as to pretend that the cell is but the identical form of the bee, which posts itself in the wax, and by the friction of its body, a blind manœuvre, obtains an impress of itself, a hollow, an identical cell. A baseless hypothesis, which the least reflection would show to be improbable, even if observation did not contradict it.

In reality, their work is extremely various, and diversified in numerous different ways.

In the first place, the combs are pierced in the centre by corridors or little tunnels, which do away with the necessity of traversing two sides. Economists in everything, the bees are specially economical of time.

Secondly, the form of the cells is by no means identical. They prefer the hexagon,—the form which is best adapted to secure the greatest possible number of cells in the smallest area. But they do not slavishly bind themselves to this form. The first comb which they attach to the framework would cling to it very insecurely, and only by its projecting edges, if it were composed of six-sided cells. They therefore make it with five sides only; and fashion it of pentagonal cells with broad bases, which attach themselves solidly to the wood on a continuous line. The whole is agglutinated and sealed, not with wax, but with their gum, or *propolis*, which, as it dries, becomes hard as iron.

The great royal cellules, or cradles of the future mothers, which may be seen by the side of the combs, are not six-sided, but of the form of an oblong egg,—which secures the royal favorites considerable ease, and a great facility of development.

Finally, you may, with a little attention, detect important differences among the ordinary hexagonal cells, though at the first glance they all seem alike. They are small for the industrious gleaners, larger for the artistic wax-makers, and largest for the males. This size is generally obtained by means of a little rounded fragment which is deposited in the bottom, and renders it slightly circular,—I was about to say pot-bellied (*ventru*). As the house, so the tenant; the male will come into the world a squat, obese figure,—predestined to this form by that of its cradle.

Thus, of their own accord, they vary the configuration and extent of the cellules. And they vary them yet more, according to the obstacles they encounter. If room be denied them, they reduce the size of their hexagons in due proportion and with extreme address. This fact Huber verified by some ingenious experiments. He bethought himself of deranging their operations by placing, instead of wood, a plate of glass against the wall of the hive where they were building up their cells. From the distance they saw this smooth shining crystal, to which nothing could be fixed; and taking their measures accordingly, they curved their cake in such a manner that it went past the glass and joined on to the wood. But, to carry out the alteration, it became necessary to change the diameter of the cells; to enlarge that of the convex portion, and diminish that of the concave. A delicate problem! and yet it was readily solved by the skilful architects.

In mid-winter, says Huber again, in their season of inertia, an over-heavy slab of wax fell away, but was checked *en route* by the cakes beneath. An avalanche seemed imminent! But the bees invented buttresses and barriers in strong mastic, which, supporting the fallen cake and propping up the sides of the hive, prevented the dangerous ruin from dragging down the inner edifice. Then, to prevent the occurrence of similar misfortunes, they created some novel architectural works in the shape of flying buttresses, bulwarks, pillars, cross-beams, and the like.

Novel! Ay, this is a sufficient refutation of Buffon's theory. That machines or automata could invent, is a thing not easily explicable. Yet the sovereign authority of this great dictator of natural history would have prevailed, perhaps, over facts and over observation, if, towards the close of the last century, the bees themselves, by an unforeseen stroke, had not definitively cut the Gordian knot.

It was about the epoch of the American, and shortly before the outbreak of the French Revolution. An unknown creature then made its appearance over all Europe,—of a frightful figure,—a great strong nocturnal butterfly, marked very plainly in tawny-gray, with a hideous death's head. This sinister being, which none had seen before, alarmed every countryside, and seemed an omen of the most terrible misfortunes. Yet, in truth, those who were terrified by it had brought it into Europe. It had come in the grub condition with its natal plant, the American potato,—the fashionable vegetable which Parmentier extolled, Louis XVI. protected, and which spread in all directions. The savants baptized the insect with a somewhat horrifying name—the *Sphinx Atropos*.

And terrible indeed *was* this new creature, but only for the honey. Of this it was remorselessly greedy, and to attain it was capable of everything. A hive of thirty thousand bees could not daunt it. In the depths of night, the rapacious monster, profiting by the hour when the approaches to the city are less carefully guarded, with a gloomy but subdued sound, as if stifled by the soft down which covers it (and all other nocturnal insects), invaded the hive, swooped down on the combs, devoured and plundered, gutted and destroyed the magazines, and slew the infant bees. In vain they awoke, and flew to arms; their sting could not penetrate through the soft elastic padding which clothed the sphinx,—like the cotton armor worn by the Mexicans in the days of Cortez, and impenetrable by Spanish weapons.

Huber meditated on the best means of protecting his bees against this shameless brigand. Should it be by gratings, or doors? And how? He could not determine. The most skillfully devised barriers have always the inconvenience of impeding the great movement of ingress and egress, which takes place at the threshold of the hive. Their impatience regarded as intolerable the obstructions, which could not fail to embarrass them, and against which they might break their wings.

One morning, Huber's faithful assistant, who seconded him in his experiments, brought information that the bees themselves had already solved the problem. In different hives they had conceived and attempted various systems of defense and fortification. Here they constructed a wall of wax, with narrow loopholes, through which the *great* enemy could not pass. There, by a more ingenious expedient, without creating a single impediment, they built up some inter-crossing arcades at the gates, or tiny cloisters one behind the other, but running in different directions,—that is to say, to the void left by the first corresponded the substance of the second. Thus was secured a number of openings for the impatient buzzing crowd, which might go in and out as usual, with no other difficulty than that of moving in a slightly zigzag fashion. At the same time, a complete barrier was obtained against the great and *big* enemy, which could no longer enter with expanded wings, nor even glide uninjured through the narrow corridors.

It was the *coup d'état* of the brute creation, the revolution of the insects, executed by the bees, not only against their plunderers, but against the calumniators who had denied their intelligence. The theorists who had refused to believe in it, the Malebranches and the Buffons, were compelled to own themselves beaten. They had to adopt the reserve of eminent observers, like Swammerdam and Réaumur, who, far from questioning the genius of insects, furnish us with numerous facts in proof of its flexibility, of its rising to the measure of great dangers, of its scorn of routine, and of its power to make unexpected progress under certain circumstances.

Chapter IX. How the Bees Create the People and the Common Mother

In the life of the bees, all things are brought to bear on the welfare of the infant. Let us see, then, this object of love. Let us see what is lying at the bottom of the cell; her who has just been created, the little virgin of toil.

She is born in a condition of singular purity; so much so that she is not even provided with the organ of the inferior necessities. On a delicate mixture of honey and flower dust, which is constantly renewed, you see nothing at first but a comma, then a C, a spiral. But she already lives, is organized, and active; so that on the eighth day, like a skilful spinner, she weaves her network of metamorphosis.

Her nurses, that she may enjoy a complete repose at the sacred moment, take the precaution to close up her cell; erecting over it a little dome, velvety, and of a tawny color. For ten days she is a nymph, enveloped in a veil of exceeding whiteness and great delicacy, through which you can discern a miniature of mouth, eyes, wings, and feet. Twenty-one days suffice for her development. Then she scratches an opening in the little dome, and thrusts through it her head; next, with her fore-feet resting on the rim, she strenuously endeavors to disengage her whole body. It is a great effort; but the honey is close at hand to recruit her energies. At the first cell she falls in with she plunges into it her proboscis, and initiates herself into life.

She is still humid, gray, and very weak. So she hastens to get dry in the sun, to harden her soft and rumpled wings. There she is welcomed by her numerous kinswomen, who stroke and lick her amorously, and bestow on her a maternal kiss.

No creature is more richly endowed with implements, or more obviously intended for an industrial speciality. Each organ reads her its lesson, and informs her what she has to do. Lighted by five eyes and guided by a couple of antennæ, she carries in front, projecting beyond her mouth, an unique and marvelous instrument of taste,—the proboscis, or long external tongue,—which is of peculiar delicacy, and partly hairy that it may the more readily absorb and imbibe. Protected, when at rest, by a beautiful scaly sheath, the proboscis puts forth its fine point to touch a liquid; and this point wetted, draws it back into its mouth, where lies the internal tongue, a subtle judge of sensation, and the final authority.

To this delicate apparatus add some coarser attributes which indicate their own uses: hairs on every side to catch up the dust of the flowers, brushes on the thighs to sweep together the scattered harvest, and panniers to compress it into pellets of many colors. All these conjoined form the insignia of her trade.—Go, my daughter, and become a reaper!

Thou wilt desire nothing else, and thou wilt be fit for nothing else. The fairy virgins who prepared thy cradle, and feed thee daily, will bring thee up to be what they have been. Sober, laborious, and sterile, they practice a rigid economy; in them and in thee they maintain the pure flame of virginity by fasting, or at least by very scanty nourishment, while they banquet splendidly the future mother, though still a child, and are lavish towards the numerous, and, for the most part, useless tribe of males.

It is here we reach the fundamental strata of the City, the aristocracy of devotion and intelligence. The wax-makers, or bee-architects, if they consulted the wishes of the living queen, would never train up an heiress to her throne. She is blindly jealous, and as soon as the successor is born would have her put to death. They do not listen. Those firm sage heads, remembering that we all die, take counsel on the necessity of perpetuating the race. And, accordingly, by the side of the cells, or close little cradles which receive all the children of the republic, they build some spacious chambers, fifteen, nay, twenty times larger, in which the ordinary egg, favored by the conditions of ease and liberty, may enlarge and develop at will all its natural faculties. The more certainly to ensure the superior growth of the chosen egg, they prodigalize upon it a stronger and more generous food, which shall give full liberty to its sex, and endow it with fecundity. Such is the efficacy of this potent liquor, that if the nurses accidentally let fall a drop or two on the neighboring cradles, the little bees, rejoicing in the chance, participate in the queen-mother's fecundity, although in an inferior degree.

The Insect

Madam,

Kings I have made, but never willed to be one.

[J'ai fait des rois, madame, et n'ai pas voulu l'étre.]

This dramatic line perfectly characterizes the disinterestedness of these prudent nurses. They bestow all the world's gifts on their favorite,—a beautiful and ample habitation, a superior regimen, and that paradise of women—motherhood!

To the others, on the contrary,—to their sisters, who are born resembling them,—narrow cradles, coarse food, incessant work, and pain! These will go into the fields to sweat for the people and the mother; those, confined at home, will build incessantly, and attend to the young. No recreation is allowed to them; I do not think they have, like the ants, fêtes and gymnastic games. Their entire feast will be labor (from which the queen-mother is excused). To one alone they give love, and for themselves preserve nothing but wisdom.

The characteristic attribute of this child of grace, of whom the whole multitude is enamored, is certain beautiful long legs of gold, or rather of transparent amber, of a gilded yellow. This rich color lends nobility to her belly, and is also found on the edge of her dorsal rings. Elegant, *svelte*, and noble, she is freed from the drudgery of dragging the industrial apparatus which overloads the worker,—brushes and panniers. Like all the bees, she carries a sword,—I mean the sting,—but never uses it except in a personal combat; nor has she many occasions, being so surrounded, beset, and overwhelmed with an excess of love.

This mother is very timorous, a trifle is sufficient to terrify her; at the slightest danger she takes to flight, and conceals herself at the bottom of the hive. Her head is not very large, and the unique function which so distinguishes her, is not one of those which tend to expand the brain. The others have more opportunity of acquiring knowledge and varying their accomplishments. The little gleaners gather a wide experience Of the country and of life. The bee-architects, who, moreover, attend to a thousand unforeseen domestic affairs, are compelled to think and develop their intelligence. The mother has but two duties to fulfill.

On a sunny day in spring, about three hours after noon, she issues forth, and out of a myriad males or more she selects a spouse, carries him off a moment on her wings, and then rejects him, mutilated; he does not survive his felicity. She re-enters her hive, and all is ended. She is impregnated for four years, the ordinary term of her existence. No loves can be briefer or more chaste. All her toil, by day and night, without distinction of season,—except for three months of lethargy in rigorous winters,—is to lay eggs everywhere, and without cessation. She flies from cellule to cellule, and in each deposits an egg. Nothing more is required of her. She was born for this destiny, and her people prosper in proportion to her fecundity. If she fell barren, all would languish,—as well as the activity, the labor, and the love which every one bestows upon her. The sentiment displayed towards her is not so much of a personal character as the idea of utility, of the preservation and perpetuity of the people, which very visibly prevails.

This mother, say our authors, has a somewhat giddy head. Like all individuals who have nothing to do, she is volatile and capricious. At the end of a year's incubation and sedentary life in the depths of the hive, a desire seizes her for the open air, to see a little of the world, to visit new countries. She has, nevertheless, a more serious motive than they say. She sees the spacious chambers which are being built for the young mothers who will replace her. She feels that her rivals are concealed there, and grows fiercely jealous. Incessantly she prowls around, and but for the assiduous guard which protects them, and keeps her away, she would dart her sting through the thin partitions. Conceive, then, what must be her rage when the young captives, ignorant of her fury and

their danger, make imprudent efforts to escape from their cradles, hum and sing aloud their little cicala song, which is peculiar to the mother of the bees, and so clearly announces to the queen the presence of the pretenders? The foresight of the bees, which, to guard against all accidents, has thus reared up the young mothers, involves them then in difficulty. A frightful combat impends, a wholesale massacre; the old queen-mother, were she allowed, would not spare one of those odious females. Separation is preferable to civil war. The aged sovereign, agitated and distraught, runs everywhere, and seems to say: "Let those who love me, follow me." She raises a song of departure, and all labor is suspended.

Determined to follow her, numbers of the bees make the necessary preparations, and eat a supply of food which will last them several days. The excessive agitation is manifested by a sudden change of temperature; from 28° C., the heat of the hive mounts up to 30° or 32°,—a condition of things intolerable to the bees, for to respire easily is a peculiar feature of their organization. In the extreme heat they are all bathed in sweat. Therefore they must either set out or die. The mother sallies forth, and they rush headlong after her. They buzz and whirl for a moment round the abandoned home, and then dart a little further away, describing in the air the most fantastic and incredible flights. The air is darkened with them. At length some settle upon the branch of a neighboring tree, then numerous others take their places, along with the queen. They cling to one another, and droop downwards in a large cluster. tranquility is re-established. The other bee communities having taken the alarm, and fearing the invasion of the fugitives, have guarded their gates, and reinforced their ordinary posts; but now, seeing them settled, they breathe freely, and return to their occupations.

Meanwhile some prudent and faithful messengers are despatched from the cluster to examine the neighboring localities best adapted for a new establishment. M. Debeauvoys was the first to observe this act of prudence, this special and prudent mission of inspection for the information and guidance of the new colony. A hollow tree, or a cavity in the rock, protected from the north wind, and near a brook where they can conveniently drink, are the conditions which weigh most with our prudent emigrants. A hive fully prepared and already furnished with honey they do not regard with indifference. They are very decisive in their movements, being directed by an excellent sense.

Shall we affirm that they have quitted without regret the native land where they toiled so successfully? And that, having once forsaken it, they think of it no more? By no means. The mother especially,—"giddy" as they call her,—has her fancies for return, and twice—nay, thrice—persists in going back, carrying with her the too devoted colony.

What would befall if, in these home-visits, she found herself face to face with the new queen whom the non-emigrating people have substituted in her place? There would be a combat. And this, too, happens without emigration, when, spite of all the efforts that are made to prevent her, a young mother, having forced her way through the wall of her apartment, reveals to the old queen the detested object of her jealousy. A duel then infallibly takes place. However, as each knows the other to be armed with a mortal dart, their natural cowardice would moderate their fury, and limit the struggle to a few harmless shocks, and an innocent wrestle, like the pugilistic display of paid athletes. But the people who gather round and look on from a near point of view are very grave, and mean the affair to be so. Division in the community would be the greatest of all evils. Moreover, they are so economical and temperate for themselves, so parsimonious for others, that they take into consideration, I am sure, the enormous cost that would result from the establishment of a couple of queens. Each one of them, royally nourished as they are, is a serious trouble to the republic. The State would be ruined if it had to pay a double budget. Therefore one of them must die. And hence arises a strange spectacle, completely characteristic of the singular spirit of this people: the object of adoration, recently gorged, and brushed, and caressed,—if she recoil, is led back to the combat, is impelled and driven into it, until one of the two antagonists contrives to leap upon the other, and from its bended and superjacent abdomen plunges into the latter's entrails the irremissible poignard.

Unity is thus secured. The survivor, who, if conquered, would have been flung aside without regret, now that she is victorious becomes the idol and living deity of the commonwealth; but let her remember, on the express condition of perpetuating the people and proving continuously prolific.

Let us suppose a deplorable misfortune,—that every mother has perished. What then becomes of the orphaned world? Does it fall, as some have asserted, into complete demoralization? Does such a calamity entail a furious anarchy, a universal pillage of the people by the people themselves? By no means, says M.

Debeauvoys. A few hours of trouble, pain, wrath, and apparent delirium follow. The bees flutter to and fro in great agitation, and suspend their work; for a moment they even neglect the nurslings. But a people so grave and dignified at bottom soon resume their dignity, and remember what they owe to themselves. The mother is dead? Long live the mother! We know how to create another. What we were yesterday, so are we to-day.

The last will be first. They turn to the youngest child of the people, who has barely opened her shell, who has not had time to undergo the confinement of a narrow cradle, who has not yet grown lean on the scanty fare of an artisan. This fare is not honey, but merely the dust of flowers which naturalists call *bees' bread*. Those who have been previously fed upon poorer fare will remain little; they no longer possess the faculty of transformation.

But this young bee, so soft and so tender, will become whatever you will; and in order that she may develop into a true female, a bee of love, and a prolific mother, what is necessary? Liberty. Let them provide her with a vast cradle where her young life may float, and agitate, and develop, at ease. It will cost three cradles destroyed to provide for hers, and the lives of three infants, who will perish before birth; but what matter, if in a year she supplies the nation with ten thousand?

The consecration of the mother of the people is that living nourishment which the people extract from themselves, and in which they mingle their bee-sweetness with the balmy essence of the flowers. A strong and noble nourishment, rich in the intoxicating perfume of aromatic herbs, richer in the virginal love concentrated upon it by thirty thousand sisters for the behoof of the marvelous child who belongs to them all.

On the third day the child sees its cradle extended by an ornament intended to make it still freer,—a pyramid reversed. On the fifth only do they seal it up, to the intent that she may sleep peacefully, and accomplish her metamorphosis in peace. And then the anxiety increases. They guard the beloved sleeper who will be to-morrow the common soul, and will inspire by her love the labors of the people. They guard her, and they wait upon her, but with the haughty dignity of a people who adore only their own handiwork, chosen by them, nourished by them, created by them, and to be unmade by them. It is their pride that at need they know how to create a god.

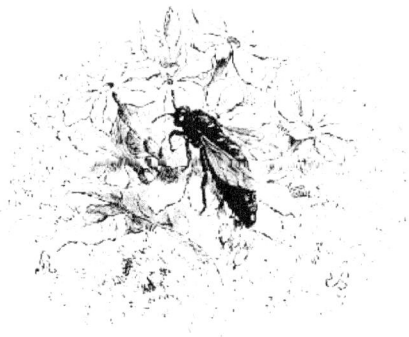

Conclusion

The bee and the ant reveal to us the lofty harmony of the insect.

Both, in their high intelligence, are of superior rank as artists, architects, and the like. The bee is more, a geometer; the ant is before all remarkable as an educator.

The ant is frankly and strongly republican, having no need of a living and visible symbol of the community, lightly esteeming and governing with sufficient rudeness the soft and feeble females who perpetuate the race. The bee, on the other hand, more tender apparently, or less reasoning and more imaginative, finds a moral support in the worship of the common mother. For her community of virgins it is, so to speak, a religion of love.

Among both the ants and bees maternity is the social principle; but fraternity also takes root, flourishes, and springs to a glorious stature.

Our book, begun in a profound obscurity, terminates in a fulness of light.

To form a correct judgment of insects, you must examine and estimate their achievements and their societies. If their organization rank so low as has been said, so much the more are they to be admired for accomplishing such noble works with such inferior organs.

Observe that the most advanced works are executed by those (as, for example, the ants) who have no special implements to facilitate them, but must supply the want by skill and invention.

Were they not so diminutive, what consideration we should extend to their arts and labors! Comparing the cities of the termites with the cabins of the negro, the subterranean galleries of the ants with the little excavations of our Tourangeaux of the Loire, how we should dwell on the superior skill of the insects! Is it stature, then, which changes your moral judgments? What are the proportions which will merit your esteem?

Let us add, that if this book do not modify the opinion of the reader, it has greatly modified our own. This, in the course of our labor, has undergone a considerable change. We thought we were going to study things, and found them *souls*.

Close daily observation, initiating us into their ways and habits, developed in our minds a sentiment which animated our study, but also complicated it,— respect for their persons and lives.

"What say you? An ant's existence? Nature holds them cheaply, renews them incessantly, prodigalizes lives, sacrifices them to one another."

Yes, but because she makes them. She bestows life and withdraws it; has the secret of their destinies, and that of the compensations in the course of possible progress. But as for us, we have no power over them, except to make them suffer.

This is a grave reflection. We are not talking here of any childish sensibility. On the contrary, neither children nor men of science cherish any such feeling. But a man—man accustomed to reason with himself and estimate his acts—will not lightly deprive any creature of that gift of life which it is utterly out of his power to confer on the most insignificant. This consideration impressed us strongly. And at first a person, a woman, more impressionable and more scrupulous than myself, who had come hither with the design of making a collection of the insects of Fontainebleau, hesitated, deferred the task; and then, having interrogated her conscience, felt compelled to renounce it. Without uttering a word of censure upon scientific collections, which are absolutely indispensable, it is certain that we ought not to find a pastime in death. Note that many of these creatures are much less important in form and color than by attitude and movement, which cannot be preserved at the extremity of a pin!

Our first discussion of this kind was in reference to the fate of a very remarkable butterfly (a sphinx, if I mistake not), which we caught in a net to examine for a moment. I had admired it for several days, coming and going among the flowers,—not, like most of its race, flying hap-hazard, but choosing them discreetly, and then, with a very fine, very long and arrowy proboscis, sucking by small sips, and very quickly withdrawing, as if acted upon by a steel spring. The movement was one of incomparable grace, of coquettish sobriety; just as if it said: "Enough for to-day,—enough! But, to-morrow!" I have never seen anything more graceful.

The Insect

It is only a gray butterfly, and not at all remarkable. Who that sees it dead would divine that, in charming nimbleness, it is the favorite of Nature, in which she has exhausted all her grace?

We opened the net. And not long afterwards we had the pleasure of seeing the same butterfly, which, in bad weather, came one evening to take shelter with us, and found a resting-place in our chamber. In the morning, wishful to enjoy the sunshine, it flew away.

I ought to add, moreover, that all the shipwrecked unfortunates of the latter end of autumn, guided by a very sure but very surprising instinct, willingly came to our house,—some on a temporary visit, others to remain with us. A young bullfinch, in a bad condition, and who had evidently met with more than one adventure, arrived all bewildered, and even on the first day ate from our hands. The same thing happened with a still more miserable creature,—a little tiny red-tail, which had been barbarously deprived of its head-feathers that it might be sold for a nightingale. This creature, so ill-treated by men, which might justly have been afraid of them, not only took at the very first the seed from our hands and lips, but would not sleep except on the mistress's finger.

As for insects, their domestication is impossible. But many, nevertheless, seem able to live with man, to appreciate peaceable people and mildness of character. Last winter, two pretty red lady-birds had taken up their residence on our table, among our books and papers, which were being constantly moved about. What to give them, we knew not; they passed the whole season without eating, or appearing to receive any injury. The warmth of the apartment seemed agreeable to them.

A strong September wind is now blowing, and, this very day, has cast in upon us a beautiful reddish-colored caterpillar. Though she had not come of her own accord, but in spite of herself, we felt that we ought to respect misfortune. We did not know from what plant she had been torn, but supposed from her motions that she had been carried away at the moment she had begun to spin. We presented her with a variety of leaves; but none of them pleased her taste. She moved to and fro, displaying an extraordinary agitation. We supposed she wished to find rest upon a branch, but the rain fell in torrents. As many caterpillars and larvæ work underground, we brought it some earth. But this, too, was useless. Thinking she might like a web at a time when she was engaged in weaving, we placed her on the lace-work of a cushion which lay in the window; but the lace was cold and coarse, and did not please her. Moreover, the wind, the little wind which entered, would have cruelly frozen her during a whole winter. Finally, by a feminine marvel of intuition, we concluded that, since she was about to weave silk, she would like the silk-velvet lining of our microscope.

Plainly, it was the very thing she herself would have chosen. Installed in the evening, by the morning she had made herself at home in this soft, warm, and sheltered place. She had already spun, and hastily extended her threads to right and left, as if fearing she might be disturbed. Then, during the day, her work having been respected, she saw that she had miscalculated her measurements, and that her cocoon was too short; she destroyed a third of it, to resume the fabric from that point on better proportions.

Behold, then, microscope, and scalpel, and all our instruments expelled. What could we do? The confiding animal had taken up a position at our fireside, and would not withdraw from it. Life had driven out Science. Grave study, wait! for awhile thou art adjourned. During the winter we respected the sleep of the chrysalis.

Illustrative Notes

NOTE 1

The Meaning of this Book.—It has sprung wholly from the heart. Nothing has been given up to the intellect, nothing to systems. We have abstained from entering into scientific disputes.

If the following formula should seem to you too systematic, pass over it. We have not sought to embody a dogma in it. We would only simplify, if possible, the point of view, and place it in the reader's power to embrace the whole significance of the book.

The point of departure is violent. It is the gigantic and necessary war waged by the insect upon all morbid or encumbering life that might prove an obstacle to life. A terrible war, an infernal toil, which, ensures the safety of the world.

This powerful accelerator of the universal passage should destroy like fire. But to secure the sharpness of action such a mission requires, it is necessary that its own transformations be accelerated, its life compressed; that from love to death, and death to love, it revolve in a burning circle. However brief may be this circle, it cannot be accomplished but at the cost of painful metamorphoses, which resemble a series of successive deaths.

Among most insects, marriage means the death of the father; maternity, the death of the mother. Thus the generations pass away without knowing one another. The mother loves her daughter, anticipates her birth, often immolates herself for her sake, but will never see her.

This cruel contradiction, this harsh denial which Nature opposes to the most pathetic aspirations of love, apparently inflames and irritates it. It gives everything unreservedly, knowing that it is for death. It draws from it two powers; on the one hand, unheard *tongues of light and color*, ravishing phantasmagorias, in which love is not translated, but expands in rays, and pharos-fires, and torches, and burning sparks. It is the appeal to the rapid present, the lightning and the thunder of happiness. But the love of the to come, the foreseeing tenderness for that which not yet is, is expressed in another fashion by the astonishingly complex and ingenious creation of a storehouse of implements, whence all our mechanical arts have derived their most perfect models. Usually this grand apparatus of tools serves but for a day; it enables them at the moment they forsake the orphan to improvise the cradle which shall continue the mother, shall perpetuate the incubation when the mother ceases to exist.

But how? Must she indeed perish? Can there be no exception to the pitiless law? In hot climates, especially, many mothers may survive. What if these mothers united together to deceive destiny, by associating so many brief existences in one common and lasting life in which their children should find an eternal mother?

How shall we elude death?—Let us create society.

The society of mothers. The insect is essentially a female and a mother. The male is an exception, a secondary accident,—frequently, too, an abortion, a caricature of an insect.

The dream of the female—maternity, and the safety of her child—the preservation of the future—leads her to create the community, which secures her own safety.

This society can only perpetuate itself by ensuring its existence against the season of sterility. Hence results a need of accumulation. Hence proceed labor and economy.

But Nature, eluded by the effort and the toil,—I was going to say, the virtue,—does not lose its rights. Beaten on the one side, on the other it reacts upon the commonwealth, and grievously oppresses it. This self-protecting society, while rescuing immense multitudes from death and prolonging the common existence, multiplies the mouths to be fed, and is often overloaded. If its members would not die of famine, they must live on a very scanty regimen, must preserve alive a limited number of fertile females, and condemn the majority, or nearly the whole of the females to celibacy. Reared for virginity and labor, sterilized from the cradle in their maternal powers, they are by no means of barren intellect. The extinction of certain faculties seems to strengthen the others.

Such is the institution, ingeniously severe, of aunts or adoptive mothers. With too little sexual feeling to desire love, they possess enough to wish for children, to love and adopt them. They are both less than mothers, and more than mothers. Should invasion or ruin befall the hive or the ant-hill, the true mothers consult their own safety in flight; the devoted aunts or sisters know no other thought but that of saving the children.

Elevated by this factitious maternity and disinterested love above itself, the insect surpasses all other creatures,—even those which, like the mammals, are evidently superior in organization. It teaches us that organism is not everything, and that there is a potency in life which acts strongly beyond the range and in despite of the organs. Those species which, like the ants, have no special instruments to facilitate their work, are invariably the most advanced.

The noblest work of the world, the most elevated goal to which its inhabitants tend, is the community,—by which I mean a society strongly consolidated. The only being, besides Man, who seems to reach this goal, is undoubtedly the Insect.

No other creature approaches it. The most sublime and charming, the Bird, is, through these very qualities, also the most individual. Its society is the family; its community, the nest; its associations are only collocations of nests for the sake of security. Those mammals which, approach us so nearly, and impress us so strongly by their advanced organization,—I mean, the beaver,—show wonderful powers of combination for the execution of their task; but, when the work is done, they retire to their own houses and families, isolated by the very tenderness of their domestic affections. The assembly of the beavers is, as it were, a colony of builders and engineers, where each one lives apart; but they are not citizens, and it is not a city.

The city is only to be found in the insect world. Separated from man by many degrees in organism, the insect approaches him more closely than any other being in the supreme work of his life,—which is, to live for the many. It has not those touching signs of close relationship which render the higher animals so interesting to us. It has no blood; it has no milk. But I recognize it as akin by one loftier attribute: it has the social sense.

An ignorant dogmatism had long asserted that the very perfection of these insect-societies depended on their automatism. But modern observation has proved, that if the conditions are varied, and unforeseen obstacles and difficulties placed in their way, they confront them with vigor and calm sense, and with the resources of an unfettered ingenuity,

It is a world of *method*, which, at need, can show itself *unrestrained.*

A world which, presently, in its original mission of combat and destruction, seemed to us an atrociously fatal force; but which afterwards, by the influence of its maternal devotion, became a world of social harmony, preaching a lofty morality.

But is *maternity* all? No; the community of life introduces the insect to the threshold of a still higher rank of sentiments. Even among those which are isolated—among the necrophori, for example, and the pilulary scarabæi—*fraternal* co-operation has a beginning. They render mutual services, and fly to the assistance of one another, co-operating in certain works. Among the sociable insects the feeling is carried to a considerable height; the bees feed one another, mouth to mouth, and stint themselves to supply their sisters. A very safe, and by no means romantic observer, saw an ant dressing the wound of another ant which had lost an antenna, by pouring on it some honey-dew to close it up and protect it from the air.

See now how far we have advanced from our starting-point, where the insect appeared to us a pure voracious element, a machine of absorption.

A great, a sublime metamorphosis, more marvelous than that of the moultings and transformations which guided the egg, the grub, the nymph, to the assumption of wings.

It is a world strange to man, but singularly parallel to our own, though having no mutual mode of communication. We invent scarcely anything which has not previously—though for a long time unknown to us—been invented by the insect.

What have the great animals discovered? Nothing. Apparently their warmth of life, and their red blood, obscure their mental light.

On the contrary, the insect world, free from a heavy apparatus of flesh and blood intoxication, more subtly sensitive, and moved by a nervous electricity, seems a frightful world of spirits.

Frightful? No. If terror sit at the threshold of science, safety is found in its *penetralia*. At the first glance the living energy of the invisible may startle us; and with a shudder of alarm we may contemplate in the animalcule the likeness, some flashes of the individuality, or a certain undefinable something which seems like a counterfeit, of man.

These gleams, which so troubled the great Swammerdam, and made him recoil with dread, are precisely the circumstances that give me encouragement. Yes; all see, all feel, and all love: a miracle truly religious! In the material infinite which deepens under my eyes, I recognize, for my reassurance, a moral infinite. The individuality hitherto claimed as a monopoly by the pride of the chosen species, I see generously extended to all, and conferred even upon the least. The gulf of life would have seemed to me deserted, desolate, barren, and godless, had I not everywhere discovered the warmth and tenderness of the Universal Love in the universality of the soul.

NOTE 2

Our Authorities.—In a book which puts forward no scientific pretensions, the book of an unlearned writer dedicated to unlearned readers, we do not hesitate to confess that our method of study was very indirect. If we had commenced with subtle classificators or minute anatomists, or with dry manuals of instruction, perhaps we should have been checked at the first step. But we approached this science on its attractive side—through the great historians of the insect, who have united the delineation of its habits with the description of its organs. Our mind had received a strong and decisive blow (if we may so speak) from the hooks of the two Hubers on the Bees and the Ants. The impression was so great, that thereafter we read with interest what one does not usually read continuously, Réaumur's six quarto volumes of *Mémoires*—an immortal book, which must always be a standard authority. Neither the contemptuous reaction of Buffon, nor the anatomical works, of superior exactness on special points, which have since been produced, should cause it to be forgotten. Réaumur was, as it were, the central point of our studies, and from him we went back to the illustrious masters of the seventeenth century, Swammerdam and Malpighi; next, we descended to those of the eighteenth, the Lyonnets, Bonnets, and Geers; finally, to our modern writers, Latreille, Duméril, Lepelletier, Blanchard,—to the fertile and audacious school of the Geoffroy Saint-Hilaires and the Audouins, gloriously supported by Ampére and Goethe. While profiting by the noble treatises which sum up the main results of the science, like those of Lacordaire, we by no means neglected the admirable monographs of the present, century,—those of Léon Dufour (scattered through the *Annales des Sciences Naturelles*, and other collections), the grand work of Walckenaër on the Spiders, the colossal labor of Strauss on the Cockchafer—a monument of the first class, which can only be compared to Lyonnet's treatise on the Caterpillar. As for details drawn from travelers, we shall hereafter have an opportunity of referring to them. We shall also acknowledge our debt to foreign writers,—to Kirby, Smeathman, Lund, and others. For the anatomy of the insect, as for general anatomy, we cannot too strongly recommend the admirable and usefully enlarged specimens prepared by our excellent master, Dr. Auzoux.

NOTE 3—Book i., Chap. iii.

On Insect Embryos, Invisible Animalcules, Infusorias as the Predecessors or Forerunners of the Insect, &c.—The work of the *vermets* has been observed, in Sicily, by M. de Quatrefages.—As for the microscopic fossils, the infusorias,

&c., their great *coup de théâtre* has been Ehrenberg's discovery. See his *Mémoires* in the *Annales des Sciences Naturelles*, Second Series, vols, i., ii., vi., vii., viii. In volume i., p. 134, for 1834, he specifies the point at which Cuvier left the science, and how much his discovery has added to it.

Upon the living world, upon the processes at present in operation for the creation of little spheres, on those humble constructors who accomplish such great things, we owe all our information to the English voyagers, the Nelsons,[19] the Darwins, and others. They are minute and very simple observers, generally timid in their assertions, which have been of the boldest character, they having seen the very heart of the mystery, and caught Nature in the act. Read Darwin (whose researches have been most ably summed up by Sir Charles Lyell) for information on the prodigious manufacture of chalk, divided alternately between the fishes and the polypes, which are building up islands with it, and will soon construct continents.

England alone, that immense *poulpe* whose arms enfold the earth, and who incessantly *feels* and examines it, could observe it thoroughly in its distant solitudes, where at its ease it continues its everlasting procreation. The great theories formerly advanced in explanation of the cataclysms, epochs, and revolutions of the earth, will lose, perhaps, something of their importance. For we know now that everything is in a state of constant change.

Does Europe perceive that quite a complete literature has sprung from Great Britain in the last twenty years? I describe it as an immense commission of inquiry into the condition of the globe, undertaken by the English. They alone could do it. And why? Because other nations *travel*, but only the English *reside*. They daily recommence at all points of the earth the life-study of a Robinson Crusoe: and this is done by a crowd of isolated observers, led abroad by commercial speculation, and hence so much the less systematical in their inquiries.

---

[19] "Nous devons tout aux navigateurs Anglais, aux Nelson, aux Darwin," etc.

The Insect

NOTE 4—Book i., Chap. iv.

(*Love and Death.*) *On the Female Apparatus.*—Réaumur,—and, in fact, every writer,—has admired the manner in which the weapons of war become the instruments of maternal love. M. Lacase, in a very beautiful thesis, the result of independent observations, and a continuation of the analogous works of an eminent master, Léon Dufour, has treated this subject with great anatomical preciseness. An original and important point of his labor is, undoubtedly, his demonstration, conformably to the views of Geoffroy Saint-Hilaire, Serres, Audouin, and others, "that the very various armors which prolong the abdomen imply the modification, or even the sacrifice, of one or two of its posterior rings." Thus Nature apparently operates upon a fixed, amount of substance, only increasing one part at the expense of others, which are shortened or transformed.

NOTE 5—Book i., Chap. v.

The Chilly Offspring of the Insect.—"But," the reader will exclaim, "what labor! How terrible a law of continuous efforts to be imposed on young beings, as yet but ill provided with tools, and without, that superb arsenal of implements which at a later stage we admire in the insect. How protracted are the means devised for their defense, which would be much sooner accomplished if they were born less soft, a little firmer, and somewhat less impressionable."

Yes; but in that case they would be just so far unfitted for the essential circumstance which ensures their development. Nature wishes them to be soft, ay, and very soft, that they may more easily undergo the moultings and painful changes which are imperative upon them,—which moultings, if the insect-substance were hard, would inflict upon it the most severe injuries. By instinct they are aware of this, and dread extremely lest their bodies should harden. The *processionary* caterpillars, for example, though covered thickly with hair, conceal themselves from the sun under ample curtains. And they are also mindful to issue forth only in the evening, when the damp and misty air may preserve their salutary humidity.

NOTE 6—Book i., Chap. vii.

The Appearance of the Perfect Insect.—The anatomy of the insect has been the theme of one of the greatest disputes of our time. Some one having visited Goethe, soon after the French Revolution of July 1830:—"Well, well," inquired the illustrious sage, "have they settled the question?" And as the traveler seemed to think he referred to the political question, "Oh, it is something of far greater importance!" said Goethe; "I refer to the great duel between Cuvier and Geoffroy."

The world took part in it. Strauss and others remained faithful to Cuvier. The great physicist Ampére, in an anonymous article inserted in the first volume of the *Annales des Sciences Naturelles*, adopted the opinions of Geoffroy, Audouin, and Serres, and even expressed them with a juvenile audacity that these anatomists, in their modesty, had not displayed.

All the complex details of their proceedings had been extracted and prepared [by Madame Michelet] for the present volume with a patience and persevering love such as could be inspired only by a true and tender religion of Nature. Barbarian that I am, I must sacrifice this arduous labor, which, perhaps, would not be much relished by the public to whom I address myself.

The place which the insect occupies in the animal creation is very clearly defined in Lacordaire's excellent *résumé*:—"Equal to the vertebrates in the energy of its muscular fibre, scarcely inferior to them in the organization of its digestive canal, superior even to the bird by the quantity of its respiration, it falls below the molluscs through the imperfection of its system of circulation. Its nervous system is less concentrated than that of many of the crustacea." (Lacordaire, vol. ii., p. 2.)

Has the insect a brain? It is a disputed question. The nervous apparatus which, in the molluscs, has not found, so far, a centre, tends, it is true, in the insect, towards centralization. Two longitudinal strings of nerves, which run through the entire length of the body, abut on the nerves of the head, which are not massed as in the higher animal. In the wasp, however, has been discovered a firm, whitish substance, strongly resembling the brain. But this would seem exceptional. Even in the head of insects remarkable for their intelligence, you will find only simple nervous ganglions, not differing in any respect from those which compose the two threads.

This inferiority of organization does but render more surprising the superiority of the insect in art and sociability to all other animals, even to the principal mammals (with a single exception). Here at the highest point of the ladder, there at the lowest, it occupies, on the whole, a middle place; and is, as it were, in the scale of existence, an energetic mediator between life and death.

NOTE 7—Book ii., Chap. i.

Swammerdam.—We refer to the inaugurator and martyr of our science, the creator of the instrument which has enabled men to follow up his discoveries,—a great inventor in many senses,—specially for the preparation of anatomical specimens. The reader should study his *Biblia Naturæ*, in Boerhaave's edition, ornamented with fine illustrations (two vols. folio), and not in the incomplete French abridgment, published in the *Mémoires* of the Academy of Dijon, which gives the scientific results, but no trace of the man.

We do not undertake to write the history of Entomology. A good abridgment will be found at the end of M. Th. Lacordaire's *Introduction à l'Entomologie.*

NOTE 8—Book ii., Chap. iv.

The Insect as Man's Auxiliary.—The ingenious work which I here confute, and which, assuredly, cannot be read with gratification, is entitled,—*Les Insectes, ou Rèflexions d'un amateur de la chasse aux petits oiseaux*, par E. Gand, *Lecture faite à l'Académie d'Amiens* (26th December 1856).

A remark which I make a few pages further on, in reference to the necessity of a popular teaching of natural history, well deserves to gain attention. The wealth and morality of the world would be doubled if this teaching could be universal. M. Emile Blanchard's important work, *Zoologie*

Agricole (in folio, 1854), gives the very useful history of the principal insects injurious to our ordinary or ornamental plants. M. Pouchet, in his excellent *Mémoire* on the Cockchafer, enumerates the principal authors who have described the destructive insects. The United States Congress has entrusted to Mr. Harris the preparation of a history of them.

NOTE 9—Book ii., Chap. v.

Light and color.—My description of tropical climates is borrowed from a large number of travelers,—Humboldt, Azara, Auguste, Saint-Hilaire, Castelneau, Weddell, Charles Waterton, and others. For Brazil and Guiana, I have been greatly indebted to the exceeding courtesy of M. Ferdinand Denis, whose knowledge of those countries is so perfect.

Paris possesses several fine collections of insects, besides that of the Museum. One of the best-known is Doctor Bois Duval's (lepidoptera). An establishment exclusively devoted to the sale of insects may be found at No. 17 Rue des Saints-Péres. The magnificent collection to which I refer on page 176, is that of M. Douë, who most readily showed it to us, and explained it with infinite complaisance.

The anecdote which concludes chapter xii. (*The Ornament of Living Flames*) is related, in reference to the women of Santa Cruz in Bolivia, by the always accurate Dr. Weddell. The Indian phrase, "Replace it whence thou borrowedst it," is recorded by Waterton.

The Insect

Renovation of Human Arts by Study of the Insect.—Who has not seen that for a long time the art of decoration has made no progress, does but incessantly repeat itself? When a particular subject has lasted ten years, men think to rejuvenate it with a few variations. In a life of half a century I have several times seen this rotation of fashion, which would appear singularly monotonous if we did not possess in so high a degree the gift of forgetfulness.

The decorative art, instead of seeking its renovation in the things of old, would profit greatly by drawing its inspiration from the infinity of beauties distributed throughout Nature. They abound and superabound:—

1st, In the highly accented forms of tropical plants. Ours only produce their effect in masses, and on a grand scale.

2nd, In those of a great number of the lower animals, radiata, and others; in many of the little floating molluscs, living and imperceptible flowers, the design of which, when enlarged, might suggest some very original ideas.

3rd, In certain parts of the most despised creatures; as, for example, in the eyes of the fly.

4th, In the forms, designs, and colors one detects in the thickness of the living tissue; as, for example, on lifting with the scalpel the strata of the wing-sheath of the beetles. Nature, which has so embellished the surface, has hidden, perhaps, still more beauty in the depth. Nothing is finer than the vital fluids, when seen in the mobility of their circulation, and in the delicate canals where that circulation is accomplished and defined. They speak to us less eloquently, and impress us less forcibly by the splendor of the glittering leaves among which they circulate, than by the expressive forms in which we divine the mystery of their life. These are their visible energies.

The Spider.—These two chapters are mainly the result of our own observations. We have profited, however, by several authorities; especially by the capital and classical work, the grand labor of Walckenaër,—which is of importance both for the description, classification, and moral history of the Spiders.

Azara tells us that in Paraguay the natives spin the cocoon of a great orange-colored spider fully an inch in diameter. Sir George Staunton, the English ambassador to China, in his "Travels in Java" (vol. i., p. 343) informs us that the epeiras of Asia weave such stout webs that they can only be cut with a sharp-edged instrument; at the Bermudas, their webs are capable of arresting the progress of a bird as big as a thrush (Richard Stafford, *Coll. Acad.*, ii., p. 156).

Doctor Lemercier, our learned bibliographer, has lent to me (from his personal collection) a rare and very clever *brochure* by Quatrefages on the hygrometrical sensibility of spiders, on their prescience of variations of the temperature—which we might very well turn to advantage—and on the skilful exposure of their webs.

The formation of their beautiful and poetical autumn-webs, which are called *Virgin's Threads*, is very clearly explained by Des Étang, in the *Mémoires de la Société Agricole de Troyes*, for 1839.

In reference to the spider's most terrible enemy, the ichneumon, some curious details are given in the fourth volume of the *Memoirs* of the American Society. In order to preserve it for its little ones, it does not kill its victim, but, if one may so speak, etherizes it by pricking it, and distilling into the wound a venom which apparently paralyzes it.

My remarks on the terror of the male in his amorous advances are based upon those of De Geer, and Lepelletier, in the *Nouveau Bulletin de la Société Philomathique*, pt. 67, p. 257.

Finally, the master-work of the spider, the ingeniously constructed house and door of the *Mygale* of Corsica, has been completely described and drawn by an observer whom one can trust implicitly,—Audouin (followed by Walckenaër, and others).

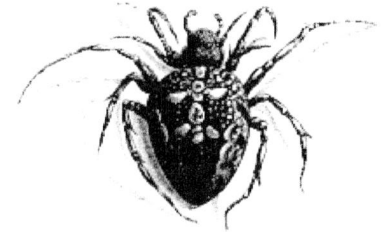

NOTE 12-Book iii., Chap. i.

The Termites.—The beautiful illustrations of Smeathman would merit reproduction, and the translation of his book (ed. 1784), now very rarely met with, ought to be reprinted. The interesting additional details collected by Azara, Auguste, Saint-Hilaire, Castelneau, and others, might be added, so as to make a complete monograph.

The Insect

It is by no means a matter of slight import to recognize that the true and grand principle of art, so long misunderstood in the Middle Ages, has been always followed to the very letter by creatures of so low an order, in their surprising constructions.

The fact I have related in reference to the subterranean mining of Valencia by the termites, will be found in Humboldt's "Travels in Equinoctial America."

As for La Rochelle, read the interesting chapter in M. de Quatrefages' *Souvenirs d'un Naturaliste.*

NOTE 13—Book iii., Chap. ii.

The Ants.—The migrations of the tropical ants, say Azara and Lacordaire, sometimes last over two or three days. They are to be compared in continuousness and frightful numbers only to the clouds of pigeons which, in North America, obscure the sky for several days in succession (see Audubon). Lund (*Annales des Sciences Naturelles*, 1831, vol. xxiii., p. 113) gives a curious picture of these ant-migrations. They are terribly warlike, and the Americans amuse themselves by opposing in a duel the *visiting ant* (Atta) to the *Araraa* ant. The latter, though the weaker, prevails through the potency of its poison.

As for our European ants, my brother-in-law, M. Hippolyte Mialaret, transmits to me a curious fact, which, I believe, has not before been observed. He gave them a medley of various kinds of grain,—wheat, barley, rye,—which they employed in their buildings. Having opened the ant-hill, he found the grains carefully classified, and distributed on different stories,—wheat, for example, on the second, barley on the third,—the different kinds being nowhere mixed.

An excellent Italian dissertation by M. Giuseppe Gené would induce one to believe Huber mistaken in his assertion that the mother ant can by her unaided self found a community. After her fecundation she retires into a corner, where she plucks off her wings, and waits. There some prowling ants discover, feel, and recognize her, her and her eggs sown on the ground, with much prudence and even visible mistrust. Afterwards they explore the country round about with an infinite circumspection, always coming back to the mother, and hesitating long before they decide. At length, their numbers increasing, they definitively adopt her, and set to work.

The indomitable perseverance of the ants is celebrated in a beautiful Oriental legend of I know not what Asiatic prince,—Tamerlane, I believe. Beaten and defeated several times in one campaign, he was seated, almost despairing, in the depth of his tent. An ant mounted the side. Several times he made it drop, but it invariably reascended. He was curious to see how long it would persevere, and twenty-four times threw it to the ground without discouraging it. Then he grew tired, and moreover he was full of admiration. The ant conquered. So he said: "Let us imitate it. We too will conquer as the ant has done." But for the ant, the hero had missed the Empire of Asia.

NOTE 14—Book iii., Chap. iii.

Flocks of the Ants.—Nearly every plant nourishes grubs, which are embellished with the most varied, and frequently the most dazzling colors. The rose-tree aphis, when I examined it through a microscope, seemed to me of a very pleasant bright green. Thrown on its back, it displayed a very big belly, and a very small ungainly head, which appeared to be neither more nor less than a sucker, while it agitated all its limbs. On the whole, I took it to be an innocent creature, which should inspire no repugnant feeling. One can understand how the ants absorb the honey-dew upon its body. (See Bonnet and others, in reference to their prodigious fecundity.)

NOTE 15—Book iii., Chap. v.

The Wasps.—Before speaking of this terrible species, in which, perhaps, we see revealed the loftiest energy of nature, I ought to have spoken of its modest neighbor, the drone. Réaumur, who is not sufficiently known as a writer, and who frequently displays much grace of style, says, very pleasingly, that the poor drones, in their rough little societies, when compared with the royal communities of the wasps and bees, are mere rustics or savages, and their nests so many hamlets, but that we find a pleasure, even after having visited great capitals, in resting our eyes on the simplicity of villages and villagers. (Réaumur, *Mémoires*, vol. vi., p. iii. preface, and p. 4 text.) Notwithstanding their simplicity, the drones are industrious, and have their characteristic manners and virtues. The poor males, so despised elsewhere, are more happily employed here in a society where the lofty speciality of art, not being so strikingly developed in the females, proves less humiliating; they are almost the equals of their spouses, who do not massacre them, as the wasps and bees do their destined husbands.

The Insect

NOTE 16—Book iii., Chap. viii.

The Wax-making Bees. An Aristocracy of Artists.—I here follow, in the main, the authority of M. Debeauvoys, in his *Guide de l'Apiculteur* ("The Bee-keeper's Manual"), ed. 1853. In this little but important book he has made the all-important distinction which escaped Huber's notice, and separated the great wax-making architects from the little gleaners and nurses. But I ask his permission to trust rather to M. Dujardin on the general character of the bees. They are, undoubtedly, choleric, and of a very dry temperament; the liqueurs and perfumes of the flowers excite them, and compel them frequently to quench their thirst. But in themselves they are sufficiently gentle, and can even be tamed. M. Dujardin, having renewed every day the provisions of a poor hive, was readily recognized by the bees, who flew towards him, and ran over his hands without stinging him. The annual destruction which they consummate of their males is a common law with them; the wasps, and other necessitous tribes, living in dread of famine at the epoch when the flowers disappear. In America they are looked upon as the sign of civilization. The Indians see in the bee the type of the white race, and in the buffalo the precursor of the red. (Washington Irving, "Tour in the Prairies.")

The bees, as sisters and aunts, remind one of the Germany of Tacitus:— "The aunt is there held in higher esteem than the mother." It must have resembled a country of bees.

M. Pouchet, whom I have already cited several times, has been good enough to furnish me with a very interesting anecdote of the mason-bees:—

"In Egypt and Nubia, which I traversed some few months ago, these hymenoptera and their buildings are so abundant that the ceilings of certain temples and those of some hypogea are entirely covered with them, and they absolutely mask the sculptures and hieroglyphics. These nests frequently form there a succession of layers; and in certain localities they are superimposed one upon another in sufficient numbers to form a kind of stalactite suspended to the vaulted roofs of the monuments. In their construction the bee makes use of Nile mud only; and when she has deposited therein her progeny, she seals them up with a delicately wrought cover, which the young bee, after having undergone its various metamorphoses, lifts off and flies away. But these nests are often broken up by a species of lizard, which, by means of its singularly sharp nails, climbs to the ceilings. There it wages incessant war against the mason-bees while they are building their nests, or rather it may be seen crashing through the walls to devour their young progeny."

NOTE 17—Conclusion,

A Feminine Intuition.—A great question of method which the future will clear up, is, to know how far woman will one day master the sciences of life, and to what extent the study of these sciences will be shared between the two sexes. If sympathy for animals, long and patient tenderness, the persevering observation of the delicatest objects, were the only qualities which this study demanded, it would seem as if woman ought to make the best naturalist. But the life-sciences have another and a far gloomier aspect, which repels and affrights; and it is so, because they are at the same time the sciences of death.

However, in this very century, the grand and leading discovery, all-important for the knowledge of the higher insects, belongs to a maiden, the daughter of a scientific naturalist of French Switzerland, Mademoiselle Jurine. She has found that the bee-workers, who were thought to be *neuters* (of neither the one nor the other sex), were really females, attenuated by their exceedingly narrow cradles and inferior regimen. Now, as these workers form nearly the whole people (except five or six bred as queens, and a few hundred males), it follows that the hive of twenty or thirty thousand bees is female. Thus the predominance of the feminine sex, the general law of insect life, has obtained its supreme confirmation. There are *no neuters*; neither among the bees, nor the ants, nor all the superior tribes of insects. The males are a small exception, a secondary accident. I feel able to assert that, on the whole, *the insect is female.*

Mademoiselle Jurine's discovery has also revealed to us the true character of the maternity of adoption, an admirably original characteristic of these insects, and the elevated law of disinterestedness and sacrifice which is the ennoblement of their communities.

An undoubtedly inferior, but still distinguished merit to that of accomplishing great discoveries, is that of representing animals to us by pen or pencil in their true forms, their movements, and the general harmony of the things with which they are associated. No art seems to belong more naturally to woman. A woman has commenced it.

The illustrious Audubon has won just admiration for his representation of the bird in its complete harmonies, its animal and vegetable medium, on the plants which feed, near the enemy which assails it. But it has been too generally forgotten that the model of his harmonious paintings, which present us with so true a picture of life, was furnished by a woman, Sybille de Mérian. Her handsome volume (*Métamorphose des Insectes de Surinam*, folio, in three languages, ed. 1705), was the first in which this admirable method was invented and skillfully applied.

She is called "*Mademoiselle*," though she was married. The name of "*dame*" was in her time still restricted to women of noble birth. And she remains "Mademoiselle;" is never cited except under her maiden name. Her books, from their pure science and great perseverance, give one the idea of a person lifted above the world of persons, and wholly devoted to art and nature.

I have dedicated to her a word or two, but without speaking of her life. A native of Bâle, the daughter, sister, and mother of celebrated engravers, and herself an excellent painter of flowers upon velvet, she long resided at Frankfort and Nurenberg. She experienced great misfortunes, her husband being ruined and having separated from her. She then sought refuge in a mystical society, analogous to that which had formerly consoled Swammerdam. The religious spark of the new science, *the theology of insects*, as a contemporary terms it, here produced a strong impression on her mind. She was acquainted with Swammerdam's great idea, the unity of metamorphoses, and with that which Malpighi had flung in the face of astonished Europe in his book on the silkworm: "Insects have a heart."

What! they have a heart, like us! Which, like ours, throbs and stirs at the impulse of their desires, their fears, or their passions! How touching an idea! How well adapted to influence a woman!—But is this a fact? Many long denied it, but doubt has been impossible since the truth was demonstrated in 1824 in M. Strauss's treatise on "The Cockchafer."

Madame de Mérian, then, started from the silkworm. But her curiosity and artistic eagerness embraced everything. Contrasted with her dull and sombre Germany, Holland, with its rich American and Oriental collections, appeared to her like the great museum of the tropics. There she established herself, and with her pencil made its collections her own. Those faëry cemeteries, glittering with the beauty of the dead, did but whet in her the desire to investigate life in the region where it most luxuriates. At the age of fifty-four she set out for Guiana; and, during a two years' residence in its dangerous climate, collected the drawings and paintings which were to inaugurate art in natural history.

In this branch of labor, the stumbling-block of the artist, who is an artist and nothing more, is that he may do very well, but make Nature coquettish, add the pretty to the beautiful, and flourish those graces and daintinesses which secure for a scientific treatise the favor of fashionable ladies. Nothing of this kind is discernible in the work of Sybille de Mérian, but on every page a noble vigor, a masculine gravity, a courageous simplicity. At the same time, a close inspection, especially of the illustrations colored by her own hand, discovers in the softness, breadth, and fulness of the plants, their lustrous and velvety freshness,—the tones either dead or enamelled, and, as it were, flowered, which the insects offer,—the tender, conscientious hand of a woman who has labored upon the whole with a reverence inspired by love.

We have seen, in our chapter on the *Fire-Flies*, the astonishment of the timid German in a world so new, when the savages brought her its living materials,—venomous herbs, lizards, and snakes, and fantastic serpents. But the very strangeness of this nature, the emotions of the painter trembling before her models, the restless attention with which she sought to seize the changeful physiognomy and mysterious manners, while keenly agitating her heart, did but awaken her genius. Never satisfied by her representations of fugitive realities, she believed she could make each insect properly known only by painting it under all its forms (caterpillar, nymph, butterfly). And this not contenting her, she placed beneath it the vegetable on which it fed, and by its side the lizard, serpent, or spider which fed upon *it*. Thus, the mutuality and exchange of nature was clearly shown; you saw clearly that formidable circulation, which, in tropical climates, is so rapid. Each of those fine plates, so harmonious and so complete, instructs not only by its truthful details, but inspires a profound sympathy with life, which is a very different and much more valuable teaching.

One thing strikes me, which, however, this love explains. She has painted side by side those creatures which devour one another. They draw close together, each faces its antagonist, and you conclude that a frightful duel is imminent. But she has generally concealed the tragic struggle. She has shrunk from painting death.

How much more terrible would have been her task had she advanced further, had she opened and dissected her models, and forced her feminine pencil to the lugubrious painting of anatomical detail!

And here we recognize the precise limit at which women are arrested in the study of the natural sciences. They are incapable of confronting it on *both* sides. Michael Angelo has finely said:—"Death and life are but one. They are the work of the same master and the same hand." But women do not submit. Between them and death no compact is possible. This is very easily understood; they themselves *are* life in all its prolific charm. They are born to give it. Whatever breaks the charm is a horror to them. Death, and especially pain, are not only antipathic, but almost incomprehensible. They feel that only happiness and joy should attend upon woman. Pain inflicted by a woman's hand appears to them very justly as a horrible contradiction.

In the natural sciences there are three things they may master, the three things of life: the *incubation* of the new being,—that is, the tenderness of its earliest care; the *education*, the *nourishment* (to speak as our fathers did) of the young adults; finally, the *observation* of manners, and the subtle intelligence of means of inter-communication with all species. By the aid of these three woman's arts, man may conciliate and gradually appropriate the inferior species, and even many of the insect species. To them belong entirely the arts of domestication. If childhood were less cruel, or at least not harshly insensible, it might share these womanly cares. For Woman, as a soft and tender child, full of pity, is the mediator of all nature.

But as for death, as for pain, as for the lights which science draws from them, do not speak of them to Woman. Here she halts, leaves you on the road, and will go no further forward.

She asserts—and the assertion may appear of some real weight, even to the sedatest minds—that science, of late years, has marched by two contrary roads: on the one hand, demonstrating by the study of manners and of organs that animals are not a world apart, but far more like ourselves than had been generally supposed; and on the other, when it has so clearly proved their great resemblance, and consequently their capacity of suffering, it ordains that we shall inflict upon them the most exquisite and most cruelly protracted agonies.

Science, on this terrible side, closes itself more and more against women. Nature, while inviting them to penetrate it, checks them at the same time by their excessive tenderness of feeling, and by the reverence for life with which she herself has inspired them.

Of all creatures, insects seemed the least worthy of being trained (or domesticated). They were sought only for their colors. Nevertheless, whoever sees in the pursuit nothing but a simple pleasure, will perhaps reflect for a moment when he learns that impaled insects frequently endure their torture for whole years! (See Lemahoux, and, particularly, the excellent *Bulletin de la Société Protectrice des Animaux*, September and October 1856.)

In proportion as women understand the maternal instincts of the creatures I have described, their infinite tenderness, and their ingenious prevision for the objects of their love, it will become impossible for mothers to immolate *these* mothers, and put them to the torture!

Last Words

The originating sentiment of the studies of which this book is the outcome, is also that which induced their suspension. Their primary attraction was found in Huber's revelation, in his vivid manifestation of the individuality of the insect. But that which at the first glance had seemed so paradoxical and incredible, was discovered, when verified, to fall below the reality. The spectacle of so many labors and efforts for the common good, the sight of all these meritorious existences, imposes a duty upon our conscience, and renders it more and more difficult to treat as a *thing* the being which wills, and toils, and loves!

Printed in Great Britain
by Amazon

56157947R00112